A History (and Future) of the Budget Process in the United States

Paul Winfree

A History (and Future) of the Budget Process in the United States

Budget by Fire

palgrave macmillan

Paul Winfree
Heritage Foundation
Washington, DC, USA

ISBN 978-3-030-30958-9 ISBN 978-3-030-30959-6 (eBook)
https://doi.org/10.1007/978-3-030-30959-6

This Palgrave Macmillan imprint is published by the registered company Springer Nature Switzerland AG.
The registered company address is: Gewerbestrasse 11, 6330 Cham, Switzerland

To Jade, Amos, and Ezra

Acknowledgments

This book began with a series of lectures that I gave following my time working on the US Senate Committee on the Budget. I am grateful to my many colleagues serving Congress, including those who have been with the Congressional Budget Office and Congressional Research Service, as I have learned so much from them over the years. I owe a special thanks to my friend Chris Colvin for his initial encouragement to write the book and insights along the way. Research for the book would have been impossible without the incredible preservation of resources at the Library of Congress and National Archives. The book benefited greatly from the impeccable research assistance of Jessica Schultz and Victor Xiao. Conversations with many colleagues, especially Jack Spencer and Katie Tubb, were critical to the development of this project. Support from Rachael Wolpert and Altagracia Gutierrez has been essential in completing the manuscript. I am grateful to those who read the manuscript at different stages, including James Wallner, Kevin Kosar, and Adam Michel, and to the external reviewers, who all provided valuable contributions. Thanks also to my parents, William (Bill) and Barbara Winfree, for their encouragement. Finally, I am indebted to my wife Jade Winfree, who has provided much more than the constant support and countless conversations that made this all possible.

Contents

CHAPTER 1

Introduction

This book tells the story of the budget process in the United States. The language, policy, and power of government is money. And the United States has a unique, but ever evolving, system for determining how money is spent when compared to other modern governments. Through the course of this book we will seek to understand the budget process and how it is central to understanding how the federal government functions.

The *powers of the purse* granted to the Congress are enumerated under the Constitution. The lack of a legal guide for exactly how to delegate the powers, and under what conditions, has led to a budget process marked by power struggles over the last 230 years. This book covers the transformation of American government through the lens of shifting power over who controls what flows in, and out of, the purse of government.[1]

Additionally, the history of the budget process is also about the people who have influenced the evolution of the budget system; their individual histories, personalities, relationships, strengths, weaknesses, conflicts, victories, and tragedies. This book tells the story of a process that was constantly evolving, the people who had the most influence over it, and where it is today.

It could be easy to dismiss most action that took place before the enactment of the Congressional Budget Act of 1974, establishing the modern budget process, since before that there at first appears little consistency. On close investigation, there are themes that cycle throughout our budget

P. Winfree, *A History (and Future) of the Budget Process in the United States*, https://doi.org/10.1007/978-3-030-30959-6_1

history. Certain issues have always been controversial. For instance, debt has always been a contentious political issue—either on the periphery or at the epicenter. The size and purpose of the federal government was debated from the very beginning. Taxes have always been politically unpopular and a subject of great debate. And the use of tariffs and taxes beyond revenue generation has always been a point of contention. However, the specific circumstances of different periods have shaped the ideas regarding each issue. Although general controversy around debt or taxes may be timeless, many of the arguments developed during the different periods are difficult to generalize to our current or future circumstances. All of these issues are addressed within their temporal context; they influence the future, but are difficult to generalize.

One theme that applies to the US government in general, and budgeting specifically, was conflict and ambiguity built into the system from the beginning. In order for the process to succeed in achieving a desired end, whether it was to provide money for the government or increase the nation's creditworthiness, the system requires cooperation between equal branches who are constantly vying for power. Often times the budget process gets caught between disagreements of competing parties.

Other times, such as during national crises, there has been a tendency to consolidate power, usually in the presidency, to streamline budgeting decisions. But there are also many examples of Congress taking back power based on what they considered to be overreach based on those past actions, regardless of how necessary at the time.

The history of the budget process reflects a combination of electoral politics as well as micro- and macroeconomic policy. It involves decisions about spending, taxes, tariffs, and debt management. It is also impossible to tell a history of the budget process without monetary policy which has had a significant influence on fiscal policy in every period.

There already exists a significant literature on the history of the budget process. Aaron Wildavsky's formative work *The Politics of the Budgetary Process* (1964) suggests that the budget process is best understood as a development around political rather than simply economic determinations.[2] Practitioners have argued something similar, such as David Stockman, Reagan's Director of the Office of Management and Budget, who claimed in *Triumph of Politics* (1986) that budgeting decisions and politics are inseparable.[3] Both Wildavsky (1964) and Lindblom (1959) argue that the budget process developed incrementally in response to events of the time.[4]

The intrinsic political struggle can be broken down into what Schick (1980) has described as the "parts against the whole" or what Stewart (1989) has called "distributional" versus "aggregational" problems.[5] Distributional problems are, essentially, electoral and result in the determination of "who gets what." Aggregational are "what happens when all the budgetary pieces are added together."

Throughout much of our early history, spending bills were just an accumulation of the resolution of distributional problems. However, most budget process reforms since 1921 can be seen as an attempt to resolve aggregational with distributional problems. Stewart (1989) suggests that the budgetary conflicts can be interpreted as rising from the tension this resolution has created. In this book, aggregational problems include debt management and macroeconomic policy.

Wildavsky (1988) suggests that budget outcomes are a compromise between groups with different preferences, including preferences toward debt. Over time, these preferences have shifted. This includes the evolution of macroeconomic policy itself. Prior to the 1960s, presidents and Congress could generally agree. Therefore, adjustments to spending, revenue, and overall macroeconomic policy were made on the margin to meet some end.

Savage (1988) suggests that budget policy setting is symbolic. This has driven the political pursuit of balanced budgets from Presidents Washington to Reagan. However, as this book will argue, this pursuit has also been economic. Prior to the 1930s and the influence of John Maynard Keynes on macroeconomic policy, balanced budgets were seen as an effective debt management tool, especially in world where seigniorage was not always an option. Thus, spending and tax policy often influenced one another; although this relationship has broken down since the 1960s with deficits now playing a larger role.

In fact, we find ourselves in a period where persistent deficits may not be as economically destructive as implicitly assumed. Blanchard (2019) has suggested that when rates at which the government borrows money are lower than the rate of economic growth, as they have been for considerable periods of time in the United States, we might not need to worry so much about deficit financing because debt can be rolled over. To the extent that a gap between real and potential output exists, the negative effects of debt on welfare may be limited.[6] In fact, the concept of rolling over debt as a beneficial strategy is not new to American fiscal policy. Alexander Hamilton suggested rollover as an effective debt management strategy in the 1790s.

At the same time, there is a growing literature suggesting the fiscal austerity (i.e., deficit reduction strategies) may result in positive economic growth. Alesina, Favero, and Giavazzi (2018) and Giavazzi and Pagano (1990) both argue that large decreases in government spending can and have increased economic growth as they can be accompanied by market liberalization, debt stabilization, as well as other factors.[7] These differing analyses highlight only one divergence in the economic literature that might affect a prescribed economic policy path.

This book suggests that both politics and economics have been critical to determining the evolution of the budget process. John Neville Keynes (1917), the father of John Maynard Keynes, suggested that economic events help shape economic theory.[8] There is an interdependence between theoretical positions guiding policy and historical events. The same is true for understanding the historical arch of the budget process which has been driven simultaneously by politics, economic events, and economic theory. Similar to Wildavsky, Lindblom, and many others this book suggests that incremental development is mainly responsible for the development of the process although some events (World War I and the Great Depression, for instance) have led to substantial changes. However, budgetary outcomes may not be as incremental as experienced through the extensive growth in the federal government during the twentieth century.[9]

When the budget process has been successful, the structure does not have material effects on the actual outcomes. As many budget analysts have said over a long time, process does not guarantee outcomes. The structure itself is endogenous to the institutions, personalities involved, the time period, the various economic theories, and exogenous factors. Historically, the budget process has evolved quickly to deal with challenges of the day, whether war or economic crises, but it is not very effective in helping to resolve fundamental disagreements whether they are political or economic. At this point, the budget process breaks down and it's no longer helpful to policymakers in helping focus their cumulative attention on goal setting and execution.

Rivlin wrote: "There will be little progress in reducing the complexity of the budgeting process until Congress realizes that it can contribute more to changing the future of the nation by directing overall policy, than by controlling details."[10] But this sadly ignores the history of the process. Congress has almost never ignored the details. Asking them to change their ways is probably too much. The part must come before the whole.

Today, there are many disagreements on both the distributional and the aggregational levels. As the nation's goals have become more complicated, as the government has grown in size and scope, and as the federal budget has evolved to symbolize additional concepts that elicit controversy, the budget process has broken down entirely. This book examines the evolution of the budget process with attention to what caused division and unification driving the evolution over time.

Chapter 1 examines the consequential issues from the Washington to Madison Administrations, the economics and politics of debt management for the new country, the development of appropriations bills, Congress's response to a powerful Treasury, and early struggles over whether the legislative or executive branch actually has the power to make spending decisions.

Chapter 2 examines the evolution of public finance in response to external threats and during the Civil War, the innovation of federal debt to finance a war when other loans and taxes were unavailable, recasting tariffs as a way to raise money and protect domestic industry, the application of the sinking fund to retire debt, paying off the debt under Jackson, and attempts to distance federal finances from banking crises.

Chapter 3 explores the period from immediately after the Civil War until World War I, the development of the Congressional appropriations process under a new committee structure, the early progressive reformers, the standardization of accounting, the rise of the income tax and Federal Reserve system, and the beginning of the executive budget process.

Chapter 4 illustrates the evolving role of the budgets beginning with the Great Depression and aftermath of World War II, the legislative budget, the empowerment of the Bureau of the Budget, and the influence of Keynesian economics on budgeting.

Chapter 5 details how the unified budget process created additional goals for the budget besides the allocation of resources, how the growth in government influenced both budgeting and structural reorganization, the debt limit, the full employment and stable prices budgets, and the onset of structural budget deficits.

Chapter 6 details Congress's new role within the executive budget process through the Congressional Budget Act, Reagan's economic policy driven by small government and low taxes, the balanced budgets of the 1990s, the growth in government under no fiscal restraint during the 2000s, and the return to concerns over the deficit during the Obama Administration.

Chapter 7 discusses the current state of the budget process and its relationship with economic policy while recommending that we ask too much of the budget process and should incorporate a decentralized system of economic policy setting.

Before diving into Chap. 2, which begins in 1789 with the first Congress and Washington Administration deliberating how they plan to increase confidence in the new nation by managing debt, it's imperative to know a little bit about the experiences of the Founders. They were not starting with a blank slate in establishing a new financial system for the new government. The Founders had a sophisticated knowledge of other government financial systems, such as Great Britain, and experience with the colonial governments. At the same time, they had nearly a decade of experience under the Articles of Confederation. The rest of this prologue is dedicated to setting the stage for the budget process, or lack thereof, and the actors experience with the weaknesses of the Articles of Confederation.

Debt and Government Finance Before the Constitution

The US government under the Articles of Confederation was unequipped to handle the task of managing public credit and debt accumulated during the War of Independence. The early government had significantly weakened its financial position by distancing itself from what were seen as the oppressive powers of a central government through overly decentralized power. The consequent inability to raise revenues and efficiently establish the terms for loans became a significant threat to the national security of the new country. Particularly as its prior parent nation, which had previously afforded protection and safety from outside forces, had become its new belligerent.

In Great Britain power was divided between the Crown and Parliament, including a division of power over the allocation of money and the collection of revenues. The Founders would, in almost every way, use the Constitution to improve upon this division made to the British system of representative government starting in the early 1600s through the Glorious Revolution of 1688. Therefore, it is important to understand the basics of the system that the Founders were adapting from under the Articles of Confederation government.

The House of Commons orchestrated a series of budgetary reforms leading up to the beginning of the English Civil War in 1642. These reforms were intended to give Parliament additional powers of oversight over the Crown's habit of unilaterally taxing and spending. To this point, the English monarch had been able to remain financially independent of the legislature by charging fees and land rents. For example, in 1635, King Charles I famously ordered the levying of a tax on both coastal and inland towns to provide money for building ships (known as "Ship Money"). The King based this practice on a historical precedent, when the Crown's authority to tax was used during times of war. However, it was used in this instance to address financial problems without calling a new Parliament.

Under certain circumstances, such as going to war, the Crown was able to request "aid and supplies" from Parliament. "Aid and supplies" functioned with broad authority by giving the Crown additional powers to tax and spend for specific purposes. Parliament would, by way of legislation, provide the Crown with the power to tax and also yield control over how the resources were spent.

From 1620 to 1689, Parliament made three process changes that would empower the legislature over the Crown within regards to financial decision-making.[11] The first change was the creation of the Committee on Supply in 1620. The purpose of the Committee on Supply was to provide oversight over the estimates provided by the Crown for various activities. The Committee on Supply would also authorize the amount available to the Crown based on these assessments. The second change happened in 1641, when the House of Commons created the Committee on Ways and Means. The new committee functioned in tandem with the Committee on Supply in order to develop the "ways and means," or tax revenues, to pay for authorized activities. The third and final change occurred in 1689, when the English Bill of Rights made it illegal for "levying money for or to the use of the Crown by pretence [sic] or prerogative without grant of Parliament." This built on the Petition of Right of 1628, which had declared any direct tax not authorized by Parliament to be illegal.[12] However, the Crown retained the power, along with Parliament, to initiate tax and spending legislation through direct requests. These three changes would magnify Parliament's oversight and, ultimately, its control over government's finances. Furthermore, with a knowledge of modern English history and government, the Founders of the United States would have been well aware of not just Parliament's role in the financial decisions but also the reasoning behind the evolution of the process.

In fact, the colonial governments in the British North American colonies were, characteristically, reflective of the same relationship between

Parliament and the Crown.[13] A governor would serve the executive functions (and were many times a royal appointee), whereas the local legislatures maintained the same control over the money as one would find in the parent country. In most places, the legislatures wielded powers similar to the House of Commons, who maintained control over appropriating resources and formulating tax policy to be executed by the governor. Some colonial legislatures would further tie the hands of their governors or their delegates by appointing their own representatives to execute the financial decisions.

However, there were several unique characteristics of the colonial governments that restrained the seats of power. In many states, detailed authorizations and limitations were attached to any new money provided to colonial executives in an effort to restrict its use to only very specific purposes. Tax collections for the governor's appointments and general use were curtailed. The phrase "no other use of purpose whatsoever" began appearing in the legislation that specified the use of funds.[14] This raised enough of a fervor amongst the royal representatives in the colonies and ultimately prompted Parliament to pass the Stamp Act in 1765, in part, to provide a dedicated revenue source to the royally appointed executives whose fiscal powers had been stripped.

In Great Britain, and in many of the colonial governments, the involvement of the upper house (e.g., House of Lords and Senate) in the budgetary process was merely a formality. In reality, they would neither originate spending or tax bills nor amend them later in the process. This phenomenon became the basis for contention during the Constitutional Convention of 1787, when the attendees disagreed on the involvement of the upper and lower houses in the nation's fiscal authority. The dispute resulted in the compromise reflected in Article I, Section 7: "All bills for raising Revenue shall originate in the House of Representatives, but the Senate may propose or concur with Amendments as on other Bills." Even today, the House usually begins the appropriations process, even though there is not a prohibition on the Senate for sending the House a spending bill first.

The Confederation government did not reflect either Parliament or state governments in either structure or power. Under the Articles of Confederation, there was no executive (e.g., governor) or executive branch. Rather, basic tasks of administration were first handled by committees, and then by departments created under the legislature and constituted by elected members who were not necessarily members of Congress.

For instance, Congress initially created a group of standing committees to oversee financial decision-making, until it superseded those committees with a Board of Treasury in 1779. The Board of Treasury comprised five members, of whom only two were members of Congress.[15] Finally, in February 1781, the Board of Treasury was replaced by the Department of Finance with Roger Morris elected as its superintendent.

The Articles of Confederation permitted Congress to borrow money, but they were required to ratify the terms of each loan. As a result, agents of the government could be negotiating loan agreements in European markets to cover even the most necessary of expenses, such as interest on debts accumulated during the War of Independence.[16] Nonetheless, that money could not be disbursed until Congress both approved the agreement and apportioned the money to states.

Though the Articles conferred the power to borrow, Congress did not have the power to tax and impose duties. Rather, Congress would ratify the loan while also apportioning the cost of servicing the debt to the states based on the property value of each state. This consequently gave the state legislatures an implicit veto over the terms of the loan agreements as well as their payments. Meanwhile, despite the possibility of a single state's veto unraveling the nation's ability to pay, officers were negotiating loan agreements overseas on behalf of the entire Confederation at a time when it took a typical mail ship over a month to travel the roughly 3000 nautical miles from the English Channel to America.

James Madison expressed his concerns about this process in a letter to Edmund Randolph, a Virginian delegate to the Confederation Congress, in September 1782:

> *Mr. Adam [John Adams, then Ambassador to the Dutch Republic] we are informed has contracted with a mercantile House in Holland for the negotiation of a loan of 5 million guilders, or about 10 million livres, for which he is to give 5 perCt. interest, and 1 ½ perCt. for commission & other douceurs & charges, which will raise the interest to about 6 perCt. The Principal is to be discharged in five annual payments, commencing with the 10th year from the date of the loan …. The contractors however made it a condition that none of the money should be paid to the U.S. until the contract should be ratified by Congress …. How far amount will by that time have augmented is uncertain. The Contractors seemed to be tolerably sanguine but not absolutely sure, of getting the whole sum. The partial subscription already secured, is a most seasonable relief to the department of finance which was struggling under the most critical difficulties.*[17]

Madison goes on to detail for Randolph that the Rhode Island General Assembly had adjourned for the season without consenting to a proposal from Congress to amend the Articles and empower the government to impose a 5 percent import duty. This was after Robert Morris had made a personal plea to the Governor, William Greene, to remain in session so that Congress could ratify the agreement and make progress toward securing $1,200,000 to cover interest payments on past debts.[18] Eleven states had already ratified the amendment, but unanimous consent was required for adoption. Rhode Island would reject the amendment in November 1782.[19]

Further illustrating how contentious dealing with debt and public credit had become was a September 1783 report by the General Court of Massachusetts. This report justified the state's refusal to adopt the terms of a Plan for Restoring Public Credit put forward by Morris based on other policy decisions carried in the Confederation Congress's proposal. In this case, Massachusetts was concerned about congressional pay, the number of civil officials in the government, and pay to former members of the continental army.

That same month, Robert Morris expressed his concerns to John Adams, who had just negotiated the Treaty of Paris, formally ending the War of Independence. Morris penned, "the necessity of strengthening our Confederation providing for our Debts and forming some federal Constitution begins to be most seriously felt; But unfortunately for America the narrow and illiberal Prejudices of some have taken such deep Root that it must be difficult and may prove impracticable to remove them."[20] Morris would leave his post as superintendent of the Department of Finance within the year citing frustration over dealing with the states over paying past debts.

Richard Peters also took up his frustration in an anonymous article published on September 18, 1783, in the *Philadelphia Journal, and the Weekly Advertiser*. Peters, a delegate from Pennsylvania to Congress, wrote under the name "The North American" that if debts were not paid and public credit maintained, American dignity and security would be at stake. Specifically, he predicted that France and Holland, the largest creditors of the United States, might begin confiscating American ships as payment. Peters wrote that such actions would be "a measure ever in their power – which must be the result of disappointment in a regular and pacific mode – and which (if ever adopted) will record our infamy as well as our impotence."[21]

The very real problem of securing credit and managing payments of past debts under the Confederation was further captured in a letter to the state governments and drafted by Jefferson in March 1784:

> *When the army were furloughed they had the promise of three months' pay and as there was not money in the treasury, the Superintendent of finance was under the necessity of issuing his notes to discharge this and other demands. The notes becoming due, part of them were redeemed with money supplied by the several states; but this being inadequate, the financier drew bills on Holland for the deficiency. A considerable portion of these drafts have been paid by loans obtained there on the credit of the United States. But the letters from our bankers to the Superintendent of finance inform that they had been under the necessity for the want of funds to suffer so many of his bills to be protested for non-acceptance as with the damages on protest in case of non-payment will amount to the sum of 636,000 dollars.*
>
> *We expect the return of these bills under a protest for non-payment, and should there not be money in the treasury of the United States to discharge them, your excellency may easily conceive the deplorable consequences.*[22]

Jefferson's letter warned the states that the nation's slipping public credit had come back to haunt them. Without support from the states, bankruptcy would loom over their heads. This, as Jefferson notes in a letter to Morris, would result in "fatal effects" for the United States.

Securing public credit was seen as both a necessary task for securing the position of the country, and the nation's core weakness. From his home Mount Vernon, George Washington wrote to James Warren in October 1785 that "we have it in our power to be one of the most respectable Nations upon Earth … if we would pursue a wise, Just, & liberal policy towards one another – and would keep good faith with the rest of the World. That our resources are ample, & encreasing [sic], none can deny; But whilst they are grudgingly applied, or not applied at all, we give a vital stab to public credit, and must sink into contempt in the eyes of Europe."[23] Public credit was the metric of good faith and the knife's edge on which the country was balancing.

The energy exhumed over managing the debt continued to plague the young nation. Meanwhile, other policy disagreements also entered into the process and thus tied up deliberations on debt management. In a December 1786 letter to James Madison, Speaker of the House Edmund Pendleton (who was then a member of Virginia's House of Delegates) wrote to Madison questioning the appearance of an excessive number of government officials as well as the funding of a military at a high level during peace time. Pendleton told Madison, "We ought to preserve our rank amongst Nations, but should it not be the virtues of Justice & economy, suited to our infantine States, and not by Aping the vices of Opulent Nations, realize the Fable of the Frog, swelling to attain the size of the Ox at one effort & produce distruction [sic]."[24]

In Aesop's fable, a young frog is stomped on by an ox while drinking water from a pond. An older frog comes to ask what happened and the other frogs tell him that a monster has crushed their friend. The older frog draws air into his belly and says, "was he this big?" The other frog says he was bigger, and the older frog continues to puff himself up until finally he bursts. In his reference to this tale, Pendleton was suggesting to Madison that the United States not try to compete with the European nations in what he considered to be extravagancies of government and an excessive military, for such a pursuit would inevitably lead to their own downfall.

In Federalist No. 15, an appeal to the people of New York to ratify the Constitution, Alexander Hamilton posed the following rhetorical question: if public credit is so indispensable, why has the country come to "abandon its cause as desperate and irretrievable?" He would go on to argue in Federalist No. 30 that the power to directly raise revenues was the key to good credit. This was the weakness of the Articles of Confederation; there was too much risk associated with relying on the states to raise money. Without the power to tax, the United States was plagued with poor credit. This jeopardized the existence of the United States in real terms and quantified in credit markets.

The time had come for a new type of government to deal with public credit. Perhaps one of the most succinct articulations of this need was illustrated by Thomas Jefferson in a letter to James Madison dated May 3, 1788. Jefferson's letter written while he was Minister to France was indicative of the sentiment concluded by many after more than seven years over the Articles of Confederation. Jefferson begins his letter by noting the necessity of credit even from the perspective of a skeptic:[25]

> *While [in Amsterdam], I endeavored to get as well as I could into the state of national credit there: for tho' I am an enemy to the using our credit but under absolute necessity, yet the possessing a good credit I consider as indispensable in the present system of carrying on war. The existence of a nation, having no credit, is always precarious.*

Jefferson goes on to suggest that Britain, America's recent enemy, was strengthened by its management of debt:

> *The credit of England is best. Their paper sells at par on the exchange of Amsterdam the moment any of it is offered, & they can command there any sum the please. The reason is that they ever borrow without establishing taxes for the paiment [sic] of the interest, and they never yet failed one day in that paiment.*

Jefferson believed that the "first act" of the new government under the Constitution should be to prove that the United States was a good investment:

> *The first act of the new government should be some operation whereby they may assume to themselves this station. Their European debts form a proper subject for this. Digest the whole, public & private. Dutch, French & Spanish, into a table, shewing [sic] the sum of interest due every year, & portions of principle paiable the same years.*

Finally, Jefferson concluded that the United States must be able to more effectively manage its debt and interest payments in order to survive as a nation:

> *The new government should by no means be left by the old to the necessity of borrowing a stiver before it can tax for it's [sic] interest. This will destroy the credit of the new government in it's [sic] birth.*

By the time Thomas Jefferson's letter had reached James Madison, seven states had ratified the new Constitution. Five more states would ratify the Constitution before Secretary Hamilton issued his First Report on Public Credit, which prompted earnest decision-making over the issues of debt and other fiscal responsibilities of the new government. But there became a consensus that the strength of the nation was tied to its unified financial position.

While the first experiment to construct a new government had failed to provide enough centralized power to meaningfully manage the finances of the new nation, the Founders had learned a great deal about what would be necessary to provide for a sustainable government. Public credit was tied to international standing. The new government under the Constitution would need to quickly develop a system for managing its finances, and creditworthiness, if it was going to remain unified and independent.

Notes

1. Henry Shuman, *Politics and the Budget: The Struggle Between the President and the Congress* (Englewood Cliffs, NJ: Prentice-Hall, 1984). Shuman offers a good summary of more recent history and the inherent political power struggles between the president, Congress, and other institutions involved with the budget process.
2. Aaron Wildavsky, *The Politics of the Budgetary Process* (Boston, MA: Little, Brown and Company, 1964). Many others have analyzed the connection between politics and the budget, including Rubin (2013), Sharkansky (1969) Fisher (2009), Ippolito (2012), and Witte (1985). Wildavsky (1975) finds that both political and economic factors are important for determining domestic agency budgets. Koven (1988) suggests that ideology affects budgeting decisions which can create either a system of political accountability or a budget derived based on "emotion and passion" thus threatening credibility.
3. David A. Stockman, *The Triumph of Politics: Why the Reagan Revolution Failed* (New York, NY: Harper & Row, 1986).
4. Aaron Wildavsky, *The Politics of the Budgetary Process* (Boston, MA: Little, Brown and Company, 1964); Charles Lindblom, "The science of 'muddling through'," *Public Administration Review* 19, (1959).
5. Allen Schick, *Congress and Money: Budgeting, Spending, and Taxing* (Washington, DC: The Urban Institute, 1980); Charles H. Stewart, III, *Budget Reform Politics: The Design of the Appropriations Process in the House of Representatives* (New York, NY: Cambridge University Press, 1989).
6. Oliver Blanchard, "Public Debt and Low Interest Rates," *American Economic Review* 109, no. 4 (2019): 1197–1229.
7. Alberto Alesina, Carlo A. Favero, and Francesco Giavazzi, "What Do We Know about the Effects of Austerity?" *AEA Papers and Proceedings, American Economic Association* (2018): 524–530; Francesco Giavazzi and Marco Pagano, "Can Sever Fiscal Contractions be Expansionary? Tales of Two Small European Countries," *NBER Macroeconomics Annual 1990, Volume 5, by Oliver Jean Blanchard and Stanley Fischer* (1990): 75–122.
8. John Neville Keynes, *The Scope and Method of Political Economy, 4th ed.* (London: Macmillan, 1917).
9. Similar to LeLoup (1983) and others, this book does not imply that incrementalism is preferable as a normative strategy over a comprehensive approach to the federal budget.
10. Alice M. Rivlin, "Reform of the Budget Process," *The American Economic Review: Papers and Proceedings of the Ninety-Sixth Annual Meeting of the American Economic Association* 74, no. 2 (1984): 133–137.

11. Courtenary Ilbert, *Parliament: Its History, Constitution, and Practice, 3rd ed.* (London: Oxford University Press, 1948); K.C. Wheare, *Government by Committee* (London: Oxford University Press, 1955); Kenneth Bradshaw and David Pring, *Parliament and Congress* (Austin, TX: University of Texas Press, 1972).
12. S.J. Niefield, "The Development of the Budgetary Systems of the United States," *FinanzArchiv/Public Finance Analysis* 13, no. 4 (1951/1952): 606–614.
13. Jack P. Greene, "Political Mimesis: A Consideration of the Historical and Cultural Roots of Legislative Behavior in the British Colonies in the Eighteenth Century," *The American Historical Review* 75, no. 2 (1969): 337–360.
14. David R. Kennon and M. Rebecca Rogers, *The Committee on Ways and Means: A Bicentennial History, 1789–1989* (Washington, DC: U.S. Government Printing Office, 1989).
15. Albert S. Bolles, *Financial History of the United States from 1774 to 1789, Vol. I* (New York, NY: Augustus M. Kelly Publishers, 1969).
16. For more on American debt during the early period and European capital markets, see Perkins (1994).
17. James Madison to Edmund Randolph, September 16–17, 1782, in *The Papers of James Madison*, vol. 5, ed. William T. Hutchinson and William M. E. Rachal (Chicago: The University of Chicago Press, 1967), 126–130.
18. Ibid. see note 11.
19. Douglas A. Irwin, "Revenue or Reciprocity? Founding Feuds Over Early U.S. Trade Policy," in *Founding Choices: American Economic Policy in the 1790s* by Douglas A. Irwin and Richard Sylla (Chicago, IL: University of Chicago Press, 2010).
20. John Adams, *The Adams Papers: Papers of John Adams*, vol. 15, ed. Gregg L. Lint, C. James Taylor, Robert F. Karachuk, Hobson Woodward, Margaret A. Hogan, Sara B. Sikes, Mary T. Claffey, and Karen N. Barzilay (Cambridge, MA: Harvard University Press, 2010): 300–301.
21. *The Philadelphia Journal and Weekly Advertiser*, September 17, 1783.
22. Thomas Jefferson to Robert Morris – with Draft of Circulation Letter to the States, March 30, 1784, in *The Papers of Thomas Jefferson*, vol. 7, ed. Julian P. Boyd (Princeton, NJ: Princeton University Press, 1953), 53–56.
23. George Washington to James Warren, October 7, 1785, in *The Papers of George Washington, Confederation Series*, vol. 3, ed. W. W. Abbot (Charlottesville: University Press of Virginia, 1994), 298–301.
24. Edmund Pendleton to James Madison, December 9, 1786, in *The Papers of James Madison*, vol. 9, ed. Robert A. Rutland and William M. E. Rachal (Chicago: The University of Chicago Press, 1975), 201–204.

25. Thomas Jefferson to James Madison, May 3, 1788, in *The Papers of James Madison*, vol. 11, ed. Robert A. Rutland and Charles F. Hobson (Charlottesville: University Press of Virginia, 1977), 33–38.

References

Adams, John. The Adams Papers: Papers of John Adams, vol. 15, June 1783–January 1784, edited by Gregg L. Lint, C. James Taylor, Robert F. Karachuk, Hobson Woodward, Margaret A. Hogan, Sara B. Sikes, Mary T. Claffey, and Karen N. Barzilay. Cambridge, MA: Harvard University Press, 2010.

Alesina, Alberto, Carlo A. Favero, and Francesco Giavazzi. 2018. "What Do We Know about the Effects of Austerity?" AEA Papers and Proceedings. American Economic Association. 524–530.

Blanchard, Oliver. 2019. "Public Debt and Low Interest Rates." American Economic Review 109 (4): 1197–1229.

Bolles, Albert S. 1969. Financial History of the United States from 1774 to 1789. Vol. I. 3 vols. New York, NY: Augustus M. Kelly Publishers.

Bradshaw, Kenneth, and David Pring. 1972. Parliament and Congress. Austin, TX: University of Texas Press.

Fisher, Patrick. 2009. The Politics of Taxing and Spending. Boulder, CO: Lynne Rienner Publishers, Ltd.

Giavazzi, Francesco, and Marco Pagano. 1990. "Can Severe Fiscal Contractions be Expansionary? Tales of Two Small European Countries." In NBER Macroeconomics Annual 1990, Volume 5, by Oliver Jean Blanchard and Stanley Fischer, 75–122. Cambridge, MA: National Bureau of Economic Research.

Greene, Jack P. 1969. "Political Mimesis: A Consideration of the Historical and Cultural Roots of Legislative Behavior in the British Colonies in the Eighteenth Century." The American Historical Review 75 (2): 337–360.

Ilbert, Courtenay. 1948. Parliament: Its History, Constitution, and Practice. 3. London: Oxford University Press.

Ippolito, Dennis S. 2012. Deficits, Debt, and The New Politics of Tax Policy. New York, NY: Cambridge University Press.

Irwin, Douglas. 2010. "Revenue or Reciprocity? Founding Feuds Over Early U.S. Trade Policy." In Founding Choices: American Economic Policy in the 1790s, by Douglas Irwin and Richard Sylla. Chicago, IL: University of Chicago Press.

Jefferson, Thomas. 1953. "Letter to Robert Morris – with Draft of Circulation Letter to the States, 30 March 1784." In The Papers of Thomas Jefferson, vol. 7, edited by Julian P. Boyd, 53–56. Princeton, NJ: Princeton University Press.

Jefferson, Thomas. 1977. "Letter to James Madison, 3 May 1788." In The Papers of James Madison, vol. 11, edited by Robert A. Rutland and Charles F. Hobson, 33–38. Charlottesville: University Press of Virginia.

Kennon, David R., and M. Rebecca Rogers. 1989. The Committee on Ways and Means: A Bicentennial History, 1789–1989. Washington, DC: Government Printing Office.

Keynes, John Neville. 1917. The Scope and Method of Political Economy. 4th. London: Macmillan.

Koven, Steven G. 1988. Ideological Budgeting: The Influence of Political Philosophy on Public Policy. New York, NY: Praeger.

LeLoup, Lance T. 1983. "The Myth of Incrementalism: Analytical Choices in Budgetary Theory." In Public Budgeting and Finance: Behavioral, Theoretical, and Technical Perspectives, by Robert T. Golembiewski and Jack Rubin. New York, NY: Marcel Dekker.

Lindblom, Charles. 1959. "The science of 'muddling through'." Public Administration Review 19: 79–88.

Madison, James. 1967. "Letter to Edmund Randolph, 16–17 September 1782." In The Papers of James Madison, vol. 5, edited by William T. Hutchinson and William M. E. Rachal, 126–130. Chicago: The University of Chicago Press.

Niefield, S.J. 1951/1952. "The Development of the Budgetary Systems of the United States." FinanzArchiv/Public Finance Analysis 13 (4): 606–614.

Pendleton, Edmund. 1975. "Letter to James Madison, 9 December 1786." In The Papers of James Madison, vol. 9, edited by Robert A. Rutland and William M. E. Rachal, 201–204. Chicago: The University of Chicago Press.

Perkins, Edwin J. 1994. American Public Finance and Financial Services. Columbus, OH: Ohio State University Press.

Rivlin, Alice M. 1984. "Reform of the Budget Process." The American Economic Review: Papers and Proceedings of the Ninety-Sixth Annual Meeting of the American Economic Association 74 (2): 133–137.

Rubin, Irene S. 2013. The Politics of Public Budgeting: Getting and Spending, Borrowing and Balancing. Seventh. Washington, DC: CQ Press.

Savage, James D. 1988. Balanced Budget and American Politics. Ithaca, NY: Cornell University Press.

Schick, Allen. 1980. Congress and Money: Budgeting, Spending, and Taxing. Washington, DC: The Urban Institute.

Sharkansky, Ira. 1969. The Politics of Taxing and Spending. Indianapolis, IN: Bobbs-Merrill.

Shuman, Howard. 1984. Politics and the Budget: The Struggle Between the President and the Congress. Englewood Cliffs, NJ: Prentice-Hall.

Stewart, Charles H., III. 1989. Budget Reform Politics: The Design of the Appropriations Process in the House of Representatives, 1865–1921. New York, NY: Cambridge University Press.

Stockman, David A. 1986. The Triumph of Politics: Why the Reagan Revolution Failed. New York, NY: Harper & Row.

The Philadelphia Journal and Weekly Advertiser. September 17, 1783.

Washington, George. 1994. "Letter to James Warren, 7 October 1785." In The Papers of George Washington, Confederation Series, vol. 3, edited by W. W. Abbot, 298–301. Charlottesville: University Press of Virginia.

Wheare, K.C. 1955. Government by Committee. London: Oxford University Press.

Wildavsky, Aaron. 1964. The Politics of the Budgetary Process. Boston, MA: Little, Brown and Company.

———. 1975. Budgeting: A Comparative Theory of Budgetary Processes. Boston, MA: Little, Brown, and Company.

———. 1988. The New Politics of the Budget Process. Glenview, IL: Scott, Foresman & Co.

Witte, John F. 1985. The Politics and Development of the Federal Income Tax. Madison, WI: University of Wisconsin Press.

CHAPTER 2

Debt Is the Price of Liberty

On January 14, 1790, a letter was delivered to Speaker of the House Frederick Muhlenberg at Federal Hall in New York. The new federal capital wouldn't move to Philadelphia until later that year, and the center of government was still in the heart of Wall Street. The letter arrived six days after George Washington had delivered his first annual address to Congress. A modest 1088 words, President Washington's address called for the maintenance of peace through the provision of a "common defense," a standardization of currency and measurement to help the economy grow, and the promotion of science and literature.

Washington began his address with a succinct congratulation to Congress on the "present favorable prospects of public affairs." The second of these favorable circumstances (which fell behind a mention of North Carolina's ratification of the Constitution more than a month earlier) was the "rising credit and respectability of our country." Washington elevated these noteworthy accomplishments worthy of a young and growing nation. He closed his remarks with a message to the House of Representatives. The House had adopted a resolution in September requesting a plan to manage the credit, and debt, of the United States.[1]

The failure of the Articles of Confederation to secure good credit for the country was the genesis of the stronger federal government built through the Constitution. The Articles had placed limitations on raising revenues to pay the interest on existing war debts had hamstrung the

P. Winfree, *A History (and Future) of the Budget Process in the United States*, https://doi.org/10.1007/978-3-030-30959-6_2

nation. But now sky was the limit. The new government had the authority to tax and manage debt but no obvious system guiding their new powers.

Recalling the years governed under the Articles, Washington called the establishment of public credit "a matter of high importance to the national honor and prosperity."[2] There was widespread agreement that something had to be done. The letter delivered to Muhlenberg contained a plan devised by Alexander Hamilton to do exactly that by giving faith to potential investors overseas and at home and encourage an influx of credit to the infant country.

Hamilton's proposal is known today as the "First Report on the Public Credit" to differentiate it from the other three related parts of his economic agenda issued to Congress between 1790 and 1795.[3] The plan laid out several principles for establishing credit, which would increase the value of debt available to foreign and domestic investors on behalf of the new nation. Hamilton also argued that the debt securities would serve other important purposes, such as functioning as tradable commodities where their value was tied to the nation's creditworthiness.

To Hamilton, debt was not only a necessity, but also a natural resource akin to gold or oil, with the power to fuel the nation's young economy through trade. Hamilton called debt an "indispensable resource" during "times of public danger, especially from foreign war." Hamilton went on to advise that "transfers of stock or public debt are there equivalent to payments in specie; or in other words, stock, in the principal transactions of business, passes current as specie." In addition to its monetary functions, debt could also prove to be an advantageous tool for real economic stimulus. "Trade," Hamilton claimed, "is extended by [debt]," so "agriculture and manufactures are also promoted by it." Furthermore, Hamilton contended that debt could help increase the value of land, reversing an earlier trend; after the War of Independence, land began depreciating, driven, in part, by a scarcity of money. With debt available as a money substitute, land prices could rise again. However, the integral ability of debt to spur investment and guard against stagnation across industries was derived from having a debt that "by being well funded, it has acquired an adequate and stable value."

To establish such credit stability, Hamilton asserted that state debt would need to be consolidated by the federal government in order to build confidence in the new American Republic and its creditworthiness. This would provide the nation with more leverage within credit markets than any one state could receive on its own. However, it would also weaken any individual state's position—a point not lost on others in Washington's Cabinet and Members of Congress.[4] Should the possibility arise for a common defense, consolidated debt management would allow the country as a whole to negotiate terms rather than rely on each state's ability to borrow on its own. Hamilton explicitly argued that through ratification of the Constitution, all state debt should be assumed by the new government or "as valid against the United States under it, as under the confederation." This bold statement was a rhetorical tactic by Hamilton, for his call for an "assumption" of state debt by the federal government became a strong point of contention between himself and James Madison, an author of the Constitution and then Congressman from Virginia.

Hamilton also proposed the equal treatment of all creditors under the principle of full payment regardless of when they purchased the debt certificate. This was distinct from a plan Madison later suggested that would pay back these certificates at face value only if they were the original purchaser.[5] Madison's plan was intended to exclude those who were involved in debt speculation. Hamilton's proposal would instead pay them back at face value with a reasonable amount of interest. Doing otherwise, he stated, would have been unfair to those who had purchased certificates of indebtedness when the future of the country was uncertain, and thus placed a bet toward America's success in secondary markets:

> *To discriminate the merits of these several descriptions of creditors, would be a task equally unnecessary and invidious. If the voice of humanity plead more loudly in favor of some than of others, the voice of policy, no less than of justice, pleads in favor of all. A WISE NATION will never permit those who relieve the wants of their country, or who rely most on its faith, its firmness, and its resources, when either of them is distrusted, to suffer by the event.*

Not only did Hamilton lay out the arguments of maintaining debt, but he also presented a compelling case for servicing debt obligations rather than paying them down. An objective of maintaining good public credit was showing creditors that the public financial system had a command over the debt service. A dedicated revenue source to pay interest costs would have been most appropriate. To Hamilton, this revenue would come from a series of tariffs, including on Madeira wine, sherry, other wine, spirits at all proofs, a number of teas, and coffee. Different levels of taxation, Hamilton argued, should be applied to different drinks based explicitly on the policy of modifying human behavior or a progressive tax on luxury items:

> *That the articles which have been enumerated, will, better than most others, bear high duties, can hardly be a question. They are all of them, in reality – luxuries – the greatest part of them foreign luxuries; some of them, in the excess in which they are used, pernicious luxuries. And there is, perhaps, none of them, which is not consumed in so great abundance, as may justly, denominate it, a source of national extravagance and impoverishment. The consumption of ardent spirits particularly, no doubt very much on account of their cheapness, is carried to an extreme, which is truly to be regretted, as well in regard to the health and the morals, as to the economy of the community.*

Hamilton justified these new duties by suggesting they would reduce the negative externalities associated with excess consumption of alcohol. Therefore, Hamilton argued that his plan would not only boost the economy through the accumulation of debt, but would also guard against the social ills that could depress the system.

Unlike the Confederation Congress, the more fiscally empowered Congress created by the Constitution had the authority to levy taxes and duties on imports. Hamilton believed that this was a critical part of any plan to secure public credit. Having good credit was also necessary to ensure that the nation could be taken seriously on the world stage. To Hamilton, having control over debt management was both a clear signal of a highly preforming economy and the bedrock of maintaining the principles ratified within the Constitution itself:

> *This reflection derives additional strength from the nature of the debt of the United States. It was the price of liberty. The faith of America has been repeatedly pledged for it, and with solemnities, that give peculiar force to the obligation. There is indeed reason to regret that it has not hitherto been kept; that the necessities of the war, conspiring with inexperience in the subjects of finance, produced direct infractions; and that the subsequent period has been a continued scene of negative violation, or non-compliance. But a diminution of this regret arises from the reflection, that the last seven years have exhibited an earnest and uniform effort, on the part of the government of the nation, to retrieve the national credit, by doing justice to the creditors of the nation; and that the embarrassments of a defective constitution, which defeated this laudable effort, have ceased.*

Secretary Hamilton was not alone in his assessment of how to secure a better standing with credit markets. A great debate had raged over how to both support public credit and manage debt in the preceding seven years since the Treaty of Paris was signed and independence won from Great Britain. How the country dealt with its debts was the primary fiscal challenge of the time and, arguably, remains so today.

Public credit was, and is, an indication of the perceived strength of a nation at home and abroad. How a country manages debt provides insight into the strength of the government, its finances, its economy, and its ability to protect itself. It's true that the framers of the Constitution varied on their positions regarding the qualities of debt expounded upon by Hamilton. Nevertheless, for many of the Founding Fathers, debt was the price of liberty.

However, in the First Report on Public Credit, Hamilton explicitly criticized the government run under the Articles of Confederation and set the tone for change. He had anticipated his critics and built an argument for a new budgetary system based on the unifying principles articulated in the Constitution and foundational to the new nation. In order to accomplish all that Washington had laid out in his first address to Congress, public credit was essential. Hamilton's plan was, in many ways, the first budget of the federal government.

First Acts of the New Government

Reports may have been the blueprints for the new government, but laws were needed to build its foundation. When the first Congress convened on March 4, 1789, it got to work on creating departments, providing money, imposing tariffs to generate revenues, and establishing the infrastructure involved with the management of debt. Processes involving all of these issues that were distinctly American would take shape with time. But many of the early systems of government functions, especially debt management, closely resembled those of Great Britain. The United States was learning how to manage its own resources in an evolving global system where it would compete for political relevance, trade, and credit.

On September 2, 1789, President Washington signed a bill creating the Department of Treasury which also established the offices of the Secretary, the Comptroller, an Auditor, a Treasurer, a Register, and an assistant to the Secretary. The official duties for most of the new posts involved maintenance and oversight of revenue collected and spent. However, the

Secretary's job was to provide ideas or proposals on improving the "management" of revenues and public credit. He was also to provide Congress with accounting statements.

The Secretary of the Treasury had a slightly different role than the other members of Washington's Cabinet. The Department's charter gave the Secretary a legal responsibility to report directly to Congress, providing revenue and expenditure estimates, as well as other reports on the public credit. At the time, only the Departments of War and Foreign Affairs had also been authorized by Congress and neither had such strict reporting requirements as the Treasury. The unique structure of the Treasury Department suggests that Congress intended for the Secretary to act as an executive agent within the legislature. If true, the direct reporting structure is similar to how Roger Morris reported to Congress under the Articles of Confederation.

Congress passed the first bill providing appropriations for the new government exactly twenty-seven days after the Department of Treasury was established. The bill was prepared by the House using estimates they had received from the Treasury. The appropriations act contained a meager 143 words and provided "sums not to exceed" $639 thousand, or what we would call budget authority today. This would be equivalent to about $66 billion in 2017 if measured relative to the size of the economy.

According to the *Principles of Appropriations Law* published by the Government Accountability Office, Congress's authority on appropriations law, an appropriation consists of two things: a direction to an officer of the government to make a payment for a specific purpose or to an entity, and a source of funds for that payment.[6] This first appropriations act was no different. The money was to be collected from import tariffs and requisitions made on states. The payments provided in the bill were to fund civil activities taken on by the government under the Articles of Confederation, the War Department, obligations made by the now exhausted Treasury Board, and pensions provided to veterans from the War of Independence.

The ratification of the Constitution boosted confidence in the prospects of the United States. The new federal government was seen by the markets as having critical powers that hamstrung the country during the Articles of Confederation. The weakness of the Articles had put public finance at a critical point during the 1780s. As the certainty of the new government came into being, the value of public securities rose from 15 cents on the dollar to 30 cents during 1789.[7]

Meanwhile, Hamilton's First Report on Public Credit sparked debate and deadlock in Congress over the assumption of states' debts, with then Secretary of State Thomas Jefferson and James Madison as his primary opponents. Over the next few months, the two opposing parties came to a compromise that would adopt Hamilton's proposal in exchange for relocating the capital to an area along the Potomac River between Virginia and Maryland. The compromise was codified by the adoption of the Residence and Funding Acts enacted in July and August 1790.[8]

Earlier that year, on August 4, 1790, Congress passed its first bill which provided money to pay interest on the debt, its principal, and to service any future loans. Specifically, the act provided a permanent appropriation by making available residual money from import tariffs and proceeds from western land sales, and it gave the president the authority to enter into new loan agreements. The bill also enumerated the assumption of $21.5 million in debts from the states. Virginia, the Carolinas, and Georgia would have $9.8 million in debt assumed by the new federal government. Debt assumed from Maryland, Delaware, Pennsylvania, and New Jersey totaled $4 million. The remaining $7.7 million in debt was from New Hampshire, Massachusetts, Rhode Island, Connecticut, and New York.

To manage the retirement of debt, Congress would approve the first quasi-sinking fund on August 12.[9] The main purpose of this fund was to raise the value of government securities as had been advocated in Hamilton's *First Report on the Public Credit*. The fund's commissioners, responsible for overseeing the management and ultimately the paying down of debt, would be the Vice President, Chief Justice, Secretary of State, Secretary of Treasury, and Attorney General.

Sinking funds were a popular piece of public finance during the eighteenth century and embraced by the American public who "were in a mood to welcome anything that promised to eliminate debt quickly."[10] Sinking funds were dedicated to the "sinking," or the amortization, of the national debt, and financed through dedicated revenue. For instance, in 1716, finance minister Robert Walpole introduced a sinking fund in Great Britain to help manage debt.[11] This sinking fund evolved in the 1740s as Parliament directed certain taxes to the retirement of debt and charged the fund with covering the interest on new loans.[12] However, sinking funds were also political in nature. Specifically, they provided the public with confidence in the idea that debts would be repaid even though the revenues were habitually raided to pay for new spending.[13]

However, the theory of sinking funds evolved in 1772 when Richard Price, a lecturer in London at the Old Jewry Presbyterian meeting house, wrote a widely read pamphlet called an "Appeal to the Public on the Subject of National Debt."[14] Price was influential in both defending the colonies during the American Revolution and later with helping the British government determine a response to the public's "general alarm" over the doubling of debt because of the war.[15]

Price's unique contribution to the idea of a sinking fund was to use interest, rather than only residual tax revenue, to buy additional debt. Price believed that by borrowing money at simple interest rates, the government could then use it toward purchasing government stocks at compounded rates. However, steady operations of the sinking fund were critical to success. Therefore, Price's proposal required that the government buy debt in times of both deficit and surplus regardless of war and peace.

In 1786, Parliament set aside £1 million per year to purchase debt with the intention of using any interest to buy more debt.[16] The sinking fund's operations were also turned over to a board to keep it from being raided by other officials who were short on cash. But sinking funds have several critical flaws. The main problem with Price's plan, as a number of later observers pointed out, was that that the interest from the stocks were based on proceeds from taxes and not on the earnings of the government.[17]

Almost three decades later, in 1813, a mathematics professor named Robert Hamilton published a book called *The National Debt*, which criticized both Price's theory of how a sinking fund should operate and its implementation by the British government. In his critique, Hamilton pointed out that only excess revenue could result in the discharge of debt. He also highlighted the illusory nature of Price's idea to use compound interest to purchase debt. *The National Debt* successfully convinced Parliament to start changing their practice of public finance. By the end of 1829, Parliament had abandoned Price's concept completely as they "denounced a sinking fund fed by loans" and "laid down the axiom that funds for the extinction of debt should not be raised by the creation of it in another shape."[18]

But both Robert Morris and Alexander Hamilton would propose sinking funds based on the state of public finance in Britain in the 1780s and 1790s.[19] In July 1782, Robert Morris outlined a proposal to address the slipping public credit.[20] Morris's plan was twofold: Congress would need to first retire all paper money that was issued during the war, and afterward, develop dedicated revenue to fund the interest on the debt. Morris proposed a 5 percent tariff, a land tax, a poll tax, and an excise tax on distilled liquors. Morris's plea for dedicated taxes to fund the debt would fall to the uncooperative states; however, Congress responded with a resolution calling on any surplus revenue received from the states to be applied toward a sinking fund.[21] Later in the same session of Congress, they would resolve that it was necessary to establish permanent taxes or duties to retire the debt.[22]

By 1790, things were different. Congress now had the power to tax, an authority granted by the Constitution. The first quasi-sinking fund was to be financed by revenues from excess tariffs on imports and tonnage in a single year, as well as any proceeds from western land sales.[23] Because there was no significant permanent appropriation (western land sales generated only a small sum of revenue), the sinking fund did not look exactly like that of Richard Price's vision. However, much like the executive authority encouraged under Price's sinking fund, the president was also authorized to borrow up to $2 million at an interest rate not exceeding 5 percent to be used for the purchase of additional debt.

Finally, it is imperative to say that the impetus for the first quasi-sinking fund was Hamilton's First Report on Public Credit where he mentions the idea of a sinking fund along with a proposal to amortize debt on a thirty-four-year cycle.[24] In the bill enacted in August 1790, Congress authorized repayment of up to 8 percent of the debt at 6 percent interest, which would have repaid debt on a twenty-four-year cycle.[25] Jefferson, a commissioner of the new sinking fund, believed that debt should be repaid within one generation or within nineteen years.[26]

In his Second Report on Public Credit, sent to Congress on December 14, 1790, Hamilton would reference the passage of these two debt bills, marking a significant legislative victory for the Treasury Secretary. In that report, he explicitly tied his case for a national bank to the execution of the debt bills passed that August. At this point, however, Hamilton did not believe that a national bank was necessary outside of providing specie. Hamilton advocated that Congress should direct the president to buy up to $2 million in stock (or roughly one-fifth of the total shares) in the new bank on behalf of the US government. He additionally outlined the management structure of the bank, which would be run by a twenty-five-man board of directors, five of which would be chosen by the government.

Edmund Randolph, the Attorney General, had been previously critical of plans to institute a national bank that had been supported by John

Francis Mercer, a delegate to the Confederation Congress for Virginia and later governor of Maryland. In a letter to James Madison in November 1782, Randolph's disapproval of a bank was based on the question of whether it was effective or necessary.[27] Randolph had recognized that banks brought opportunities, like lending and printing money to expand trade, but also created downside risks such as going out of business.

Jefferson, too, was skeptical.[28] His specific criticisms included that the national bank would crowd-out the development of state banks and would likely empower the wealthy living in Northern cities. Jefferson also argued that the Constitution lacked the explicit authority granting Congress the power to create a bank. However, in February of 1791, legislation creating the first national bank would pass Congress, met with much less resistance than Hamilton's earlier proposal to assume state debts.

During this time, Congress also began a process of making ad hoc appropriations based on its work with the Treasury and the executive departments themselves. On behalf of the Treasury Department, Hamilton would submit itemized requests to Congress. Meanwhile, executive officials would make their own petitions of Congress through an uncoordinated but still routine process. The Committee of the Whole House would debate these requests and, often, approve the operations of the executive.

Over a five-year period, the House redirected roughly 300 petitions to Hamilton from individuals who were seeking money through these spending bills.[29] The House would evaluate each claim based on Hamilton's assessment. This is yet another example of how Congress considered Hamilton an employee, if not a member, of the legislature.

The spending bills also began to evolve in complexity. The appropriations bill for 1790 included direction for a new lighthouse to be built at Cape Henry, Virginia using money from tariffs on imports and tonnage. It also included reimbursements for Jehoiakim M'Toksin, who had assisted General Sullivan as an interpreter in his expedition in New York during the War of Independence. M'Toksin had petitioned the House for compensation earlier than February. The bill contained payments to other individuals to fulfill their petitions as well.[30]

By 1791, Congress was appropriating money to carry out war with Native American tribes, money to compensate wounded veterans, and money to pay for servicing the debt.[31] There would never again be an appropriations bill as short, limited, or open ended as the bill providing money for the first year of the new government. Congress began using appropriations to enact their will on the policy of the federal government.

This included dictating to the departments how much money was available for specific goods or activities.

Under the second Congress, beginning with the spending bill for general operations in 1792, deficiency appropriations began to appear. Deficiency appropriations are payments to departments based on previous appropriations that fell short. In its first appropriations bills, Congress had provided similar reimbursements based on select petitions. For instance, people who had worked on behalf of the government had received payment for their goods or services previously rendered. But in 1792, Congress additionally began back paying departments for previous appropriations that fell short. Over the next seventy years, these deficiency appropriations would rise in significance as executive branch departments learned to push their own constitutional authorities by relying on deficiency appropriations.

In January 1792, Hamilton issued a report calling for a permanent sinking fund to address the debt. In May of that year, Congress passed a bill expanding revenue available to the fund. That bill also allowed government stock held by the administration to draw interest and "thus bound the government to a policy of amortizing, even if it compelled at the same time to create new debt at higher interest."[32]

Toward the beginning of his tenure at Treasury, Alexander Hamilton tried to manage each of the loans separately.[33] However, he ran into complications. His fix was to issue government stock based on the general authority granted by Congress.

At the same time, the national debt became a growing concern as the sinking fund proved to be ill-equipped to meet its purpose. Between 1790 and 1794, seven loans were made by banks in Holland for purchases of the sinking fund at a total of $9.4 million. However, about $3 million was used for general expenses as the young government found itself short on cash with a high demand for resources. This was exacerbated by a financial market panic in 1792 induced by a credit bubble.[34] By 1795, President Washington called on Congress "for a definitive plan for the redemption of public credit."[35]

Hamilton's response to Washington's call was the Final Report on the Public Credit. And Congress's response to Hamilton's report was its near-complete adoption on March 3, 1795, in "An act making further provision for the support of Public Credit, and for the redemption of Public Debt." The bill further expanded the appropriations available to the sinking fund and made them permanent until the entire national debt was extinguished. Furthermore, the resources would be treated as private property and unavailable for other uses. Finally, the bill gave foreign creditors the ability to exchange government stock for new stock valued at one half a percent higher than what they had on hand. This was intended to extricate the Treasury Department from debt while turning over management to the sinking funds commission. However, conversion was also seen by critics of the system as a path to permanent indebtedness.[36]

Despite the fact that Hamilton called the 1795 sinking fund "a main pillar in the fabric of our public credit," the exchange of stock was generally a failure.[37] During the latter half of the Washington Administration, most of the French debt was converted to the new stock. But the Dutch, who had matured stock, failed to convert. This put the Treasury on the hook for $12.2 million in debt that they had not accounted for when establishing the revised sinking fund in 1795. The fund's troubles were exacerbated by the fact that the United States Bank could not lend to meet the demand of the growing government, forcing the commission to borrow additional money from European credit markets. Finally, the sinking fund was undermined in 1796 when United States Bank stock, the dividends of which provided a primary source of revenue for the fund, was sold.

In 1802, several revisions were made to the sinking fund based on the recommendations of Treasury Secretary Albert Gallatin. One of these revisions was a provision of what amounted to $10 million in dedicated funds to the sinking fund. Additionally, the commissioners of the fund were granted the authority to refinance the Dutch debt through a series of short-term loans.[38] The reforms also converted all debt service over to the sinking fund. The fund would begin reducing the debt until new stock was created two years later for the Louisiana Purchase.[39]

When Gallatin reviewed the status of the debt repayment policy through the sinking fund at the end of 1811, it was judged to be fairly successful—even at a time when the country was expanding, and the civil government was growing. From 1791 until the Mexican American War, the domestic budget grew at a steady exponential rate.[40] Meanwhile, the inherited debt from the American Revolution through 1791 that amounted to $76.8 million was reduced by the Washington and Adams Administrations by $4 million. However, an additional $7.2 million was added. During the Jefferson and early-Madison Administrations, over $46 million of the inherited debt was reduced through the sinking fund though more than $11 million was added for the Louisiana Purchase.

Hamilton's Fall and the Rise of Congressional Committees

Congress and the Treasury Secretary had spent the early years of the new government developing a budgeting process that was largely defined by the immediate demands placed on the government. And it seemed to be a success. Public credit was improving, and the House of Representatives was working with Hamilton to establish a fiscal policy and process. However, the system functioned primarily because of the individuals involved.

In his fourth annual address to Congress, Washington reported that the government had been able to secure new loans from creditors in Antwerp and Amsterdam, which were "confirmations of the high state of our credit." Furthermore, Washington noted that "a strong hope that the state of the national finances is now sufficiently matured to enable you to enter upon a systematic and effectual arrangement for the regular redemption and discharge of the public debt.... No measure can be more desirable, whether viewed with an eye to its intrinsic importance or to the general sentiment and wish of the nation."

Along with the new process avoiding any perception of financial emergency, new dramas ascended through long-standing disagreements over executive power. Early in 1794, William Giles, a Congressman from Virginia, attempted to censure Secretary Hamilton, suggesting that he had exceeded the legislative authority to secure loans on behalf of the government and had operated independently of the president. In response to this political question about Hamilton's actions, the House determined "a committee, consisting of fifteen members, be appointed to inquire whether, any, or what, further or other revenues are necessary for the support of public credit; and if further revenues are necessary, to report the ways and means."[41]

The intention of this new committee was to provide explicit oversight over both the government's finances and the Treasury. Members of the House sought to prohibit Hamilton from speaking directly on his reports to the entire legislature while the select committee of ways and means had him appear at least once during the Third Congress. Control over the purse was at stake and Hamilton was a threat.

But by this time, Hamilton had otherwise permanently changed the country's fiscal policy and outlook, both directly and indirectly, under his five years at its helm. Hamilton had proposed increasing tariff rates to protect domestic manufacturers and Congress had obliged. There were now channels for managing public debt which gave investors additional confidence in the new nation. There was a system for providing detailed estimates on how much money was being generated by different types of revenues and what the government would cost. Finally, there was a national bank that issued its own notes, made loans, and expanded the money supply. Hamilton had believed that all of these things were necessary to drive economic growth and domestic production while ensuring good credit for years to come.

However, Congress was beginning to assert itself in new ways over what they understood were their enumerated responsibilities. Congress was taking back its power over the country's fiscal system through their oversight of Hamilton and their resolve asserted through appropriations. Hamilton left the office in January 1795. His Comptroller of the Treasury, Oliver Wolcott, Jr., would take over as Secretary the next month.

While Treasury was undergoing its regime change, a highly controversial international conflict, and subsequent resolution politically complicated the appropriations process. On November 19, 1794, representatives from the United States and Great Britain entered into the Treaty of Amity, Commerce, and Navigation. Known as Jay's Treaty, the agreement sought to end long-run disputes regarding implementation of the Treaty of Paris which had ended the War of Independence and various practices of the two countries during the period following the war.

Jay's Treaty was extremely unpopular with the American public and enthusiastically criticized by former members of Washington's Cabinet, including Jefferson, who had resigned as Secretary of State at the end of 1793. The treaty granted the United States admission to British markets but significantly restricted access to lucrative trading centers in the British West Indies. Furthermore, the treaty allowed the British, who were at war with France at the time, to confiscate goods both to and from the United States from France. Other outstanding issues, such as the resolution of outstanding British debt granted to the states before the War of Independence, were sent to arbitration. President Washington submitted the treaty to the Senate in June 1795 in an attempt to finally resolve the issue of peace with Britain.

The treaty passed the Senate with a final vote of 20 to 10 on June 24. However, the House would still need to provide money for the implementation of the treaty. What transpired was the first real conflict over the

House's role in implementing treaties and the extent to which its power of the purse could be exercised. Was the House able to assert its own will over the Senate in financing treaty obligations? What information would the House have access to in its own deliberations over funding treaties? These questions would be addressed in the ensuing battle over politics and the weight placed on precedent from treaties.

At the end of the first session of the Fourth Congress in March 1796, Edward Livingston, a Congressman from New York, offered the following resolution asking that President Washington turn over documents associated with Jay's Treaty:

> *Resolved, That the President of the United States be requested to lay before this House a copy of the instructions given to the Minister of the United States who negotiated the Treaty with Great Britain, communicated by his Message of the first instant, together with the correspondence and other documents relative to the said Treaty.*[42]

Washington wrote to Hamilton that he had considered complying with the House resolution.[43] However, the new Secretary of State, Timothy Pickering, drafted a letter for Washington declining the request based on constitutional delegations of authority. Specifically, the letter stated that the Constitution had granted the President with the authority to negotiate treaties with the advice and consent of the Senate. Furthermore, the letter highlighted the benefits of secrecy over negotiating such matters. The House took the President's letter reasonably well and voted on April 7 to approve of his message.

However, the appropriations situation was unresolved. The office with control over the money held both fiscal and political power. In this case, it was the House that held the power—or at least, that was what they believed. On April 14, Congressman Samuel Maclay of Pennsylvania offered a motion to make it the policy of the House that based on Washington's letter that it was not "expedient at this time to concur in passing the laws necessary for carrying the said Treaty into effect."[44] In a letter to Jefferson on April 18, Madison wrote that the opponents of Jay's Treaty had rallied around this position and that debate over the appropriations had started.[45]

The following day, April 19, a frustrated Vice President Adams wrote to his wife Abigail about how members of the House were inappropriately using their power over money to force their will over a treaty:

> *The Pride of Madison, Giles, Baldwin, ill broking the Superiour Powers of the Senate, Emulating the Dignity and Lustre of Members of that Body, ardently Struggling to Rival an Elsworth a King &c These are feelings that our Lawgivers in framing our Constitution did not advert to.—The Elections of the two Houses by such different Bodies as the People & their Legislators, will always leave this difficulty in full force. The Leading Members of the House, such as Madison & Baldwin should have been e'er now senators.*[46]

As Adams points out, the Constitution does not have a direct role for the House in the treaty process. But the House had found a way to assert themselves regardless. Meanwhile, Adams became very pessimistic about the situation: "Some persons still think the H[ouse] will comply – But there is an Inveteracy and Obstinacy on this occasion as I scarcely ever Saw."[47]

On April 20, New York Senator Rufus King wrote to Alexander Hamilton that the merchants of Philadelphia had started a petition in support of funding the treaty, but that the opponents had their own petitions as well.[48] Hamilton would involve himself in a similar petition from merchants in New York that would be sent to King with "more than 3200 signers" on April 24.[49] Hamilton also published a broadside to New Yorkers attacking Congressional opponents of the treaty for a breach of the Constitution through a usurpation of power away from the President and Senate. Hamilton placed the House's reluctance to appropriate money for the treaty in clear terms: "The truth most assuredly is, Fellow Citizens, that the Constitution and Peace are on one scale – the overthrow of the Constitution and War in the other. What do you prefer?"[50] George Washington and John Jay were heroes of The War. Why, asked Hamilton, should their intentions be questioned now that they have finally closed out hostilities with Britain?

But Hamilton's statement was more than a defense of Washington and Jay. It was an attack on the position of the Democratic Republican party. To Hamilton, the House was not making a principled statement, but rather, fighting an older political battle with Hamilton and his allies. Hamilton went on, "Do not second the ambition of a Virginia Faction, constantly endeavoring to govern the United States – a Faction of which some of your Representatives are the Dupes – and are sacrificing very essential Interests of the State of New York, the recovery of your western Posts, the Furr [sic] trade, and the Trade of the two Canadas; all which from the course of the Lakes and Rivers must necessarily fall into the lap of the City of New York. May heaven by your guide and Preserver."[51] All that was good and right was with Washington. All that was wrong was with the other Virginians.

Madison confided to Jefferson that the petitions of the merchants might "triumph over the popular sentiment."[52] In addition, Madison warned that other businesses, such as the insurance companies, had stopped conducting business to "alarm the public" over the failure to appropriate money for the treaty. Banks were collecting signatures for the petitions like "Highwayman with a pistol demanding the purse." If the appropriation fails, "the game will be played in other forms" with the Senate potentially coupling Jay's treaty with another with Spain. However, support for the opposition was slipping, while special interests grew and became mobilized.

On May 1, 1796, the New York Senator Rufus King wrote to Alexander Hamilton that the Committee on the Whole had decided to make the appropriation and thus sent the decision to the House:

> *In committee of the whole on Friday it was resolved by the casting vote of Muhlenburgh the chairman, to make provision by Law for carrying the Treaty with England into Effect. Yesterday the Resolution of the Committee of the whole passed in the House by 51 against 48. A proposition to prefix to the Resolution a Preamble declaring the Treaty to be "injurious to the Interest" of the US and assigning the short duration of its temporary articles as a reason why it should be permitted to go into Effect, was negatived by 50 against 49.*[53]

On the same day, Madison blamed the success of the treaty's implementation on the organization of special interests, especially those who were heard most loudly by the seat of power: "An appeal to the people on any pending measure, can never be more than an appeal to those in the neighbourhood of the Govt. & to the Banks, the Merchts. & the dependents & expectants of the Govt. at a distance."[54] Congress would go on to pass an appropriation of $80,808 to implement the treaty on May 6.

Preparing for War

Washington, in his farewell address, made a plea to "avoid the necessity of overgrown military establishments," which were "hostile to republican liberty." He understood that military strength was derived from economic strength, for the key to having the necessary resources when they were in need was to maintain a good public credit. Through their efforts, Washington and the other Founders had made great strides toward economic and national security. But having a strong economy wasn't sufficient. A public financial system, along with an accountable process for servicing the debt, was needed.

In the early years, appropriations for military and civil activities were handled together. For instance, the appropriations bill for 1793 provided money for the compensation of officials, rent for government offices, previous deficiencies in appropriations, firewood and stationary, and new lighthouses. It included money to hire clerks and people to oversee the western lands, to repair buoys and piers, and hydrometers for use in the ports by the customs officials to determine whether imports were contaminated with salt water. It also included money for arsenals, cartridge boxes, guns, cannon, equipment for the cavalry, and anything else that one would need to campaign in the eighteenth century. Importantly, these early appropriations bills also provided the president with borrowing authority so that he could afford to pay for all the new spending in excess of tariff revenues collected.

But in 1794, appropriations for the military and the "civil list" were split into two bills. Though, they did not start that way. On January 10, the House went into the Committee of the Whole to consider appropriations for that year. William Giles offered a resolution that had been agreed upon earlier by the Committee of the Whole to separate appropriations for the military into a different bill. His reasoning was that the resources for members of Congress, and other officials, were necessary for the conduct of government business. The passage of appropriations for the civil functions was routine and uncontroversial. Therefore, Congress should avoid tying up the authorization for spending on basic functions.[55]

Madison and John Nicholas, another Virginian, concurred with Giles's recommendation. According to the House Records, Nicholas suggested that the House immediately pass a bill to cover the costs of those in Congress, as "it was not fair to suppose that every gentleman in that House came to town with as much money in his pocket as would clear his expenses."[56] Madison, on the other hand, believed that unlike appropriations for civil activities, military appropriations would also bring debate. Military spending was too controversial to weigh down other issues.

Madison thought it was important to separate funding from the "ways and means" needed to pay for the new spending. According to a report from the *Philadelphia Gazette* on January 14, 1794, Madison said during the deliberations over the bill that issues of spending and ways and means were so distinct that they should be considered separately. He reiterated that this was why the Constitution had treated them separately. Thomas Fitzsimons, a Member of the House from Pennsylvania, responded that there was a difference between providing for borrowing authority and directing anticipatory revenues toward new spending.

Several months later, Congress would resolve this issue over appropriations by passing two separate bills for the funding of the general government (enacted March 14) and the military (enacted March 21). On March 4, the same day that the House's Committee of the Whole approved the appropriations for the military, it also approved a new loan in a separate bill for $1 million to fund the new spending.

On March 27, 1794, a bill was enacted authorizing the construction of six ships. Four of the ships would have forty-four cannons apiece while the other two would have thirty-six cannons. The bill also authorized the recruitment of sailors and set their pay and rations. This is widely seen as the act that established the US Navy. The purpose of the act was intended to provide a defense for American ships sailing who were in jeopardy of falling victim to piracy along the Barbary Coast in Africa. In fact, the act ends with an exit clause that would cease construction of the ships should these hostilities conclude. Of course, that did not happen, and the United States went on to fight two wars with the provinces of the Ottoman Empire between 1801 and 1805 as well as in 1815.

In 1796, Congress authorized the continued construction of two of the forty-four gunships and one of the thirty-six gunships authorized two years earlier. About eleven months later, on March 1797, the annual appropriations bill for the military included additional appropriations for the new Navy after the French government violated American neutrality due to frustrations over Jay's Treaty and payments regarding old debts. Specifically, the new naval appropriation contained the following:

> *For the pay and subsistence of three captains in the naval department, and for the pay of laborers employed in taking care of the frigates, the sum of five thousand dollars.*
>
> *For finishing the frigates United States, Constitution and Constellation, the sum of one hundred and seventy-two thousand dollars.*[57]

There was, however, debate over how and when to pay for the new military appropriations. Thomas Blout, a Congressman from North

Carolina, proposed the creation of a select committee of ways and means to take up the matter rather than consideration as the entire House. William Giles suggested delaying the appropriations bill until after Congress determined how to pay for the new funds. But the House decided to create the committee which began the consideration of several new excise taxes.

The cost of the US Navy in 1797 was about $8.4 billion in today's dollars measured relative to the size of the economy. However, only three ships were ready for action. By the end of Jefferson's Administration (1801–1809) the navy would grow to an annual cost of $2.5 million while the rest of the military would cost $2.8 million, or equivalent today to $71 and $80 billion measured as a share of the economy. By 1810, the Navy would also be receiving its own appropriation separate from the rest of the military even though the Department of the Navy was established as a separate entity from the Department of War in 1798.

The appropriations bill for the Departments of War and the Navy for 1810 provides budget authority down to the measure of a cent for some activities. If Congress were to use such specificity today, they would limit the budgets of departments down to a couple hundred dollars. However, Congress rarely provides any more detail beyond the tens of thousands of dollars.

There were necessary tradeoffs for supporting a military this size. In a letter sent to President Jefferson from Albert Gallatin on the eve of his confirmation as Secretary of the Treasury, Gallatin provides estimates of the amount by which the army and navy would need to be reduced in order to lower taxes and still have the ability to pay down the debt to Britain and Holland.[58] Jefferson needed the help of Gallatin, who had initially made a name for himself by opposing Hamilton's fiscal program while a Pennsylvanian legislator, in order to fulfill a campaign promise to eliminate internal excise taxes on alcohol and land while retiring all the government debt.[59] The plan established by Gallatin would retire all outstanding debt within sixteen years, but it would require downsizing the military and setting aside over 75 percent of tariff revenues for debt reduction each year.

Jefferson has been criticized with executing a policy to shrink the military during his administration on the eve of the War of 1812.[60] Compared to the end of the Adams Administration, Jefferson would reduce spending on the navy by 40 percent, although the budget for the army would grow by 25 percent. This would leave total spending on the military in 1810 at around 5 percent lower than when Jefferson took office.

At this point, there was a standing army, navy, and marines with sizable budgets. The cost of the military was driving domestic tax policy and new debt. It had also become clear that national security was a complicated matter when not under the protection of Great Britain and while threats were not going away. By 1802, the House had created a permanent committee of ways and means to consider ways to generate revenue to support the government.

In January 1812, six months before the start of the war with Great Britain, Congress passed a bill that increased the size of the military and provided additional funding. A month later, they would provide another appropriation for $1 million to raise a volunteer military corps and the regular appropriation of $4.6 million for the year. This most significant increase in any line-item from the previous year was in the expected costs of additional ordinance. In March, Congress passed another appropriation for $500,000 in support of protecting maritime commerce. Then in April, Congress passed another appropriation to assist the Quartermaster of the Department of War by providing him with skilled workers. The United States was preparing for war.

However, these preparations were not always enough to meet demand. There were routine occasions when President Madison's officials would be put in positions to purchase supplies for war without the authorization of Congress. This came to a head at the end of 1812, when Congress refused to pass an appropriation until Madison resolved management issues with Paul Hamilton, the Secretary of the Navy. Hamilton had, among other things, entering into contracts to buy equipment without Congressional authorization.

Hamilton wrote to Madison in September 1811 that he did not have enough money to properly defend the harbors in Norfolk, Virginia, and Wilmington, North Carolina.[61] But if Madison approved of increasing the strengths of armament, Hamilton said that he would proceed regardless. Madison would later ask Charles Goldsborough, a clerk for the Department of Navy, for a list of "vessels purchased and built, since the last session of Congress, without being previously authorized by Law."[62] In Goldsborough's response, he claimed the state of accounting books from the Department of Navy had been in such poor order that it was difficult to determine what had been bought and what it cost.

Though Madison had disapproved of Hamilton's management of the Navy and went so far as to request his resignation in December 1812, it was not uncommon for executives to enter into obligations without the explicit approval of Congress. In fact, on the second to last day of the Jefferson Administration, Congress had expanded the authority of departments to transfer appropriations between types of expenditures as long as the appropriations were not used by another department and Congress was in recess.[63] For instance, the president could move money from supplies to the repair of ships as long as the total appropriation for the Department of Navy did not change.

However, the same bill also required the executive departments to submit to Congress a statement of transfers as well as new contracts and purchases that had been made during the recess. This reflected a significant legislative shift in authority from Congress to the president over the control of resources. But the move was also generally aligned with the appropriations process up until this point. The Administration had all of the information on the costs of executing laws and implementing its policies. These were formulated in the requests made directly on Congress for appropriations required to run the government. The role of Congress was to function as a check on that process through the restrictions that it placed on the executive and by oversight.

The Limits of Power

On September 14, 1810, John B. Colvin wrote a letter to Thomas Jefferson with a series of questions regarding a memoir that Colvin was writing on behalf of General James Wilkinson.[64] Jefferson had left the office of the presidency a year and a half earlier. Colvin wanted to know if Jefferson believed that there were times when "officers in respectable stations" would need to act beyond the law.

The context of Colvin's letter was Aaron Burr's plan to lead a revolt to create an independent country in what are now parts of Texas and Mexico. Wilkinson had been the most senior officer in the army under Jefferson and Governor of the Louisiana Territory. He had also been known as a co-conspirator with Burr in the past. But Wilkinson was being publicly criticized for detaining those accused of aiding Burr without a trial.[65] The objective of Colvin's inquiry was whether Jefferson believed that Wilkinson acted on behalf of a greater good that transcends the law?

Jefferson had already defended Wilkinson publicly. But Jefferson's response to Colvin includes several important points, all of which are insightful to understanding the history of budgeting politics. He begins the response with:

> *A strict observance of the written laws is doubtless one of the high duties of a good citizen, but it is not the highest. The laws of necessity, of self-preservation, of saving our country when in danger, are of higher obligation. To lose our country by scrupulous adherence to written law, would be to lose the law itself, with life, liberty, and property & all those who ae enjoying them with us.*[66]

In other words, the principles of the law demand a higher defense than the law itself.[67] Jefferson then gives three examples to support his claim. First, he mentions that Washington had to destroy private property to defeat the British at the battles of Germantown and Yorktown. Second, Thomas Nelson, Governor of Virginia, "took horses, carriages, provisions & even men," to solidify the army. And third, a ship at sea takes provisions by force in order to survive.

Jefferson goes on to provide a "hypothetical" case of the president being presented with an opportunity to purchase Florida without an appropriation for Congress. However, the example was not completely hypothetical. In 1805, John Randolph, a Congressman from Virginia and Chairman of the Committee of Ways and Means had blocked an appropriation of $2 million to purchase West Florida from the Spanish in a deal that ultimately collapsed. In Jefferson's response to Colvin, he suggests that the president go ahead with the purchase without an appropriation, knowing that Congress would eventually provide the money "to have secured the good to his country, and to have trusted to their justice the transgression of the law." Acquiring Florida would prove strategic in order to secure the port at New Orleans and to protect shipping lanes.

Jefferson concludes with another historical reference to the Chesapeake–Leopard affair of 1807, in which a British ship attacked and boarded the USS Chesapeake, one of the first American frigates. Jefferson explains to Colvin that the United States did not have enough money appropriated following that episode to provide adequate protection for other vessels; however, the navy made its necessary purchases anyway. The administration then made a request to Congress for additional resources and provided a justification of expenditures, and the administration was subsequently granted an appropriation.

Jefferson's letter to Colvin has been cited many times by legal scholars debating presidential prerogative outside the Constitution.[68] That said, the Jefferson Administration did not purchase Louisiana or Florida absent an appropriation from Congress. After the ratification of the Louisiana Purchase on October 20, 1803, the House moved to provide an appropriation for $11.250 million and assumed French debts for the remainder of the balance of $15 million. By November 10, the House had both appropriated the money and authorized Jefferson to take possession of the land. In fact, Jefferson himself believed that a constitutional amendment would be required to permit the acquisition of Louisiana, a position from which he disagreed with others in his government, including Secretary of State James Madison.

Summary

Unlike in subsequent eras, the early period of budgeting history in the United States was not dominated by the legislature.[69] Rather it was defined by a divided set of responsibilities that at first relied on trust in a time of necessity. When trust broke down, Congress would use oversight and increase the level of bureaucracy, including the creation of its own institutions in the form of new committees. But power would shift back to the executive when the times called for it to do so. First, the power of the budget process resided with Washington's Administration to secure the country's standing in credit markets. And then, power shifted back toward the executive during the Jefferson and Madison Administrations to expand the territory and protect the country from foreign threats.

Furthermore, debt was generally seen as a necessary means for providing for the needs of the country. Both Hamilton and Jefferson agreed that debt retirement was the correct economic policy, but disagreed on the time frame and actual mechanics for getting it done. Far from the protectionist that he is sometimes portrayed as, Hamilton understood that the country's standing in foreign debt markets was critical to long-run hopes of success for the new country. Jefferson, on the other hand, showed how complicated the distribution of budgetary powers under the Constitution was in practice. Jefferson's dialogue would foreshadow many debates to come. The budget policy of the period was shaped by domestic politics and differing notions on the type of federal government that the young country should have, but also the economic theory of the time and external threats. This would be a continuing theme.

Notes

1. U.S. Congress, *Journal of the House of Representatives of the United States*, 1st Cong., 1st sess., September 21, 1789.

   Note: The House passed resolution reads "That the Secretary of the Treasury be directed to apply to the Supreme Executives of the several States, for statements of their public debts; of the funds provided for the payment, in whole or in part, of the principal and interest thereof; and of the amount of the loan-office certificates, or other public securities of the United States, in the State Treasuries respectively; and that be report to the House such of the said documents as he may obtain, at the next session of Congress."
2. George Washington, January 8, 1790, in *First Annual Address to Congress*, ed. Gerhard Peters and John T. Woolley (The American Presidency Project).
3. Over his five-year tenure as Secretary of the Treasury, Hamilton wrote four reports on public credit. The third report that is not discussed in the chapter recommended a mercantilist system supported by tariffs to protect domestic industry along with subsidies. The fourth report recommends many of the same proposals found in the other reports to stabilize funding for public debt and considers the importance of private credit.
4. The weakening of state bargaining power was something brought up by Jefferson, Madison, and Randolph – all Virginians.
5. U.S. Congress, *Journal of the House of Representatives of the United States*, 1st Cong., 2nd sess., February 11, 1790.
6. Government Accountability Office, *Principles of Federal Appropriations Law*, 4th edition, GAO-16-464SP (Washington, DC: March 2016).
7. Edward A. Ross, "Sinking Funds," *Publications of the American Economic Association* 7, no. 4/5 (1892): 9–106.
8. E. James Ferguson, *The Power of the Purse: A History of American Public Finance, 1776–1790* (Chapel Hill, NC: The University of North Carolina Press, 1961).
9. Ross, "Sinking Funds."
10. Donald F. Swanson and Andrew P. Trout, "Alexander Hamilton's Hidden Sinking Fund," *The William and Mary Quarterly* 49, no. 1 (1992): 108–116.
11. Ibid.
12. Ross, "Sinking Funds."
13. Ibid.
14. Goncalo L. Fonseca, "Dr. Richard Price, 1723–1791," *The History of Economic Thought*, http://www.hetwebsite.net/het/profiles/rprice.htm
15. Richard Cooper, "William Pitt, Taxation, and the Needs of War," *Journal of British Studies* 22, no. 1 (1982): 94–103.

16. Ross, "Sinking Funds."
17. Ibid.
18. Ibid.
19. Albert S. Bolles, *Financial History of the United States from 1774 to 1789*, vol. I (New York, NY: Augustus M. Kelly Publishers, 1969).
20. Ross, "Sinking Funds."
21. Ibid.
22. Ibid.
23. Swanson and Trout, "Alexander Hamilton's Hidden Sinking Fund."
24. Ibid.
25. Ibid.
26. Ibid.
27. Edmund Randolph to James Madison, November 16, 1782, in *The Papers of James Madison*, vol. 5, ed. William T. Hutchinson and William M. E. Rachal (Chicago: The University of Chicago Press, 1967), 280–287.
28. Paul Leicester Ford, *The Federalist: A Commentary on the Constitution of the United States by Alexander Hamilton, James Madison, and John Jay* (New York: Henry Holt and Company, 1898).
29. U.S. Congress, House of Representatives, Committee on Energy and Commerce, *Petitions, Memorials, and Other Documents Submitted for Consideration of Congress: March 4, 1789 to December 14, 1795*, staff study prepared for the use of the Committee on Energy and Commerce, 99th Cong., 2nd sess., 1986, Committee Print 99-A.
30. U.S. Congress, *The Public Statutes at Large of the United States of America, From the Organization of the Government in 1789, to March 3, 1845*, vol. I, ed. Richard Peters (Boston: Charles C. Little and James Brown, 1945), 105.
31. Ibid, 190.
32. Ross, "Sinking Funds."
33. Ibid.
34. Richard Sylla, Robert E. Wright, and David J. Cowen, "Alexander Hamilton, Central Banker: Crisis Management during the U.S. Financial Panic of 1792," *The Business History Review* 83, no. 1 (2009): 61–86.
35. Ibid.
36. Robert M. Jennings, Donald F. Swanson, and Andrew P. Trout, "Alexander Hamilton's Tontine Proposal," *The William and Mary Quarterly* 45, no. 1 (1988): 107–115.
37. Alexander Hamilton, "The Examination Number II [New York, December 21, 1801]," in *The Papers of Alexander Hamilton*, vol. 25, ed. Harold C. Syrett (New York: Columbia University Press, 1977), 458–464.
38. Ross, "Sinking Funds."
39. Ibid.

40. Bryan D. Jones, László Zalányi, and Péter Érdi, "An Integrated Theory of Budgetary Politics and Some Empirical Tests: The U.S. National Budget, 1791–2010," *American Journal of Political Science* 58, no. 3 (2014): 561–578.
41. Kennon and Rogers, *The Committee on Ways and Means: A Bicentennial History.*
42. U.S. Congress, *Journal of the House of Representatives of the United States*, 4th Cong., 1st sess., March 23, 1796.
43. George Washington to Alexander Hamilton, March 31, 1796, in *The Papers of Alexander Hamilton*, vol. 20, ed. Harold C. Syrett (New York: Columbia University Press, 1974), 103–105.
44. U.S. Congress, *Journal of the House of Representatives of the United States*, 4th Cong., 1st sess., April 14, 1796.
45. James Madison to Thomas Jefferson, April 18, 1796, in *The Papers of Thomas Jefferson*, vol. 29, ed. Barbara B. Oberg (Princeton, NJ: Princeton University Press, 2002), 70–71.
46. John Adams to Abigail Adams, April 19, 1796, in *The Adams Papers, Adams Family Correspondence*, vol. 11, ed. Margaret A. Hogan, C. James Taylor, Sara Martin, Neal E. Millikan, Hobson Woodward, Sara B. Sikes, and Gregg L. Lint (Cambridge, MA: Harvard University Press, 2013), 257–259.
47. Ibid.
48. Rufus King to Alexander Hamilton, April 20, 1796, in *The Papers of Alexander Hamilton*, vol. 20, ed. Harold C. Syrett (New York: Columbia University Press, 1974), 124–126; Rufus King to Alexander Hamilton, April 17–18, 1796, *in The Papers of Alexander Hamilton*, vol. 20, ed. Harold C. Syrett (New York: Columbia University Press, 1974), 121–123.
49. Alexander Hamilton to Rufus King, April 24, 1796, in *The Papers of Alexander Hamilton*, vol. 20, ed. Harold C. Syrett (New York: Columbia University Press, 1974), 136–137.
50. Alexander Hamilton to the Citizens Who Shall be Convened This Day in the Fields in the City of New York, April 22, 1796, in *The Papers of Alexander Hamilton*, vol. 20, ed. Harold C. Syrett (New York: Columbia University Press, 1974), 131–134.
51. Ibid.
52. James Madison to Thomas Jefferson, April 23, 1796, in *The Papers of James Madison*, vol. 16, ed. J. C. A. Stagg, Thomas A. Mason, and Jeanne K. Sisson (Charlottesville: University Press of Virginia, 1989), 335–336.
53. Rufus King to Alexander Hamilton, May 1, 1796, in *The Papers of Alexander Hamilton*, vol. 20, ed. Harold C. Syrett (New York: Columbia University Press, 1974), 149–151.

54. James Madison to Thomas Jefferson, May 1, 1796, in *The Papers of James Madison*, vol. 16, ed. J. C. A. Stagg, Thomas A. Mason, and Jeanne K. Sisson (Charlottesville: University Press of Virginia, 1989), 342–344.
55. U.S. Congress, *Journal of the House of Representatives of the United States*, 3rd Cong., 1st sess., June 10, 1794.
56. Ibid.
57. U.S. Congress, "An Act making appropriations for the Military and Naval Establishments, for the year one thousand seven hundred and ninety-seven," in *Annals of the Congress of the United States* (Washington, DC: Gales and Seaton, 1849).
58. Albert Gallatin to Thomas Jefferson, "Enclosure III: Estimate of Military Expenditures, 14 March 1801, in *The Papers of Thomas Jefferson*, vol. 33, ed. Barbara B. Oberg (Princeton, NJ: Princeton University Press, 2006), 280–281.
59. Patrick J. Furlong, "The History of the House Ways and Means Committee", *The William and Mary Quarterly* 25, no. 4 (1968): 587–604.
60. Julia H. Macleod, "Jefferson and the Navy: A Defense," *Huntington Library Quarterly* 8, no. 2 (1945): 153–184.
61. Paul Hamilton to James Madison, 17 September 1811, in *The Papers of James Madison, Presidential Series*, vol. 3, ed. J. C. A. Stagg, Jeanne Kerr Cross, and Susan Holbrook Perdue (Charlottesville: University Press of Virginia, 1996), 467–468.
62. Charles W. Goldsborough to James Madison, 7 January 1813, in *The Papers of James Madison, Presidential Series*, vol. 5, ed. J. C. A. Stagg, Martha J. King, Ellen J. Barber, Anne Mandeville Colony, Angela Kreider, and Jewel L. Spangler (Charlottesville: University of Virginia Press, 2004), 558.
63. U.S. Congress, *An act further to amend the several acts of the establishment and regulation of the Treasury, War, and Navy department*, 10th Cong., 2nd sess., March 3, 1809.
64. John B. Colvin to Thomas Jefferson, September 14, 1810, *in The Papers of Thomas Jefferson, Retirement Series*, vol. 3, ed. J. Jefferson Looney (Princeton: Princeton University Press, 2006), 78–79.
65. Jeremy David Bailey, "Executive Prerogative and the 'Good Officer' in Thomas Jefferson's Letter to John B. Colvin," *Presidential Studies Quarterly* 34, no. 4 (December 2004): 732–754.
66. Thomas Jefferson to John B. Colvin, September 20, 1810, in *The Papers of Thomas Jefferson, Retirement Series*, vol. 3, ed. J. Jefferson Looney (Princeton: Princeton University Press, 2006), 99–102.
67. Ibid.

68. Bailey, "Executive Prerogative and the 'Good Officer' in Thomas Jefferson's Letter to John B. Colvin."
69. Allen Schick, *The Federal Budget: Politics, Policy, and Process, Third Edition* (Washington, DC: Brookings Institution Press, 2007). Schick defines the period from 1789 until 1921 as "legislative dominance."

References

Adams, John. Letter to Abigail Adams, April 19, 1796. In The Adams Papers, Adams Family Correspondence, vol. 11, edited by Margaret A. Hogan, C. James Taylor, Sara Martin, Neal E. Millikan, Hobson Woodward, Sara B. Sikes, and Gregg L. Lint. Cambridge, MA: Harvard University Press, 2013.

Bailey, Jeremey David. 2004. "Executive Prerogative and the 'Good Officer' in Thomas Jefferson's Letter to John B. Colvin." Presidential Studies Quarterly 34 (4): 732–754.

Bolles, Albert S. 1969. Financial History of the United States from 1774 to 1789. Vol. I. 3 vols. New York, NY: Augustus M. Kelly Publishers.

Colvin, John B. 2006. "Letter to Thomas Jefferson, 14 September 1810." In The Papers of Thomas Jefferson, vol. 3, edited by J. Jefferson Looney, 78–79. Princeton, NJ: Princeton University Press.

Cooper, Richard. 1982. "William Pitt, Taxation, and the Needs of War." Journal of British Studies 22 (1): 94–103.

Ferguson, E. James. 1961. The Power of the Purse: A History of American Public Finance, 1776–1790. Chapel Hill, NC: The University of North Carolina Press.

Fonseca, Goncalo L. n.d. "Dr. Richard Price, 1723–1791." The History of Economic Thought. http://www.hetwebsite.net/het/profiles/rprice.htm.

Ford, Paul Leicester. 1898. The Federalist: A Commentary on the Constitution of the United States by Alexander Hamilton. New York, NY: Henry Holt and Company.

Furlong, Patrick J. 1968. "The History of the House Ways and Means Committee." The William and Mary Quarterly 25 (4): 587–604.

Gallatin, Albert. 2006. "Letter to Thomas; Enclosure III: Estimate of Military Expenditures, 14 March 1801." In The Papers of Thomas Jefferson, vol. 33, 280–281. Princeton, NJ: Princeton University Press.

Goldsborough, Charles W. 2004. "Letter to James Madison 7 January 1813." In The Papers of James Madison, vol. 5, edited by J. C. A. Stagg, Martha J. King, Ellen J. Barber, Anne Mandeville Colony, Angela Kreider and Jewel L. Spangler, 558. Charlottesville: University of Virginia Press.

Government Accountability Office. 2016. Principles of Federal Appropriations Law. 4th. Government Accountability Office.

Hamilton, Alexander. 1974a. "Letter to Rufus King, 24 April 1796." In The Papers of Alexander Hamilton, vol. 20, edited by Harold C. Syrett, 136–137. New York: Columbia University Press.

———. 1974b. "Letter to the Citizens Who Shall be Convened This Day in the Fields in the City of New York, 22 April 1796." In The Papers of Alexander Hamilton, vol. 20, edited by Harold C. Syrett, 131–134. New York: Columbia University Press.

———. 1977. "The Examination Number II [New York, December 21, 1801]." In The Papers of Alexander Hamilton, vol. 25, edited by Harold C. Syrett, 458–464. New York: Columbia University Press.

Hamilton, Paul. 1996. "Letter to James Madison, 17 September 1811." In The Papers of James Madison, Presidential Series, vol. 3, edited by J. C. A. Stagg, Jeanne Kerr Cross and Susan Holbrook Perdue, 467–468. Charlottesville, VA: University Press of Virginia.

Jefferson, Thomas. 2006. "Letter to John B. Colvin, 20 September 1810." In The Papers of Thomas Jefferson, vol. 3, edited by J. Jefferson Looney, 99–102. Princeton, NJ: Princeton University Press.

Jennings, Robert M., Donald F. Swanson, and Andrew P. Trout. 1988. "Alexander Hamilton's Tontine Proposal." The William and Mary Quarterly 45 (1): 107–115.

Jones, Bryan D., László Zalányi, and Péter Érdi. 2014. "An Integrated Theory of Budgetary Politics and Some Empirical Tests: The U.S. National Budget, 1791–2010." American Journal of Political Science 58 (3): 561–578.

Kennon, David R., and M. Rebecca Rogers. 1989. The Committee on Ways and Means: A Bicentennial History, 1789–1989. Washington, DC: Government Printing Office.

King, Rufus. 1974a. "Letter to Alexander Hamilton, 17–18 April 1796." In The Papers of Alexander Hamilton, vol. 20, edited by Harold C. Syrett, 121–123. New York: Columbia University Press.

———. 1974b. "Letter to Alexander Hamilton, 20 April 1796." In The Papers of Alexander Hamilton, vol. 20, edited by Harold C. Syrett, 124–126. New York: Columbia University Press.

———. 1974c. "Letter to Alexander Hamilton, 1 May 1796." In The Papers of Alexander Hamilton, vol. 20, edited by Harold C. Syrett, 149–151. New York: Columbia University Press.

Macleod, Julia H. 1945. "Jefferson and the Navy: A Defense." Huntington Library Quarterly (University of Pennsylvania Press) 8 (2): 153–184.

Madison, James. 2002. "Letter to Thomas Jefferson, 18 April 1796." In The Papers of Thomas Jefferson, vol. 29, edited by Barbara B. Oberg, 70–71. Princeton, NJ: Princeton University Press.

———. 1989a. "Letter to Thomas Jefferson, 23 April 1796." In The Papers of James Madison, vol. 16, edited by J. C. A. Stagg, Jeanne K. Sisson and Thomas A. Mason, 335–336. Charlottesville: University Press of Virginia.

———. 1989b. "Letter to Thomas Jefferson, 1 May 1796." In The Papers of James Madison, vol. 16, edited by J. C. A. Stagg, Jeanne K. Sisson and Thomas A. Mason, 342–344. Charlottesville: University Press of Virginia.

Randolph, Edmund. 1967. "Letter to James Madison, 16 November 1782." In The Papers of James Madison, vol. 5, edited by William T. Hutchinson and William M. E. Rachal, 280–287. Chicago: The University of Chicago Press.

Ross, Edward A. 1892. "Sinking Funds." Publications of the American Economic Association 7 (4/5): 9–106.

Schick, Allen. 2007. The Federal Budget Process: Politics, Policy, Process. 3. Washington, DC: Brookings Institution Press.

Swanson, Donald F., and Andrew P. Trout. 1992. "Alexander Hamilton's Hidden Sinking Fund." The William and Mary Quarterly 49 (1): 108–116.

Sylla, Richard, Robert E. Wright, and David J Cowen. 2009. "Alexander Hamilton, Central Banker: Crisis Management during the U.S. Financial Panic of 1792." The Business History Review 83 (1): 61–86.

U.S. Congress. 1789. Journal of the House of Representatives of the United States. 1st Cong., 1st sess., September 21.

———. 1790. Journal of the House of Representatives of the United States. 1st Cong., 2nd sess., February 11.

———. 1794. Journal of the House of Representatives of the United States. 3rd Cong., 1st sess., June 10.

———. 1796a. Journal of the House of Representatives of the United States. 4th Cong., 1st sess., March 23.

———. 1796b. Journal of the House of Representatives of the United States. 4th Cong., 1st sess., April 14.

———. 1809. An act further to amend the several acts of the establishment and regulation of the Treasury, War, and Navy departments. 10th Cong., 2nd sess., March 3.

———. 1849. "An Act making appropriations for the Military and Naval Establishments, for the year one thousand seven hundred and ninety-seven." In Annals of the Congress of the United States. Washington, DC: Gales and Seaton.

———. 1945. The Public Statutes at Large of the United States of America, From the Organization of the Government in 1789, to March 3, 1845. Edited by Richard Peters. Vol. I. Boston: Charles C. Little and James Brown.

U.S. Congress, House of Representatives, Committee on Energy and Commerce. 1986. Petitions, Memorials, and Other Documents Submitted for Consideration of Congress: March 4, 1789 to December 14, 1795. Committee Print 99-A, Washington: 99th Congress, 2nd Session.

Washington, George. 1790. First Annual Address to Congress. Edited by Gerhard Peters and John T. Woolley. The American Presidency Project, January 8.

———. 1974. "Letter to Alexander Hamilton, 31 March 1796." In The Papers of Alexander Hamilton, vol. 20, edited by Harold C. Syrett, 103–105. New York: Columbia University Press.

CHAPTER 3

Bounded by War

The 12th Congress convened on March 4, 1811. James Madison was in the third year of his presidency and the country was preparing for another war with Great Britain. New political stars on the horizon were on their way to the capital city of Washington. The 12th Congress would, in many ways, mark a generational shift in the politics of the era. The Founders were on their way to retirement and many members of this new Congress, who would later become famous themselves, were in their 20s and early 30s and therefore in their infancy when the country was last at war with Britain.

The new Congress was convening at a precarious time. At the end of his administration, Jefferson had imposed a trade embargo with Europe aimed at enforcing American neutrality in the Napoleonic Wars. This was followed by James Madison's own "nonintercourse" policy that had replaced the embargo, but continued to prohibit French and British vessels from American ports. The two countries retaliated by seizing American ships. In March 1810, Congress responded by passing Macon's Bill Number 2 which removed restrictions on trade but allowed the president to place another embargo in the event that Britain and France continued taking American ships and impressing American sailors into their own service.

Napoleon responded by offering to repeal France's restrictions on trade, imposed by the Berlin and Milan decrees, as long as the Madison

P. Winfree, *A History (and Future) of the Budget Process in the United States*, https://doi.org/10.1007/978-3-030-30959-6_3

continued to enforce his nonintercourse policy on Britain.[1] Madison discounted Napoleon's assurances and never implemented the policy change. However, Britain turned the tables on Madison by responding to Macon's Bill with a continuation of the confiscation policy until the French lifted restrictions on British vessels.

This decision by Britain accelerated tensions with America, which were flamed by the new members of the 12th Congress. The 34-year-old Henry Clay, a Democratic Republican from Kentucky, would become Speaker of the House as a freshman member. Clay and his political allies became known as "War Hawks," a term of contempt devised by their fellow Republican John Randolph in an attempt to differentiate the divisions in his own party by pointing out that his colleagues' want of war would jeopardize the union. Randolph believed that republicanism and Clay's push for war in defense of American honor were incompatible.[2]

However, Randolph had also broken away from party establishment while chair of the House Committee of Ways and Means from 1801 until 1807. During the election of 1800, he wrote:

> *I need not say how much I would prefer [Jefferson]… but I am not like some of our party who are as much devoted to him as the [Federalists] were to General Washington. I am not a monarchist in any sense. If our salvation depends on a single man, 'tis not worth our attention.*[3]

Randolph was a paternalist and a traditionalist, but he also sought to push for a devolution of power amassed during the Washington and Adams Administrations. Randolph would cooperate with Secretary Gallatin on nearly all of Jefferson's fiscal commitments, such as reducing the national debt and repealing internal taxes, but would break with the administration on the purchase of western Florida from Spain. This was at least, in part, based on his dislike of Madison, who he saw as a political rival, as Madison was serving as Secretary of State at the time.[4]

By 1811, President Madison was under pressure from multiple forces to deal with the growing hostilities. He was being mocked by Federalists in papers such as the *Federal Republican* and *Scourge* as being a "foolish elf" and "timorous little monkey" for his approach to foreign policy.[5] He was having trouble negotiating his way out of European wars while maintaining American commercial interests. Finally, he was up for reelection with the "War Hawks" of his party running the House.

Additional pressure mounted in December 1811 as the House debated going to war with Britain with Speaker Clay stoking the fire: "What are we to gain by war, has been emphatically asked? In reply, he should ask, what are we not to lose by peace?- commerce, character, a nation's best treasure, honor!" That same month, Ezekiel Bacon, a Congressman from Massachusetts and chairman of the Ways and Means Committee, wrote to Treasury Secretary Gallatin asking for the government's anticipated finances "calculated on the event of war." The next month, Gallatin responded with sobering news.

It had been President Madison's position that annual tax revenue cover both the operations of government and interest on outstanding debt. However, based on Gallatin's assessment, the current duties collected during a potential war in addition to revenue from land sales and bringing back the tax on salt as well as doubling the rate of certain tariffs would result in a deficit of about $3.6 million or about half of 1 percent of the gross domestic product in 1812.[6] Gallatin also requested that Congress consider reauthorizing the national bank that had been allowed to expire in 1811 on a tiebreaking vote cast by Vice President George Clinton. The bank, Gallatin argued, would be able to provide loans to government, which might prove to be valuable in war time, and issue securities that would function as a currency, thus increasing the supply of money that would be required in war.

On Tuesday, February 25, the House debated taxes to fund the war. Henry Clay moved to postpone the debate on hearing the Ways and Means Committee report on Gallatin's proposal was ready. However, after a suggestion from Thomas Newton, a Representative from Virginia, Clay moved to form the Committee of the Whole to debate a doubling of the duties. Bacon entered the debate by moving forward with Gallatin's recommendation for additional taxation though "were he to be governed solely by his own feelings or inclinations, he certainly should not be disposed to add to the long list of unwelcome taxes, whose adoption was recommended to this House."[7] However, Bacon reported that his committee supported Madison's principle of paying for the war, general government, and any interest without increasing the debt.

Bacon also spoke out against Gallatin's plan for reviving the national bank, believing that the money the bank could loan the government would fall far short of the needed capital if the country was to go into war:

> *It is well known that during the year 1796, the Government, being pressed for the payment of the loans previously effected with that bank and the bank of New York, opened a domestic loan for five millions, but were unable to obtain subscriptions only to the amount of eighty thousand dollars, and that irredeemable for more than twenty years, and were moreover compelled, in order to meet their engagements, to sell a large portion of their shares in the bank upon the best terms they were to do. The credit of the Government was as good then as it is now, and there was certainly a strong disposition in money interest of the nation to accommodate them as there is now.*[8]

The United States was at a critical juncture as it had not yet entered into war but needed to know what they might be getting into. The Congress and Madison Administration had to account not just the military strength of their potential adversary, but "at least equal importance in modern warfare, her pecuniary and financial strength" relative to the United States.[9] However, for Bacon at least, failure to raise taxes to cover expenditures for a war was detrimental to the effort because the United States was in a more precarious financial position even with all of Britain's "follies and prodigality."[10]

Bacon equated the support for the war with support for additional revenue. If the public could not support paying for the war, they would be reluctant to support the war itself. Langdon Cheves, a "War Hawk" from South Carolina who would take over the Ways and Means Committee later that year, spoke in favor of a tax on salt to raise revenues. The tax incidence, it was believed, would fall on the "agricultural part of the country" or the southern states. The tax on stills would fall on the middle Atlantic states, Kentucky, Tennessee, and Ohio. The tax on shops and taverns would fall on the northern cities. The tax on carriages would fall on the middle Atlantic states. Any direct tax, as had yet been described in detail, would probably fall on the southern or western states. The stamp tax, the duties on sugar, and the tax on auction sales, would fall on consumers in every part of the country.

Over the next few days the House voted on the various taxes for the purposes of funding the war. On the doubling of import duties, the House voted in favor 71 to 40. On increasing tonnage duties, the House voted in favor 82 to 40. But then the House began to consider several of the more direct forms of taxation, which caused a split with the position of both the Administration and the Ways and Means Committee. Speaker Clay spoke of his opposition to the tax on salt and a failed vote followed to increase the tax on domestically produced salt. A second vote on taxing imported salt also failed by three votes. However, after much debate and several War Hawks turning on the Speaker's previous position, another vote would be taken on March 2 to impose a tax on imported salt which would carry the day 66 to 54.

On March 4, the House resumed consideration of the tax plan. The new tax on stills was agreed to, as was the tax on auction sales, a tax on sugar, a tax on carriages, a stamp tax on bank notes, and a direct tax apportioned to the states. The direct tax of $3 million included a 15 percent markdown for any state that collected the taxes without administrative help from the federal government. Finally, the House agreed to the resolution, 72 to 27, to phase out all of the new taxes within one year of the war ending and not to begin collection until there had been a declaration war.

Gallatin's proposal was notionally adopted. However, the House Committee of Ways and Means would still have to report a bill and the House would be required to vote for final approval on the imposition of the new taxes. Gallatin pressured Bacon to move forward with the approved plan to raise taxes.[11] But the House failed to do so and finally voted on June 26, more than three weeks after declaring war on Great Britain, to postpone any action on new taxes until the next session. The House would avoid levying taxes to fund the new war until 1814 and 1815, resorting in the interim to authorizing loans and allowing Treasury to issue new notes.[12]

The new loans and revenues from additional taxes were not enough to bridge the financial demands of the war.[13] The Federalists and Democratic Republicans from the New England middle and Atlantic states were not enthusiastic about the war effort.[14] This charged an already controversial issue of debt fueled by Congressional loan authorizations. At the same time, the tax shortfall was inadequate to pay for interest on outstanding obligations. Beginning in 1812, Secretary Gallatin would ask Congress to consider approving the issuance of interest-bearing treasury notes.[15] Gallatin's proposal would allow the notes as payment for taxes, duties, and debts of the government. Congress acquiesced to the plan out of necessity as they were unwilling to levy taxes or re-charter the national bank. During the course of the war, Congress would authorize over $36 million in Treasury notes in denominations from $3 to $1000.[16]

The issuance of Treasury notes was extremely controversial during the war and fell quickly out of favor once peace was settled with Great Britain in February 1815. At the end of the Madison Administration,

Treasury Secretary Alexander Dallas recommended that the Treasury notes be recalled and that Congress pass an appropriation to reimburse their value in full.[17] At this point, the Second Bank of the United States had been chartered and could issue its own notes. On Madison's second to last day in office, a bill was enacted that prohibited future issuance of Treasury notes.

However, Gallatin's Treasury notes had entered as a new standard that was used to raise money in times of financial trouble to avoid direct taxation. With conflict came the increase in demand for money. Gallatin and Congress were forced to become creative without a national bank to rely on for loans or the political will to raise taxes. Treasury notes would return in the future to help fund future wars but the notes issued during the War of 1812 would prove superior to later innovations. Gallatin's idea to allow the notes to be used for taxes, duties, and debts was critical to the success of the plan. The issuance of additional notes, along with the increase in demand for the notes by banks to use as reserves, increased inflation during the period. Driven by their utility, the Treasury notes of 1812–1815 did not depreciate to the extent of other securities issued during the War of Independence and Civil War.[18]

The Sinking Fund in War

There remained $39.9 million in pre-war debt at the end of the War of 1812.[19] Meanwhile, outstanding Treasury notes totaled $18.5 million and additional debt taken on due to the war totaled $50.3 million including loans. At the time, the sinking fund contained about $2 million in the form of interest on stock, $800 thousand in revenues from western land sales, and $5.2 million in revenues from duties. All loans taken on during the war had also "contained a paragraph directing the commissioners [of the sinking fund] to pay the interest and reimburse the principle when due, and to purchase the stock at or below par whenever they should see fit."[20]

The sinking fund was under great strain given that the existing law had supported only $8 million toward to the payment of interest and extinguishment of debt. Secretary Dallas proposed several changes to relieve pressure.[21] These included a new appropriation to pay for the redemption of Treasury notes, prioritization of the $39.9 million in pre-war debt followed by a $500 million payment of temporary loans, and finally the interest on the debt. Any surplus, Dallas suggested, would be reserved for paying down the principle on war debt. Congress codified Dallas's proposal by authorizing a loan to cover the outstanding notes.[22]

Dallas also recommended increasing the revenue available to the sinking fund by $2 million—bringing the total up to $10 million available to service the debt. Based on his estimates from December 1815, this appropriation would have been sufficient to eliminate the existing debt within eighteen years. The sinking fund committee made a similar recommendation in 1816 along with a one-time appropriation of $9 million in 1817 as part of the same general reorganization that Dallas had proposed earlier.[23]

In 1817, Congress made significant changes to the sinking fund that would overhaul the earlier system dating back to the 1795 law and amended over the years.[24] These changes included repealing all former laws authorizing the sinking fund and dedicated revenue sources. The financing for the fund was replaced with a $10 million annual appropriation on a permanent basis as well as a one-time $9 million appropriation for 1817 and a $4 million for 1818. Any additional surplus over $2 million would also be directed toward the fund.

The 1817 statute also cleared the way for eliminating any semblance of the Price-style sinking fund discussed in Chap. 1. There were no longer requirements regarding how debt was managed and the ability of the commissioners to borrow on behalf of the fund had been eliminated. Importantly, the sinking fund was no longer responsible for all debt assumed by the government. This marked the beginning of the very long process to end of debt management through a sinking fund. Congress would return to the sinking fund through World War I, however, its efficacy was challenged. As a later scholar would conclude, the sinking fund "was but a needless administrative appendix that, once imported, continued with us only by sufferance, and that a later debt epoch has not revived."[25]

Protectionists in the (White) House

Tariffs were an uncontroversial source of revenue in the early United States. The first tariff bill was enacted on July 4, 1789, which taxed most imported goods at 5 percent of their value.[26] The stated intention of the 1789 tariff was not simply to generate revenue for the government but for the "encouragement and protection of manufacturers."[27] However, protectionist tariffs were far from a majority position as Congress changed import duties twenty-seven times between 1789 and 1816.

Alexander Hamilton advocated that it was the responsibility of the federal government to protect specific industries through a system of tariffs and subsidies in his Report on Manufacturers. But Congress ignored his suggestion to subsidize industry. Furthermore, Hamilton as Treasury Secretary never pushed strong protective tariffs. Rather, Hamilton considered tariffs valuable for the revenue and never sought prohibitive tariffs on industries that would significantly restrict trade knowing that good relations with European countries were also critical to the country's finance.[28]

But the War of 1812 left in its wake increased partisan and regional tensions surrounding the use of tariffs for the protection of industry. Prior to the war, Madison's nonintercourse policy had been based on a Jeffersonian policy dating back to his time as Secretary of State in that "free commerce and navigation are not to be given in exchange for restrictions and vexations; nor are they likely to produce a relaxation of them."[29] This was the case even though Jefferson had been supportive of free trade "with others mutual surpluses, for mutual wants."[30]

At the onset of the war, the captain of the US Frigate *Essex* hoisted a white flag with the words "A free trade and sailors rights" upon sailing from New York harbor. This phrase, "Free Trade and Sailors' Rights," came to epitomize the conflict and was widely embraced by the war's supporters.[31] The captain of the *Essex*, David Porter, raised the flag in an act of provocation with the intention of insulting the British with the idea that it was America who stood behind a diplomacy based on the free exchange of goods.[32]

The war, however, produced an increase in American manufacturing which strengthened their political position.[33] Manufacturers called for more protections, including higher tariffs, to protect themselves from British dumping of goods in America to drive down prices.[34] In his December 1815 message to Congress, President Madison recommended that "in adjusting the duties on imports to the object of revenue, the influence of the tariff on manufacturers will necessarily present itself for consideration."[35] Secretary of the Treasury Alexander Dallas followed with a report calling for a tariff increase to protect manufacturers.

Congress responded a few months later by raising tariffs 42 percent above their pre-war rates and established a 25 percent duty on imported cotton cloth valued at less than 25 cents per yard. Calhoun, a staunch war hawk from South Carolina, protested this response saying that it was "an immense tax on one portion of the community to put money into the pockets of another."[36] The tariff of 1816 is viewed by historians as the first significant tariff for the purposes of protection, but it is also not seen as particularly successful.

Collusion Between the Branches

The tariff of 1816 would not have come about without another war hawk, Henry Clay, as Speaker of the House. Clay's strong leadership style and ability to load critical House committees with protectionists was critical to executing Dallas's plan. In fact, throughout the period, chairmen of committees were selected because of their relationships with the executive branch.[37] This was especially true for the House Committee of Ways and Means that was responsible for both tax and spending bills.

Speaker Clay chose both Louis McLane and Samuel Smith, because of their relationship and loyalty to William Crawford, the Secretary of the Treasury under President Monroe, to lead the Committee of Ways and Means. Committees also began to lose their regional diversity under Clay. For instance, members representing southern states had significant majorities on the Ways and Means Committee from 1811 through 1829. At the same time, length of tenure began to lose its advantage for key appointments in the House.[38]

Prior to 1819, it was custom for the House Ways and Means Committee to report the recommendations from the Treasury Secretary along with the appropriations bill with places left open for the Committee of the Whole to include amounts for specific activities. Beginning in 1819, the Ways and Means Committee asserted itself by advancing the bills to the Committee on the Whole with appropriations amounts included. The House also began to separate appropriations bills for different civil activities. Rather than have one bill providing money for all civil activities, during the 1820s the House began passing separate bills for fortifications, pensions, roads, harbor infrastructure, and an Indian Department.[39]

Congressional committees also began to produce more legislation on their own. Before 1814, committees were instructed by the House to report bills with specific directions on what to include. For instance, the Committee on the Whole would instruct the Ways and Means Committee to report tax bills back based on specific parameters. The House changed the process through a resolution in 1814, which was codified in laws enacted in 1820 and 1822, allowing standing and select committees to report bills without previous instruction. This process changes significantly empowered the Speaker (who selected committee chairman and members) and the committees themselves. By the beginning of the Jackson Administration, the House began a process of referring all bills to standing committees rather than the Committee on the Whole.[40]

The Jacksonian Period

The political issues that dominated Andrew Jackson's administration, and the administrations that followed, ranged from slavery, territorial expansion, tariffs, and the national bank. During the Jackson's time in office which spanned from March 1829 to 1837, the president used his popular political position to push Congress toward enforcing his will—a move that was compatible with the principle of governance by the majority that Jackson had illustrated in his first address to Congress. This included Jackson calling on the Congress to nominate ideologically compatible members of his own party to lead committees.[41] This was an easier task to accomplish given that the seniority principle did not yet apply and the Speaker of the House made committee selections.

However, there are a limited number of events that occurred during this period that had a meaningful and lasting effect on the budgeting of the country. It has often been referenced that under the Jackson administration, the government not only ran surpluses but paid off its existing debt.[42] The public debt was $58 million the year Jackson was inaugurated which was equivalent to about 6 percent of the economy.[43] By the time he left office, almost all the outstanding debt had been retired leaving public debt at 0.02 percent of the economy. Paying off the debt was seen generally by both Jackson and the public as a validation that the establishment of the United States had been successful and, according to the political scientist James Savage, "a point of national honor and public morality."[44]

Over the same period, Congress and the administration increased spending and even reduced customs duties as part of the Tariff Act of 1832, which led to the Nullification Crisis. However, the Compromise Tariff Act of 1833, largely brought back the high protectionists tariffs with a gradual schedule to phase them down by 1842. Therefore, overall customs revenues did not decrease until 1834 but increased to pre-form levels within two years. Meanwhile, most of the increased spending occurred at the end of the administration and was almost entirely associated with increasing the size of the army that was engaged in the Second Seminole

War. Between 1835 and 1836, spending on the army increased by 111 percent.

Jackson supported the eradication of debt and increasing revenues through public land sales.[45] Land sales had long been an important, although relatively small, source of revenue. Between 1801 and 1828, the revenue generated from selling public land generated about 6 percent of total receipts. However, between 1835 and 1836, over 45 percent of total receipts came from land sales. In 1836, receipts totaled almost $51 million which was 133 percent higher than the amount collected in 1834. In the same year, total outlays were $31 million, netting a surplus of $20 million. This created the problem of what to do with the money, which was ultimately turned back to the states in the form of direct payments.

Along with the eradication of debt, which itself was inflationary, Jackson also advocated eliminating the Second Bank of the United States. In his first address to Congress, Jackson wrote that "if such as institution is deemed essential to the fiscal operations of government, I submit to the wisdom of the legislature where a national one, founded upon the credit of the government and its revenues, might not be devised which would avoid all constitutional difficulties and at the same time secure all the advantages to the government and country that were expected to result from the present bank."[46]

The President made good on his promise by vetoing a re-authorization of the bank in 1832 which in turn created a major political battle in the presidential election that year. After winning reelection, Jackson announced in September 1833 that Treasury would stop depositing money into the national bank and begin withdrawing from its accounts. This decision essentially shut down the Second Bank of the United States. The next year, Congress censured Jackson for "assuming power not conferred in the Constitution" by withdrawing the funds.[47]

Jackson's decision was supported by popular opinion but also by private bankers who had campaigned to escape the regulatory control of the Second Bank.[48] It was these private banks who would now take the deposits from the United States. During the Jackson administration, the number of private banks increased from 329 to 788.[49]

Two months after Jackson left office, in 1837, a banking panic broke out causing the first economic recession not associated with war in American history. The panic caused the demise of 27 percent of private banks and drove down the price of securities in several important sectors such as railroads.[50] Many economic historians have examined the causes of the 1837 panic, which have included Jackson's policies regarding the bank and fiscal surpluses. However, the increased demand for coin along with interbank transfers of government balances likely had a significant role to play in liquidating the reserves of New York banks.[51]

Another important repercussion of the panic of 1837 was the desire to separate government finances from that of the economy. To meet the impossible order, President Van Buren recommended the creation of an Independent Treasury. He also recommended extending the time allowed to pay import duties and government deposits in the banks, withholding the fourth deposit of the surplus from the states, and continuing to increase circulation of specie. The idea was that by only allowing specie, not bank notes, for the payment of duties they would be separating the federal government from the banking section.

It was thought at the time that a major cause of the panic was the expansion of credit by state banks after Jackson's removal of the government's deposits in the Second Bank of the United States.[52] Van Buren blamed "excessive issues of bank paper" as well as investments in unproductive land and the increase in demand for luxury items on the collapse.[53] The Independent Treasury would act as a bank regulator and as a mechanism to control future economic cycles by holding surpluses in the form of specie at the Independent Treasury rather than private banks.

The recently formed Whig party criticized the creation of the Independent Treasury, asserting that "the administration had decided to abandon its constitutional task of regulating the currency [via the Second Bank] and to adopt one currency, specie, for the uses of government, leaving the people with a depreciated currency, bank notes."[54] They believed that this was part of Van Buren's plan to impose a standard currency based on gold or silver.

The Independent Treasury was finally enacted in 1840 after a worsening recession. That same year, Whigs secured control of both chambers of Congress and William Henry Harrison was elected president. The Congressional Whigs, under Clay's leadership, had supported a new national bank. However, John Tyler, Harrison's new Vice President, did not. This mattered, of course, because Harrison would die of pneumonia thirty-one days after taking office.

Tyler had been a Democrat before joining the Whig party. But he had diverged with the party and President Jackson on nullification and removing the government's deposits from the Second Bank of the United States. After becoming president, Tyler vetoed Clay's bills to create another national bank and, after the second veto, his entire Cabinet with the exception of Daniel Webster, Secretary of State, resigned. Tyler was expelled from the party following this event in September 1841.

This break within the party, and between the presidency and Congress, drove a series of process changes. In 1842, Congress led an investigation into government operations and required that all executive departments submit annual reports in addition to the annual Treasury report on finances.[55] Meanwhile, the House created committees on accounts and public expenditures for each of the executive departments.[56] On August 26, 1842, Congress changed the fiscal year from the calendar year to July 1 through June 30 to buy more time for Congressional consideration of appropriations bills. It passed with no debate reflected in the Congressional record and by unanimous consent in the House.[57]

In response to growing debt brought on by the economic downturn, Tyler called for a new tariff in his first message to Congress. Millard Fillmore, then Chairman of the Ways and Means Committee, and Clay sought to use the president's call to enact a protective tariff. They devised a scheme to link distributions from federal land sales to the states with a new tariff. This would put pressure on federal revenues and create a false sense of necessity for a higher tariff.[58]

The Congressional Whigs passed two tariffs, one permanent and one temporary, coupled with federal land sale distributions. Tyler vetoed both bills based on the distribution requirement. The House then drafted a protective tariff above rates proposed in even the first two bills, but withheld the distribution requirement. Tyler, left with no other political options, signed the bill.[59]

However, many other bills passed during this period originated from within the Executive.[60] This was a consequence of the two-party system when one party controls both Congress and the White House. In order to reduce some of the tension this system had created, committee minority reports issued from the party not in power were created.

The era concludes under President Polk who was elected in 1844 with four primary goals. These included reducing the tariff enacted under Tyler, further distancing the government from the banking system through the Independent Treasury system, settlement of the boundary with Oregon, and acquiring territory in California. An Independent Treasury bill was enacted in 1846, however, most of the debate during this time was around tariffs. In May 1846, war broke out with Mexico. At the end of the war, Polk requested $2 million to purchase territory from the Mexican government. However, Northern members thought this could be a move to extend slavery. David Wilmot, a Democrat from Pennsylvania, offered an amendment on the $2 million appropriations bill that would prohibit slavery in any of the new territory, which was known as the Wilmot Proviso. The issue of slavery was heating up.

"Go See Secretary Chase. He Is Managing the Finances"

Sectional differences divided the parties and the Congress during the 1850s. This was accentuated by a string of relatively weak presidents, from Fillmore and Pierce to Buchanan, who were all relatively weak and served only one term apiece.

Additionally, the state of the government's finances immediately before the Civil War had not been good. Toward the end of the 1850s, the federal government was eyeing a surplus. In response, Congress reduced tariffs rates in 1857 which ended up going into effect at the same time the economy was headed toward recession. This resulted in a deficit, of about 5 percent of total expenditures, in 1858.[61]

In response to the deficit, Congress authorized a loan for $10 million on June 14, 1858 and an issuance of $20 million in Treasury notes.[62] As deficits continued to mount in 1859 and 1860, Congress authorized additional loans of $20 million and extended the terms of the Treasury notes authorized earlier through 1860.[63] Finally, another loan for $21 million was authorized by Congress in June 1860.

However, President Buchanan's Secretaries of the Treasury, Howell Cobb and Philip Thomas, had a difficult time securing the loans. Both were known as southern sympathizers while domestic tensions were mounting. Their critics were not wrong. Cobb would go on to become the president of the Confederate Provisional Congress and a general in the Confederate army after leaving the administration to return to his native Georgia where he advocated succession.[64] Thomas would be forced to resign in 1861 when New York banks refused to disperse the loans to the Treasury based on the fear that the money would be sent south and never paid back.[65]

On his way out of office, Buchanan signed the Morrill tariff act based on the illusion that it would raise revenues needed to cover the multi-year shortfall. But the tariff proved to be more about protecting domestic industries than raising revenues. Many imports that did not have a domestic presence, like sugar and tea, were largely left duty free.[66] The result of the Morrill tariffs was a reduction in customs revenues by 43 percent during 1861.[67]

Salmon Chase, whose political history was that of an anti-slavery leader of the Free Soil party turned Republican, was nominated Treasury Secretary the day after Lincoln's inauguration in March 1861. Chase brought with him a sentiment for "hard money" found amongst Democrats going back to President Jackson. However, he did not have much experience with financial policy and would represent a president who, like Jefferson, had no real interest on the fiscal mechanics of the federal government. In fact, Chase turned down the initial offer for Treasury Secretary before giving in to service for "the common good which cannot honorably be shunned."[68]

Chase's friend, Donn Piatt, would later write after his death, "Had Mr. Lincoln known of the war that was to follow his inauguration, it is not likely that he would have selected a man so entirely ignorant of finance, and all that pertains to that vexed business, as this man who had never given the subject a thought, let alone any study."[69] But Lincoln would come to rely extensively on Chase, telling those who wanted to speak with the president on fiscal matters, "Go to Secretary Chase. He is managing the finances."[70]

The situation that Chase would inherit called for drastic actions. On April 12, 1861, a Confederate artillery opened fire on Fort Sumter thus beginning the Civil War. Until that point in the year, the government had been relying on borrowing to fund three quarters of its spending. With conflict brought an increased demand for resources. The government quickly exhausted all of its revenue from taxation and began to rely entirely on borrowing for the remaining three fiscal quarters.[71]

Even without a war, the government would have run significant deficits as it was so short of revenues. Relative to pre-recession levels, total receipts into the federal government had fallen by 18 percent between 1857 and 1860. The government's income would fall again between 1860 and 1861 by 26 percent. Between April and June of 1861, the revenues from taxes and duties totaled $5.8 million and another $17 million had been generated from loans. But more money was needed. President Lincoln called for "at least 400,000 men and 400 million dollars" to fight the war. Congress convened a special session on July 4, 1861, to confront the revenue shortfall and new demands of war.[72]

That same day Chase issued a report to Congress calling on Congress to supply $319 million in additional resources for the war and normal operations, of which $80 million could be paid for with additional taxes and $240 could come from new loan authorities.[73] In addition, Chase recommended that $57 million in the new revenues could come from changes to the Morrill tariffs and another $3 million from public land sales. This would leave the additional $20 million to come from other direct taxes.

Thaddeus Stevens, a staunch and strong-willed Chairman of the Ways and Means Committee from Pennsylvania, was responsible for handling Chase's request. Stevens's committee had grown in influence over the years, overseeing spending, tax, tariff, and even banking legislation. As Chairman of the powerful committee, Stevens could command the House floor and manage the debate over his committee's work at almost any time under House rules.

Stevens and Chase not only had known each other for twenty years, but had been friends, dating back to when Chase was the governor of Ohio.[74] And Stevens, like Chase, did not have much experience in financial matters apart from his time in Congress. Six days after the convening of the July 4 special session, the House authorized a new loan for $250 million with a final vote of 150 to 5.[75] The vote occurred only after Clement Vallandingham, a Congressman from Ohio and leader of the Copperhead caucus, finished a long speech attacking Lincoln, his recent blockade of the Southern coast without Congressional approval, and loan request which he called "an extraordinary" demand.[76] By July 17th, Lincoln was able to sign the bill as Chase and Stevens had come through.

Salmon Chase would remain Treasury Secretary through June 1864. The work that he completed with this friend Stevens over that time would be critical in not just to providing funds for the war effort but to changing the structure of financing the federal government indefinitely. Specifically, his tenure marks a shift in the government's source of revenue. Between 1850 and 1860, 91 percent of government revenue was generated from customs duties. Revenue generated by customs would fall to 25 percent of total revenue by the war's end and would never exceed 60 percent again. Tax policy was changing in fundamental ways.

On August 5, 1861, Lincoln signed a revenue bill raising tariffs as called for by Chase's July proposal, apportioning a direct tax on the states, and levying a 3 percent tax on income above $800. This was the first income tax in the United States, styled from a similar proposal dating back to 1815.[77] However, the 1861 income tax never went into effect as Chase continually delayed its implementation based, in part, on its difficulty to administer.

As the year closed, public sentiment for further loans and the purchase of bonds was dwindling. The London *Economist* publication wrote that "It is utterly out of the question, in our judgement that Americans can obtain, either at home or in Europe, anything like the extravagant sums they are asking for; Europe won't lend; America cannot."[78] At the same time, spending on the war reached nearly $2 million per day by January 1862, vastly exceeding estimates made the last summer.[79]

Chase, who favored a metallurgical currency, was short on cash and desperate to fund the government's growing expenses. In his December 1861 report, Chase opened the door for government notes to replace currency issued by states or a system of new national banks. Weeks later the Ways and Means Committee would produce a bill authorizing $50 million in Treasury notes that were both payable on demand and "lawful money and legal tender in payment of all debts, public and private, within the United States."[80] A similar bill carrying the legal tender language and increasing the authorization of new notes to $150 million would pass the House and Senate in February. The "greenbacks," as the new Treasury notes were called, began replacing all other forms of currency in July 1862.

The Ways and Means subcommittee chairman on loans and currency, Elbridge Spaulding, would become known as the "father of the greenbacks."[81] But Chase came to regret even his role in the process of moving toward a fiat currency. As Donn Piatt, would later write, "Before the eminent war-treasurer died he saw the consequence of his blunder, and that a costly an oppressive system of banking had been fixed upon the people for all time to come."[82]

To meet the demand for revenue, Justin Morrill, a Congressman from Vermont and subcommittee chairman for taxation on Ways and Means, drafted a bill in 1862 that was estimated to generate $150 million by building from the income tax approved a year earlier. The bill established a two-tiered progressive tax beginning at 3 percent on incomes between $600 and $10,000 and increasing to 5 percent for those making more than $10,000. The income tax was assessed on most income, including capital gains, and included a deduction for local and state taxes.

The law also imposed a number of other taxes including a tax on inheritances and licensing fees for a number of occupations including, circus performers, confectioners, and billiard room owners (where the tax was assessed on the number of tables).[83] In order to administer the law, a shortcoming of the 1861 tax law, the Morrill bill created a new Internal

Revenue Bureau within the Treasury Department with a new Commissioner of Internal Revenue. The bill was signed on July 1 by Lincoln with these provisions intact.

However, both Morrill and Stevens did not favorably view progressive taxation as they believed it was unfair.[84] Morrill, for instance, believed that it resulted in a justifiable subversion of the system.[85] However, the Ways and Means leadership team was unable to convince their colleagues of such changes, and House rejected the idea of one tax during the deliberations of 1864. The Congress went on to amend the 1862 tax law later that year by creating a third tax bracket. The law, enacted on June 30, taxes income between $600 and $5000 at 5 percent, income between $5000 and $10,000 at 7.5 percent, and income over $10,000 at 10 percent.

Morrill and Stevens were more influential in amending existing import duties based on the demand for revenue to provide higher protectionist tariffs. The tariff schedule was amended in 1862 and then again in 1864 which left the average rate across imports at 47 percent—an increase of 27 percent. But at the end of the war, it had become impossible to keep up with the growth in spending. Between 1861 and 1865, total revenues grew by seven-fold whereas spending grew by eighteen-fold. Meanwhile, public debt increased twenty-eight-fold.

Although debt increased significantly relative to levels maintained before the war (debt as a percent of the economy was a small fraction during the 1840s and 1850s) the levels were not unheard of up until that point. Public debt was around a third of the economy following both the American Revolution and the American Civil War. And debt would fall to around 6 percent of the economy within thirty years of the ratification of the Constitution and the end of the accumulation of debt attributed to the Civil War.[86] Debt proved once again to be the necessary, but not a lasting, price of liberty.

By the end of the war, however, Congress's own legislative infrastructure was showing some strain. During the 37th and 38th Congresses, 126 bills had been reported by the House's Ways and Means Committee at a time when 653 public laws were enacted during the period.[87] Stevens had also been targeted in the past and members, including Samuel Cox from Ohio, used the committee's busy commitment overseeing taxes, spending, tariffs, and banking to weaken the Ways and Means Committee Chairman.[88]

At the end of the 38th Congress, James Garfield, another Republican from Ohio who had served as a brigadier general in the war before being elected to the House in 1863, suggested that the Ways and Means

Committee could be broken up into a committee focused on revenues and another on appropriations.[89] Before adjourning, the House adopted new rules splitting the Ways and Means Committee up. When the 39th Congress convened in December 1865, two additional Committees on Appropriations and Banking and Currency had been formed. Two years later, in 1867, the Senate would follow suit by creating their own Committee on Appropriations from the Finance Committee.

The Return of the Sinking Fund

During the decade of the Civil War, the economy was in poor shape. Commodity output grew more slowly during the 1860s than any other decade during the nineteenth century.[90] Economic historians have found that a number of contributing factors were responsible for the economy including the issuance of greenbacks, taxes, a limited number of skilled workers, and the diversion from capital investment toward savings in the form of long-term debt.[91]

It took Treasury the entire war to establish a debt financing system without relying on the greenbacks including new taxes and a diminished reliance on customs duties.[92] By the end of the war, the fiscal infrastructure that had been put into place continued to produce budget surpluses.[93] Treasury responded to the surpluses with a policy of retiring the greenbacks. This continued until Congress passed a law significantly restricting the contractionary policy in 1866. This freed up budget surpluses to retire interest-bearing debt.[94] At the same time, war debt began to migrate overseas as Europeans bought more of the government's securities.[95]

The revenue bill enacted on August 5, 1862, that included the first income tax also included a small sinking fund. The sinking fund was amended in February 1862 by prioritizing the payment of interest. This was based on a proposal made by Secretary Chase that, in many ways, inspired by Hamilton's sinking fund. However, Treasury never complied with the sinking fund act of 1862. And eventually McCulloch, who would take Chase's place as Secretary in the last months of the Lincoln presidency and under President Johnson, ignored the law and proposed his own sinking fund.

McCulloch believed that all that was needed was an annual appropriation of $200 million to retire the debt over a 30-year period rather than a complicated sinking fund. However, Congress rejected McCulloch's proposal and he spent the rest of the Johnson administration applying any surpluses to paying down the debt. This strategy did reduce the nominal level of debt over the period from 1865 to 1869 by almost $133 million. However, because of the poor economy, debt as a percentage of the economy increased slightly over the same period from 27 to 32 percent.[96]

In 1870, Congress reorganized public debt by rescinding all bonds applied to the sinking fund and folding any amount owed into the annual amortization schedule. This was executed through redemption of the "five-twenties", which were bonds bearing 6 percent interest issued in 1862, 1864, and 1865. These longer-term securities were redeemable after five years and payable after twenty.

But recession hit in 1873, which eliminated any surpluses. Treasury couldn't meet payments as required by the sinking fund law. To meet demand created by the shortfall, Congress again authorized the issuance of $26 million greenbacks.[97] Under President Grant, Secretary Bristow believed that interest on debt, followed by payments to the sinking fund, were the two most important payments to make. Others in Congress believed that the excess payments from years past could justify ignoring the sinking fund for the time being. In 1875, Congress passed a bill allowing Bristow to obtain bonds for the sinking fund by redeeming the five-twenties. This bill also permitted the sale of bonds for gold necessary to resume specie issuance. By 1877, the government was again running surpluses and the sinking fund obligations were exceeded.

By the 1880s, Congress was again questioning the relevance of the sinking fund. The sinking fund had become a commitment to retire debt even when revenues were falling and the federal government was running deficits. This was not politically popular raising questions about whether there were better uses for the government's revenues. At the same time, the mechanics of the sinking funds were too complicated if the policy was simply to pay down debt. However, they were an important part of the fiscal and budget policy between the 1790s and 1880s.

In 1883, the economist William Holman wrote that, "in the early years of our history there were high motives for frugal government, not only in the impoverished condition of a people just emerging from a great struggle, but in the desire to present a contrast between a free people administering their own affairs and the impoverishing governments of Europe."[98] But a century had passed since the end of the War of Independence and the country was on its way into recovery from the Civil War. The nation had faced the crucible and come out with a stronger self-identity. And the period that is most fundamental to what we would consider modern budget policy was just beginning.

Summary

The budgetary reforms throughout this period were, for the most part, born out of necessity or symbolism. External demands led to innovative ways to raise money to fund the federal government. However, the sinking fund continued to develop as the most important mechanism for debt management during the nineteenth century although its operations were again questioned including whether it should fall out of style once and for all time (it would not). At the same time, Congress tried new methods in an attempt to distance the federal government's finances from that of the economy following banking crises.

Tariff policy extended beyond simply the need to raise revenue for the government. Two things would happen as protectionism took hold. First, the tariff structure would cause revenue policy to become less predictable, especially around the Civil War, forcing the government to look for additional sources of funding including seigniorage and new types of debt. Second, they would create a constituency for additional government spending which would become more important in the next period. This dynamic would make the income tax inevitable.

Notes

1. Dennis Merrill and Thomas G. Paterson, *Major Problems in American Foreign Relations Volume I: To 1920* (Boston: Wadsworth, Cengage Learning, 2009).
2. Aaron Scott Crawford, "John Randolph of Roanoke and the Politics of Doom: Slavery, Sectionalism, and Self-Deception, 1773–1821" (PhD dissertation, University of Tennessee, 2012).
3. Kennon and Rogers, *The Committee on Ways and Means: A Bicentennial History.*
4. Ibid.
5. Aaron McLean Winter, "The Laughing Doves of 1812 and Satiric Endowment of Antiwar Rhetoric in the United States", *PMLA* 124, no. 5 (2009): 1562–1581.
6. U.S. Congress, *American State Papers*, vol. VI, 12th Cong., 2nd sess., Finance: Volume 2 (1812), 580; Louis Johnston and Samuel H. Williamson, "What Was the U.S. GDP Then?" MeasuringWorth, 2018.
7. U.S. Congress, *Journal of the House of Representatives of the United States*, 12th Cong., 1st sess., February 25, 1812.
8. Ibid.
9. Ibid.
10. Ibid.

11. Kennon and Rogers, *The Committee on Ways and Means: A Bicentennial History.*
12. In 1814 and 1815, Congress would authorize new taxes on domestic sugar, carriages, auction sales, wine retailers, banks, distillers, merchandise, furniture, gold or silver watches, jewelry, and a number of other items.
13. Donald H. Kagin, "Monetary Aspects of the Treasury Notes of the War of 1812," *The Journal of Economic History* 44, no. 1 (1984): 69–88.
14. Francis D. Cogliano, *Revolutionary America 1763–1815: A Political History* (New York, NY: Routledge, 2000).
15. Raymond Walters, *Albert Gallatin: Jeffersonian Financier and Diplomat* (New York, NY: Macmillan, 1957).
16. Kagin, "Monetary Aspects of the Treasury Notes of the War of 1812."
17. Ibid.
18. Ibid.
19. Ross, "Sinking Funds."
20. Ibid.
21. Ibid.
22. Ibid.
23. Ibid.
24. Ibid.
25. Ibid.
26. John M. Dobson, *Two Centuries of Tariffs: The Background and Emergence of the United States Trade Commission* (Washington, DC: U.S. Government Printing Office, 1976).
27. This is a quote from the 1789 tariff bill.
28. Irwin, "Revenue or Reciprocity? Founding Feuds over Early U.S. Trade Policy."
29. Paul A. Gilje, "Free Trade and Sailors' Rights': The Rhetoric of the War of 1812," *Journal of the Early Republic* 30, no. 1 (2010), 1–23.
30. Ibid.
31. Ibid.
32. Ibid. "The critique of traditional diplomacy encouraged many thinkers in the eighteenth century to advocate more honest relations between nations. Imbedded in the Enlightenment was a faith in nature and reason that shifted the way intellectuals viewed states …. Revolutionary Americans picked up on these Enlightened ideas and developed a new republican diplomacy based on free trade."
33. Ibid.
34. Edward Stanwood, *American Tariff Controversies in the Nineteenth Century* (Boston, MA: Houghton Mifflin, 1903).
35. Kennon and Rogers, *The Committee on Ways and Means: A Bicentennial History.*

36. Ibid.
37. Ibid.
38. Ibid.
39. Ibid.
40. Ibid.
41. Ibid.
42. Harold Faber, "The Nation: Once Upon a Time, a Budget Surplus," *The New York Times*, December 31, 1995.
43. U.S. Department of Commerce, *Historical Statistics of the United States, 1789–1945: A Supplement to the Statistical Abstract of the United States* (Washington, DC: U.S. Government Printing Office, 1949).
44. James D. Savage, *Balanced Budgets and American Politics* (Ithaca, NY: Cornell University Press, 1988).
45. Andrew Jackson, "First Annual Message to Congress," December 8, 1829, National Archives.
46. Ibid.
47. Senate Historical Office, "Senate Censures President: March 28, 1834," U.S. Senate, https://www.senate.gov/artandhistory/history/minute/Senate_Censures_President.htm
48. Bray Hammond, "Jackson, Biddle, and the Bank of the United States," *The Journal of Economic History* 7, no. 1 (1947): 1–23.
49. Ibid.
50. Peter Rousseau, "Jacksonian Monetary Policy, Specie Flows, and the Panic of 1837," *The Journal of Economic History* 62, no. 2 (2002): 457–488.
51. Ibid.
52. D. Murray Hayes, "Reactions of the Federal Government to the 1837–1843 Depression," *Southern Economic Journal* 8, no. 3 (1942): 380–390.
53. Ibid.
54. Ibid.
55. Kennon and Rogers, *The Committee on Ways and Means: A Bicentennial History.*
56. Ibid.
57. U.S. Congress, *Congressional Globe*, 27th Cong., 2nd sess., August 18, 1842, 909.
58. Kennon and Rogers, *The Committee on Ways and Means: A Bicentennial History.*
59. Ibid.
60. Ibid.
61. U.S. Department of the Treasury, *Report of the Secretary of the Treasury, on the State of the Finances, for the Year Ending June 30, 1858* (Washington, DC: William A. Harris, Printer, 1858).
62. Ibid.

63. U.S. Department of the Treasury, *Report of the Secretary of the Treasury, on the State of the Finances, for the Year Ending June 30, 1860* (Washington, DC: Thomas H. Ford, Printer, 1860).
64. Wesley C. Mitchell, "The Suspension of Specie Payments," *Journal of Political Economy* 7, no. 3 (1899): 289–326.
65. Ibid.
66. Ibid.
67. Ibid.
68. Kennon and Rogers, *The Committee on Ways and Means: A Bicentennial History.*
69. Donn Piatt, "Salmon P. Chase", *The North American Review* 143, no. 361 (1886): 599–615.
70. Ibid.
71. Mitchell, "The Suspension of Specie Payments."
72. Kennon and Rogers, *The Committee on Ways and Means: A Bicentennial History.*
73. U.S. Department of the Treasury, *Report of the Secretary of the Treasury, on the Finances, Containing Estimates of the Public Revenue and Public Expenditures, and Plans for Improving and Increasing the Revenue*, 37th Cong., 1st sess., July 4, 1861.
74. Kennon and Rogers, *The Committee on Ways and Means: A Bicentennial History.*
75. Mitchell, "The Suspension of Specie Payments."
76. U.S. Congress, *Congressional Globe*, 37th Cong., 1st sess., July 10, 1861, 57–60.
77. Sidney Ratner, *A Political and Social History of Federal Taxation, 1789–1913* (New York, NY: W.W. Norton, 1942).
78. *The Economist* (1861), pp. 927–928.
79. Kennon and Rogers, *The Committee on Ways and Means: A Bicentennial History.*
80. Ibid.
81. Ibid.
82. Piatt, "Salmon P. Chase."
83. U.S. Congress, *An Act to provide Internal Revenue to support the Government and to pay Interest on the Public Debt*, 37th Cong., Stat. II, Ch. 119, Sec. 6 (1862).
84. Ratner, *A Political and Social History of Federal Taxation, 1789–1913.*
85. Ibid.
86. Author's calculations using data from Historical Statistics of the United States, Colonial Times to 1970.
87. U.S. Department of Commerce, *Bicentennial Edition: Historical Statistics of the United States, Colonial Times to 1970* (Washington, DC: U.S. Government Printing Office, 1975).

88. Kennon and Rogers, *The Committee on Ways and Means: A Bicentennial History*.
89. Ibid.
90. Jeffery G. Williamson, "Watersheds and Turning Points: Conjectures on the Long-Term Impact of Civil War Financing," *The Journal of Economic History* 34, no. 3 (1974): 636–661.
91. Ibid.
92. Ibid.
93. Ibid.
94. Ibid.
95. Ibid.
96. Author's calculations using data from the (U.S. Department of Commerce Bureau of the Census 1975).
97. Williamson, "Watersheds and Turning Points: Conjectures on the Long-Term Impact of Civil War Financing."
98. William S. Holman, "The Increase in Public Expenditures," *The North American Review* 137, no. 320 (1883): 19–27.

References

Cogliano, Francis D. 2000. Revolutionary America 1763–1815: A Political History. New York, NY: Routledge.

Crawford, Aaron Scott. 2012. John Randolph of Roanoke and the Politics of Doom: Slavery, Sectionalism, and Self-Deception, 1773–1821. Unpublished Doctoral Dissertation, Knoxville: University of Tennessee.

Dobson, John M. 1976. Two Centuries of Tariffs: The Background and Emergency of the United States Trade Commission. Washington, DC: US Government Printing Office.

Faber, Harold. 1995. "The Nation: Once Upon a Time, a Budget Surplus." The New York Times. December 31. Accessed June 21, 2019. https://www.nytimes.com/1995/12/31/weekinreview/the-nation-once-upon-a-time-a-budget-surplus.html.

Gilje, Paul A. 2010. "Free Trade and Sailors' Rights': The Rhetoric of the War of 1812." Journal of the Early Republic 30 (1): 1–23.

Irwin, Douglas. 2010. "Revenue or Reciprocity? Founding Feuds Over Early U.S. Trade Policy." In Founding Choices: American Economic Policy in the 1790s, by Douglas Irwin and Richard Sylla. Chicago, IL: University of Chicago Press.

Johnston, Louis and Samuel H. Williamson. 2018. "What Was the U.S. GDP Then?" MeasuringWorth.

Kagin, Donald H. 1984. "Monetary Aspects of the Treasury Notes of the War of 1812." The Journal of Economic History 44 (1): 69–88.

Kennon, David R., and M. Rebecca Rogers. 1989. The Committee on Ways and Means: A Bicentennial History, 1789–1989. Washington, DC: Government Printing Office.

Merrill, Dennis, and Thomas Paterson. 2009. Major Problems in American Foreign Relations: To 1920. 7. Vol. 1. 2 vols. Boston, MA: Cengage Learning.

Ross, Edward A. 1892. "Sinkig Funds." Publications of the American Economic Association 7 (4/5): 9–106.

Stanwood, Edward. 1903. American Tariff Controversies in the Nineteenth Century. Boston, MA: Houghton Mifflin.

U.S. Congress. 1812a. American State Papers. Vol. VI. 12th Cong. 2nd sess. Finance: Volume 2: 580.

———. 1812b. Journal of the House of Representatives of the United States. 12th Cong. 1st sess. February 25.

Walters, Raymond, Jr. 1957. Albert Gallatin: Jeffersonian Financier and Diplomat. New York, NY: Macmillan.

Winter, Aaron McLean. 2009. "The Laughing Doves of 1812 and Satiric Endowment of Antiwar Rhetoric in the United States." PMLA 124 (5): 1562–1581.

CHAPTER 4

Building a Visible Government

Following the Civil War, the policy and politics of the federal government's budget began rapidly changing in several profound ways. Tariffs were falling in importance as a way to raise money. Changes in Congress included the introduction of a seniority system, longer tenure, hearings to discuss policy, more subcommittees, and "the professionalization of lobbying as an adjunct to congressional procedure."[1] High-profile corruption was occurring in both Congress and the executive, something that was especially recognized during the Grant administration. The term "pork barrel," which originally referred to a carrier for meat, took on a new meaning as a derogatory metaphor for government spending on special projects.

The progressive reformer and author Henry Adams, a contemporary of the period, wrote that "one might search the whole list of Congress, Judiciary, and Executive during the twenty-five years 1870-1895 and find little but damaged reputations." However, the perceived corruption and dysfunction would set the stage for reform. A movement that began with government accountability would be well on its way to establishing the modern budget process by the end of the nineteenth century.

Moreover, the period started with a debate over tax policy. In 1865, Congress established a commission to study post-war taxation. After the war, many members of Congress wanted to keep high protectionist tariffs

P. Winfree, *A History (and Future) of the Budget Process in the United States*, https://doi.org/10.1007/978-3-030-30959-6_4

to help domestic manufacturers, many of whom had been important to the war effort. However, other taxes were more efficient in raising revenue which created a surplus after war spending ended.

The tariff debates were common in American politics throughout the postwar period, and they symbolized a deep fracture in economic policy that could be traced back to the founding of the country. Stances on the tariff debates were often reflective of political, geographical, and economic divisions. However, until the Civil War, internal taxes had not raised enough money to be a viable replacement for revenue from tariffs. Therefore, other taxes had generally been seen as complements to tariff revenue and even symbolic of the general excesses of government.[2] However, by the beginning of the twentieth century, tariffs and income taxes would become substitutes for one another as a means of raising revenue for a growing nation.

The 1864 tax law, which was in place before the tax policy debates had begun, assessed taxes on personal income, interest, dividends, and government salaries. The component that taxed personal income would expire in 1870 (with an assessment on income earned no later than 1869); however, the tax on interest, dividends, and government salaries continued indefinitely, as the Civil War era tax law included no such expiration.

In 1870, the House Ways and Means Committee reported a bill to reduce internal taxes by an estimated 20 percent. That bill would have continued the existing personal income tax, but it would have raised the exemption from $800 to $1500. Congress debated the extension at length in a process that highlighted many underlying disagreements regarding the tax that had existed since its initial authorization.

Proponents of the income tax argued that it was a fair assessment based on the ability to pay, that it only affected a small number of people, and that it was the only means of collecting taxes from bondholders or an assessment on personal property.[3] Those who opposed the tax argued that it was a "war tax," it was unconstitutional, that it was unfairly levied on laborers in certain states, and that it offered "a premium for dishonesty" by encouraging evasion.

Despite strong opposition from the banking and manufacturing communities, the new income tax passed, limited to 2.5 percent on incomes above $2000 and to expire after 1871. Additionally, Congress assessed the 5 percent tax on dividends, interest, and government salaries for the year 1871 and ended them as well.

The income tax had been fairly successful in collecting revenue. Internal revenue collections comprised 47 percent of total revenues from 1863 until 1871. During the next decade, internal revenue collection fell to 38 percent of the total. Meanwhile, customs duties became a more significant portion, accounting for 56 percent of total revenues by 1880; however, they came nowhere close to reaching their level of importance from before the war.

Meanwhile, federal employment was growing. By 1816, the executive branch employed about 4500 people. Post Office employees accounted for about 75 percent of the total and about 10 percent were located in Washington, D.C. On the eve of the Civil War, the number of federal employees had grown to 36,100. By 1891, federal employment had grown to 150,850, although most employees were still outside of D.C. and working for the Post Office (about 63 percent). While the population had grown 8.5 times over the nineteenth century, government employment had grown almost thirty-four times. The majority of this growth was concentrated until after the Civil War.

Government debt fell following the Civil War and would continue to decrease throughout the period and even up until the onset of the US involvement in World War I. In fact, government debt as a percentage of the economy halved every decade from the 1870s through the 1890s. By 1899, debt as a percentage of the economy had fallen to 7 percent from a peak of 32 percent of the economy in 1869. Government debt continued to be an unpopular political necessity, and surpluses were applied to debt retirement without much resistance. However, during the late nineteenth and early twentieth centuries, opinions on how to best manage public debt would change.

Managing Debt in the Gilded Age

Debt management had evolved since the time when Alexander Hamilton was Treasury Secretary. However, the field of public finance was still in its infancy in the late-1800s. Meanwhile, debt remained an important political topic driving a number of debates within Congress as debt retirement remained a primary fiscal objective. It is, therefore, useful to be acquainted with the theoretical discussion of debt and the practices of debt management during this period. Government debt had once been a subject taken on not only by philosophers such as David Hume but also by Adam Smith and other early economists. However, by the 1880s and 1890s, the field of public finance had begun to break from economics and had taken shape within public administration. This corresponded with a transformation of the way experts considered government debt.

Government debt can be considered a form of redistribution. David Hume criticized government debt from the perspective that it enriches the "monied interest," or government bondholders, by taxing labor and capital. The cycle went something like this: war drove the accumulation of debt, debt was purchased by the wealthy, and then taxes were levied on the most productive members of society to finance the debt. This cycle was, as Hume put it, a "great encouragement to an [sic] useless and unactive life."

Adam Smith, the father of modern economics, also criticized government debt for empowering both the Crown and the well connected. However, in *An Inquiry into the Nature and Causes of the Wealth of Nations*, Smith points out that in England, the government received money from the merchant class, who had an interest in supporting enterprise through continued investment. On the contrary, in France, lenders to the government were landholding bachelors who "desire[d] only to live in splendor during their own time."[4] Smith thus puts a fine point on Hume's analysis that it does in fact matter who is buying the debt.

Karl Marx also paid attention to public debt, but in *Capital* he added the nuance that a powerful, debt fueled government was needed to detach workers from the means of production. After which, the state would cease to exist, as it was no longer needed. Therefore, much of his attention was placed on the class conflict created by government debt, such as the creation of an "aristocracy of finance."[5]

Adam Smith had pointed out that sinking funds contributed to a government's tendency to become indebted. As long as there was a mechanism for managing debt, governments would use debt to escape the political pressures of raising taxes on the current population. On the other hand, limits on the amount of debt permitted would encourage government saving.

Smith's view on the debt was related to his examination of mercantilism. Smith generally concluded that state involvement in primarily economic issues tended to be wasteful and inefficient. Therefore, government borrowing removed money that could otherwise be invested by the private sector. Furthermore, those who purchased government debt had less of an incentive to provide oversight over its uses than those who lent money to private citizens.

John Stuart Mill also believed that government borrowing was harmful, as it removed productive resources from the economy. Mill recommended the development of a metric that would ensure that interest rates fluctuated to reflect the amount of government loans.[6] To pay off debt, Mill recommended a one-time contribution but acknowledged that gradual retirement was more likely.[7]

The early-nineteenth-century economist David Ricardo, wrote in *Encyclopedia Britannica* that it was the appropriate policy to retire debt.[8] Furthermore, he suggested that the cost of war should be incurred based on a pay-as-you-go system. In other words, a government would levy new taxes to pay for conflict, and these new taxes adopted for the effort would be repealed after its conclusion.[9] Otherwise, Ricardo was in general agreement with the structure of a sinking fund elaborated upon by his contemporary Richard Hamilton (discussed in Chap. 1).[10] Put another way, both Adam Smith and Ricardo thought that sinking funds could increase government expenditures by increasing the debt that the government was supposed to buy back. Furthermore, sinking funds were often used to finance wars and it might be beneficial to make war financing more difficult.[11] Some years later, Keynes would defend the sinking fund for this same reason—he believed that sinking funds were an asset that provide policymakers with necessary flexibility.[12]

Around the 1880s, public finance started to fall out of fashion amongst economists and develop as its own field based on the experiences of governments and private businesses.[13] Soon, debt was seen as necessary to other public investments. For instance, Charles Bastable wrote in *Public Finance*, published in 1892, about the "fundamental difference between two classes of debt, the one contracted for non-economic ends, and the other for purposes of reproductive employment."[14] Bastable also argued that it was important for a budget system to be administered by a strong executive.[15]

At the time, the approach to government debt remained that balanced budgets were preferable, although the general disdain for government debt by public finance experts had declined by the 1890s.[16] Both finance experts and politicians had also soured on the use of a sinking fund, at least in the ways that Secretaries Hamilton or Chase had thought of such funds, for debt retirement by the 1880s (discussed in Chap. 2). That said, the government also continued its policy of debt reduction. Debt service as a percent of total spending reached 43 percent by 1873, but it then fell sharply until 1892, when it amounted to 7 percent of spending, and continued falling gradually until World War I.

Meanwhile, real government spending fell throughout the period from 6 percent of the economy in 1866 to 1 percent by 1916. Almost 60 percent of the reduction in real spending was due to the retirement of debt and reduction in debt service. Another 30 percent of the reduction was attributed to lower levels of spending on the army, even after accounting for the buildup associated with the Spanish-American War in 1898.

The process by which Congress authorized new debt had changed very little since the 1790s. Most of the time, Congress authorized new loans for a specific purpose, whether it be to fight a war or to build infrastructure, as long as the costs exceeded annual receipts. However, that would change during World War I with the enactment of the Liberty Loan and Bond Acts. The First Liberty Loan Act of 1917 gave Treasury additional flexibility to raise money during the war by replacing a specified loan authorization with new limits on bonds and certificates of indebtedness (also called "war savings certificates"), which were interest-bearing securities that matured after a year and similar to the T-bills that replaced these certificates in 1934.[17]

During the three-year period from 1917 to 1919, four more bond acts followed, including the "Liberty" and "Victory" Acts. These bills imposed an aggregate limit on bonds available for sale along with revolving authority which allowed Treasury to issue the certificates of indebtedness on a continuing basis as long as their outstanding balance at any given time did not exceed a specified amount. Furthermore, the Second Liberty Bond Act established the legal basis for Treasury securities that would be later amended on numerous occasions over the following decades.[18]

The Great Tariff Debate and the Income Tax

Tariffs had become a pressing issue in 1888 for two reasons. First, it was a presidential election year, and tariff policy had become a partisan issue after driving political debate for the last six years. Benjamin Harrison, the Republican candidate for president, was supportive of protectionist tariffs. President Grover Cleveland, the Democratic candidate running for re-election, had devoted his 1887 State of the Union message to reducing tariffs. Second, the government had been running large budget surpluses and was running out of ways to spend the extra money.

By the 1880s, government receipts exceeded spending by more than 40 percent.[19] The tariffs were responsible for a significant amount of revenue but the tax system had evolved during and after the Civil War to include a more robust system of internal taxation as well. Furthermore, gross domestic product (GDP) per capita was increasing as the economy expanded, even as immigration increased.[20] Meanwhile, the Southern states had been fairly effective at containing and even reducing the real growth in government spending.[21]

Both Democrats and Republicans proposed reducing tariff revenues, but they each had different reasons. The Democrats argued that revenue collections far exceeded demand for new resources; therefore, tariffs should be reduced in order to reduce revenues. This proposal would essentially function as a tax cut on consumers and farmers, while it would also eliminate the protection that domestic special interests received under the high tariffs.[22]

While this does not necessarily imply that Democrats were supportive of free trade, they did have a history of openness to tariff reductions. For instance, Democratic Speaker John Carlisle of Kentucky appointed William Morrison of Illinois and Roger Mills of Texas to the Ways and Means Committee in 1883 in order to revise the tariff law.[23] In his 1887 address, President Cleveland attempted to make a practical argument for free trade rather than an ideological one. Specifically, he maintained that "the question over free trade is irrelevant, and the persistent claim made in certain quarters that all the efforts to relieve the people form unjust and unnecessary taxation are schemes of so-called free traders is mischievous and far removed from any consideration for the public good."[24]

Republicans, on the other hand, recommended increasing tariffs in order to reduce imports, and thus, to put downward pressure on revenues. They argued that by cutting tariffs, imports would increase, which would actually increase government receipts. Although the heart of the argument was one of protection, Republicans had reverted back to advocating for lower government revenues, knowing both that this would be the impetus for reform and that tariffs had historically been justified for their contribution to government revenues.[25]

In 1884, the House voted on the first significant tariff reduction introduced by Morrison, who had become known as "Horizontal Bill" for his support of across-the-board tariff reductions.[26] However, the bill was defeated. By 1887, the government had paid off all of its redeemable debt and had started to use its large and growing surpluses to buy non-callable securities at high premiums.[27] At the same time, many in Congress consequently worried that if the government continued to run surpluses, it would hurt the economy by draining resources from the private sector.[28]

Spurred by the fervor that Cleveland had stirred in his 1887 address, the House took action under the leadership of then Chairman of Ways and Means Roger Mills. The Ways and Means' bill would have reduced the average *ad valorem* rate by about 27 percent.[29] The bill passed in the House with only a few dissenting votes from Democrats; however, despite the enthusiasm surrounding the bill, Congress adjourned before the Senate could consider it.[30] Meanwhile, President Cleveland lost his bid for reelection before Congress could meet again.

The electorate responded to the debate over tariffs by putting the protectionist Republicans in control of the Congress and the White House. The election led to the McKinley Tariffs in 1890. The McKinley Tariff bill increased average duties to nearly 50 percent for all imports.[31] Aiming to diffuse the political attack that tariffs helped manufactures at the expense of farmers, sponsors of the bill also included protective duties on agricultural products. However, farmers had already experienced little direct competition with foreign producers.

Revenues subsequently fell by about 4 percent as a result of the McKinley tariffs.[32] However, they were fairly unpopular and even led to a call for retaliatory interventions.[33] This was even after McKinley incorporated several policies aimed at popular appeal into the tariff bill, including the repeal of the sugar duty.[34] The negative public reaction to McKinley would send Grover Cleveland and Democrats back into control by 1892, and the new leadership reversed the tariffs in 1894.

The 1894 tariff bill, called the Wilson-Gorman tariff, was constructed on the principle of using tariffs for revenue only. During the initial consideration, President Cleveland asked James Carlisle, then Secretary of the Treasury, to develop new sources of revenue to pay for the $60–$75 million loss in revenue from the reduction of tariff rates. Carlisle would respond by proposing both an inheritance tax and a corporate income tax.

Instead of Carlisle's proposal, however, Ways and Means Chairman William Wilson of West Virginia moved forward with a personal income tax proposal drafted by William Jennings Bryan, then a Congressman from Nebraska.[35] The income tax would be set at 2 percent on personal and corporate incomes over $4000 which was expected to raise about $30 million. But before the bill was considered, the Ways and Means Committee decided to remove the income tax provision from the tariff bill and include it as part of an internal revenue bill instead. This bill would also increase the taxes on whisky, playing cards, and cigarettes. Together, these new taxes would raise about $45 million. As Speaker Charles Crisp, a Democrat from Georgia, said on the House floor, "we propose to meet the other deficiency if there be any, in the good old Democratic way – by reduction of expenditures."[36]

The Senate amended many of the tariff provisions but retained the income tax drafted by Bryan. Upon final passage, the votes in both the House and the Senate were bipartisan, divided instead by geographic regions. However, the income tax was almost immediately challenged in the courts. In the 1895 decision Pollock v. Farmers' Loan and Trust Co., the Supreme Court declared the income tax unconstitutional. If Congress was going to enact a new income tax it must do so on the basis of population and as apportioned to the states.[37]

The politics of the tariffs clearly revolved around revenues. However, at the time, the government was not in jeopardy of running large primary deficits should some tariff revenue been lost; revenues as a percent of the economy were falling. In 1880, the federal government was collecting about 3.2 percent of the economy. By 1895, revenues had fallen to 2.1 percent, and by 1910, they had fallen to 2.0 percent. However, spending was also very low. Spending as a percent of the economy was about 2.6 percent in 1880 and 2.1 percent in 1910. Still, another source of revenue would eventually be needed in order for tariff reductions to be sustainable in the long-run, even with low aggregate expenditures.

Early Administrative Reformers

The Dockery-Cockrell Commission was established on March 3, 1893, to examine the organization of executive departments, regulations, and methods used for administration. The Commission was also tasked with examining employee efficiency and compensation. To conduct this work, they hired organizational and accounting experts from the private sector. The Dockery-Cockrell Commission set an important precedent by outsourcing the review of government efficiency to experts outside of government. It also set a new standard with its high-level focus on government accountability, which would later become institutionalized. Furthermore, it was the first commission to use business practices to inform government functions.

The Commission's experts considered an "administration" as an entity acting "primarily in terms of accounting and auditing" rather than one which was organized around a president pursuing his policy agenda.[38] The Dockery Act, the Commission's main legislative achievement, altered the organization of the accounting and auditing systems used by the Treasury Department; rather than a decentralized system controlled by many auditors, a single Comptroller would oversee the auditors, who would oversee the Treasury's disbursement officers, who made payments on behalf of the government.

The law required the auditors both to examine all salaries and expenses and to certify the payment through the creation of a separate warrant.[39] This warrant would then be signed by the Secretary and the Comptroller before being given to the Treasurer to make the payment. The certification of the payment by the auditors was the official decision to make the payment. This marked a significant procedural change from the past, when the auditors would simply review the payment. The act essentially turned the Comptroller into a more powerful channel from which to prevent misuses of government resources.[40]

The Dockery Act also required the Secretary of the Treasury to provide Congress with an itemized list of spending and receipts from the previous year on the first day of each session of Congress. Previously, it had been the practice for the Treasury to submit an annual statement of finances, which included appropriations requests, to Congress. However, the Dockery Act streamlined both the accounting and auditing standards in such a way that established a new status quo used throughout much of the twentieth century.[41] In fact, the Comptroller's office (created under the Dockery Act) along with the standardization of accounting systems, would evolve into the General Accounting Office (GAO; now the Government Accountability Office) several decades later, after it was removed from Treasury and placed within the legislative branch.

The Dockery-Cockrell Commission proposed a number of other reforms to the budget process, most of which were accounting and personnel changes. However, many members of Congress had already been hesitant to embrace the Committee's recommendations. Nevertheless, the Commission represented a tentative step toward overhauling the budget process and increasing accountability.

Another influential institution in the early budget reform movement was the Committee on Department Methods, also known as the Keep Commission. Appointed in 1903, the Keep Commission was the brainchild of Gifford Pinchot, who was President Theodore Roosevelt's Chief of the Forest Service. The Keep Commission was initially intended to look for duplication in processes and responsibilities, but it instead found many inefficiencies within the executive departments. Many of the suggestions required legislation, which Roosevelt was unable to obtain, rendering much of the Commission's work initially ineffective. In fact, many of the suggested reforms did not take place until the Taft Administration came into power.[42]

The Commission was officially created on June 2, 1905, and consisted of seventy members of numerous executive departments in Washington. The managers of the Committee were Charles H. Keep (Assistant Secretary of the Treasury), Lawrence O. Murray (Commissioner of the Bureau of Corporations in the Department of Commerce and Labor), Gifford Pinchot (Chief of the Forest Service in the Department of Agriculture), and Frank H. Hitchcock (first Assistant Postmaster General).

The Keep Committee, under Roosevelt's direction, ultimately served as an investigative force emphasizing efficiency and exercising powers beyond its purview. Nevertheless, Roosevelt heeded the recommendations of the Keep Commission when he was in agreement with their proposals and often encouraged the Commission to advocate for greater executive powers. However, he disregarded their advice when they didn't see eye to eye.

There were subcommittees within the Keep Commission, each focused on specific executive tasks. These included Subcommittees on Accounting; Concentration of Routine Processes; Cost Keeping; Distribution, Recording and Handling of Correspondence; Inspection; Operation of Statutory and Miscellaneous Rolls; Organization of Editorial Work and Official Gazette; Organization of Libraries; Personnel; Salaries, Promotions, Reductions, Dismissals, Hours of Labor, and Sick and Annual Leave; Supplies; and Telephone and Telegraphic Systems.

In a letter from Theodore Roosevelt to Secretary Keep, Roosevelt outlined the objectives of the committee in order to "place the conduct of the executive business of the Government in all its branches on the most economical and effective basis in the light of the best modern business practice." These objectives included the following: to provide expert knowledge on the functions of the government; determine and recommend salaries that reflect the services performed; find a way to standardize government supplies; ensure that fiscal restrictions and regulations do "not interfere with executive discretion" and are simple and uniform across departments; modernize accounting practices; examine customs and practices within departments; look for ways to encourage cooperation in expert knowledge between departments; and encourage uniformity over efficiency.

Furthermore, recommendations from the Keep Commission would first be vetted before consulting with all the departments, and an official gazette would be published containing any executive orders or government updates. Roosevelt emphasized that there should be "brevity in correspondence and the elimination of useless letter writing." He criticized the many government bureaucrats who use their offices for "largely perfunctory letter writing," which he stated was wasteful and inefficient.[43]

On March 23, 1906, about one year after the appointment of the Keep Commission, President Roosevelt met with Gifford Pinchot informally. Roosevelt expressed that he did not want a "diagnosis" of the problem of "red tape" in the government. Rather, he wanted a recommendation for its improvement. Roosevelt also expressed that he would rather fix the problem through executive regulation than through legislation. He said, "I shall value the reports that I receive largely--not exclusively at all, but largely--in proportion as they do not call for legislation."[44]

Roosevelt also used the meeting to ask that Pinchot recommend that the President be given the power to transfer any part of the work of one department to another department "to put the departments on the best and most economical working basis." He expressed the urgency of "such a comprehensive, systematic effort to put the country's housekeeping in order." Roosevelt told Pinchot that there is less corruption in Pinchot's agency than many others, but the "inevitable tendency toward mere bureaucratic methods" exists in every government agency.[45]

The Keep Commission issued a number of reports, including recommendations for salaries, a restructuring of the federal workforce including job titles, and retirement. When the report on "Department Methods" was issued in 1907, salaries for federal employees were based on classifications made in 1853. At the time, the "organization [of executive departments and independent organizations] was compact and comparatively simple, and the work of discretion and supervision not especially exacting." However, the departments had expanded significantly since 1853. As a result, many additional jobs with new job titles were created without comparison to existing employees' pay, leading to instances where employees completing mundane tasks received higher compensation that those completing serious, technical tasks. The Commission observed that reorganization efforts to make processes and jobs more systematic were successful within departments, but no reorganization had been attempted across all departments.

The Keep Commission also recommended a bill that would start a program to provide retirement funds for federal employees that would pay for itself, serve as a mechanism to collect data, and avoid the incentive problems of other pension programs. The federal plan would provide an annuity or a one-time cash payment on retirement based on length of service. Congress ultimately did not introduce the bill.

Furthermore, the Keep Commission engaged in a three-month investigation into the Government Printing Office (GPO) that led to their discovery that the GPO purchased typesetting machines at unnecessarily high prices for political reasons.[46] A few employees of the GPO and their families purchased large shares of the printer company, Lanston, right before the GPO purchased typesetting machines from that company.[47] Seventy-two printers were purchased in order to increase the stock price.[48] The investigation was conducted on the basis of charges from a rival printer company, Mergenthaler, who argued the contract was corrupt. After its investigation, the Keep Commission recommended that the contract for seventy-two printers be canceled and recommended that President Palmer of the GPO not be held responsible; rather because of "his great age and physical feebleness," he had "become the mere plaything of his advisers and subordinates in the big printing shop."[49]

Ultimately, Mergenthaler failed to produce any evidence of corruption within the GPO, so the President (against the Keep Commission's recommendations), upheld the contract, stating, "in light of the failure of the company [Mergenthaler] to produce evidence of such corruption, it must be held that the charge was made recklessly, and the Mergenthaler company should be condemned for including such a charge in a formal communication with the President of the United States as a basis for action on his part."[50] Furthermore, after the investigation was closed, President Roosevelt asked for Palmer's resignation, also against the recommendation of the Keep Committee.[51] However, President Roosevelt deferred all other personnel decisions regarding the GPO, in light of the investigation, to the Keep Committee.[52] Roosevelt appointed a new head of the GPO, and received praise for "putting a practical printer instead of a politician at the head of the office."[53] The investigation into the GPO concluded on August 1, 1905.

The *New York Times* ran an editorial referring to the Keep Committee as "the President's personal investigating corps."[54] After the scandal discovered in the GPO, the Keep Commission was set to examine additional departments for similar scandals. By August 17, 1905, early discoveries of a scandal within the department of Agriculture had already been revealed, leading to public speculation of investigations into that department, including inaccuracies in cotton crop reporting, and within the Census Bureau. When asked about the nature of these investigations, Secretary Keep replied, "It should be understood that our investigation has nothing to do with irregularities, merely with administrative methods."[55]

Congressional Process Changes

Today, the House Rules Committee is an incredibly powerful institution within Congress because it has the ability to set the terms of debate and consideration of legislation before the entire House. This allows the majority to efficiently work through bills that have been produced by committee, or the Senate, but also closes off debate and amendments. However, the Rules Committee was not always as powerful.

The Speaker of the House has been a permanent member of the Rules Committee since 1858.[56] However, it was not until the 1880s that the Speaker began to use the committee, along with his ability to appoint committee chairmen and members, to significantly further the agenda of the majority party. Prior to the 1880s, committee chairmen had been responsible for managing the floor during the consideration of bills reported by their committees. For instance, when the jurisdiction of the House Ways and Means Committee included taxes, trade, spending, as well as the regulation of banks and money, the chairman was able to wield considerable influence over the legislative calendar.

Furthermore, the House minority had become extremely adept at using methods to slow the progress of legislation. For example, the House needed a quorum to be present in order to conduct business. In other words, more than just a simple majority of the members of the House were needed to legislate. It thus became common practice for members who were called on to vote to simply not answer the call. This tactic became known as the "disappearing quorum."

In 1883, the Rules Committee began issuing special orders governing the consideration of bills. At first, these special orders set the time for floor consideration, but evolved by the beginning of the 51st Congress (1889–1891) to end processes used by the minority to continually delay votes, including the "disappearing quorum," under Speaker Thomas Brackett Reed (these are known as "Reed's Rules").[57]

Around the same time, there were also important changes in committee jurisdiction. Between 1879 and 1885, the House stripped the

Appropriations Committees of much of their jurisdiction and gave primary authority over spending to the authorizing committees. Appropriations' responsibilities for agriculture, the military, Native Americans, pensions, and the Post Office were given to other committees. The appropriations bills for rivers and harbors, which were known for being rife with abuse, remained under the jurisdiction of the House Committee on Commerce. The Senate followed suit in 1899 when they also removed the Appropriations Committee from jurisdiction over eight of the fourteen bills.[58]

Accounting for Budget Reform

Budget process reform began as "an ongoing battle against corruption, bossism, unbridled plutocracy, and the general erosion of traditional values."[59] As John McCormick, the Speaker of the House in the middle of the twentieth century, would later say "Following the Civil War, there was a malodorous mountain of corruption, malfeasance, and sinister legislation."[60] Budgeting was about control, and it was sold as the basis for the eradication of cronyism. This was especially true at the municipal level. In fact, the budget process as we think of it today was started by a movement brought about within local and state governments that eventually spread to the national level.

Perhaps no single institution was as important in standardizing accounting models used by city auditors and comptrollers than the National Municipal League (NML), founded in 1894. The NML developed accounting standards that had great influence within city and state governments, and published its own journal called *Proceedings* to spread information.[61] In 1901, the Committee on Uniform Municipal Accounting and Statistics was established. The creation of both of these groups was an attempt to make municipal budgets more of an accounting exercise than a political tool. Rather than leaving the production of municipal budgets to the politicians, these institutions created uniform standards focused on needs, projections, and presentation of historical information in order to bring accountability to the process.

Progressive reformers adopted the NML standards while advocating for municipal budgets that would group expenditures together according to their purpose.[62] In 1906, Frederick Cleveland, Henry Bruere, and William Allen started the New York Bureau of Municipal Research (NYB) with financial support from Andrew Carnegie, J. P. Morgan, and John D. Rockefeller.[63] The three had previously worked together under Bruere's leadership on the Bureau of City Betterment to expose corruption with the New York City government.[64] Earlier, Cleveland had been a professor of finance at New York University.[65] Allen had completed a doctorate at Wharton, where he studied sanitary administration.[66] Bruere held a law degree from Harvard but had originally become interested in social work while studying under the economist Thorstein Veblen at the University of Chicago.[67]

In 1908, the NYB sponsored an exhibition in New York intended to expose the level of corruption and inefficiency brought on by the city government.[68] This exhibition, in addition to subsequent events held by the NYB in 1910 and 1911, brought large crowds and were used to turn budget decisions made by the government into news.[69] In 1916, Fredrick Cleveland wrote:

> *There are two things that make the news: one is a fight; the other is a scandal. A dog fight on the street may make news if each dog has a responsible backer. The events of a cockpit make news. Unimportant nobodies become news when they go into a public ring. The more important the parties contestant, the more important the news.*[70]

But rarely was budgeting newsworthy. As Arthur Eugene (A.E.) Buck, a member of the NYB wrote in 1924, "When a New York editor was asked to make his paper the medium for telling the people about the city budget, he replied: 'It can't be done. We do not make news; we print news.'"[71] However, exposing corruption within the system required transparency, and transparency required public debate. In an analysis of the Canadian budget system, Cleveland wrote:

> *When the head of a great government takes a position on a public platform before the chosen representatives of the people and issues a challenge to one and all to come and attack him, any issue joined becomes news that may travel on wires around the world and the next day be before every reader at his breakfast table. This is political news that cannot be kept out of the daily press. Given a parliamentary procedure, such as has been described, which is adapted to bring out everything that is scandalous and derogatory to persons of high positions and to make accusations the subject of "trial by battle," we need not be at a loss to understand why it is that "visible" government develops a press which prints political news.*[72]

The Presidential Treatment of Budget Reformers

President Taft, influenced by the priorities of the Keep Commission under President Roosevelt, sought out his own Commission to bring efficiency and unified methods across the government. Its primary goals were to improve and streamline accounting and reporting, organization, personnel, and business methods. The Commission on Economy and Efficiency, also sometimes known as the Taft Commission, was more educational and descriptive than it was reformative. While it proposed several changes in government operations, it largely spent its efforts studying existing problems. Nevertheless, the main issue it addressed was the need for a national budget system. The report contained the material foundational to the passage of the Budget and Accounting Act of 1921, almost ten years after the report.

The Taft Commission was led by Frederick A. Cleveland, Frank J. Goodnow (Dean at Columbia University Political Science department, and professor of administrative law and municipal science), Judge Walter W. Warwick (examiner of accounts for Panama Canal Commission), Harvey S. Chase (head of accounting firm in New England), and Merritt O. Chance (auditor of Post Office Department). The Commission's work elevated the role of the president, which posed a legitimate threat to Congress because he then had actionable power to reorganize the government.

Taft saw the problems with the Keep Commission, namely, its inability to accomplish many of its recommendations due to a lack of funding and Congressional friction. Thus, before organizing the Commission, Taft worked with Congress to secure executive appropriations. In 1910, the House passed a bill that established funding for the Commission on Economy and Efficiency, called "An Act Making appropriations for sundry civil expense of the Government for the fiscal year ending June thirtieth, nineteen hundred and eleven, and for other purposes." The act allocated $100,000 to the executive for the goals of the Commission. Taft later asked for "an appropriation for $75,000 and a reappropriation of the unexpected balance of the existing appropriation," and was granted these funds by Congress in the Sundry Civil Appropriations Act of 1912, approved March 4, 1911.

The Taft Commission focused on five different areas of reform to improve government functioning: organization, personnel, business methods, accounting, and the budget. Reports were published in each of these areas and were mainly focused on bringing the best practices from private businesses to the government, an effort to eliminate waste through a series of refinements to the administration. The need for a national budget was the single most significant reform.

The narrative of the report on the *Need for a National Budget* from the Taft Commission was that the government had grown too large and its actions too significant to leave so much control to Congress. Budgeting had come to reflect estimates of expenditures rather than consolidate financial and organization proposals. This suggested that the Executive was too weak to administer a government responsibly and reflected the devolution of the presidency into an agent of Congress rather than an equal branch of government.

The report suggested that tax and tariff policies were often disconnected from fiscal planning. There was no “periodical action” by the Congress on how revenues should be collected. However, experience during the nineteenth century suggests that this claim is only partly true. It would be more accurate to say that revenue policy was sometimes an afterthought intended to make ends meet. Changes to taxes, duties, debt, and other means of paying for activities were actively revisited on demand. However, they were also often phased-out once the temporary challenge (such as war) was financed.

While in Congress, James Madison had thought of budgeting in these terms as well (discussed in Chap. 1). It was, he believed, more appropriate to consider the merits of each expenditure proposal on its own distinct from the means used for finance. Once Congress had decided that an activity was worthy of resources, it would be appropriate to authorize its “ways and means” in another bill.

In the United States, the executive was responsible for carrying out the actions dictated by the Congress with the money provided by Congress. However, this had evolved into an awkward relationship; the president was unable to veto independent sections of appropriations bills and, therefore, may not have agreed with the policy of Congress. In the absence of a consolidated fiscal plan from the president, executive officers often found themselves with two masters: the president and Congress. Congress would request “operations expenditures” directly from agency officials while dictating the organization of the government. Meanwhile, the president would often instruct these same officials to withhold resources for activities that they did not agree with (an action known as impoundment). This was a recipe for dysfunction.

To progressive reformers, the absence of presidential control over revenue policy in the budget process represented a significant challenge. Specifically, the report stated that historically, the "budget is based upon the theory that the Government for whose operations expenditures must be made is already organized and discharges certain activities whose number and extend have already been determined."[73] It goes on to say that "the purpose of a budget is thus to finance an existing organization in order that it may be successfully prosecute defined lines of work."[74]

Two things needed to happen in order to reform or reorganize the federal government to meet the evolving challenges of the day. First, the concept of a budget needed to be redefined to consist of both a consolidated fiscal plan and necessary changes in law to implement that plan. Second, the president, "as the constitutional head of the executive branch," needed to exercise more control over that process.

In *The Need for a National Budget* report, the Taft Commission outlined the requisites for an executive budget process that have largely informed the process that we still have today. The Commission declared the president "the constitutional head of the executive branch of government" and that he should submit a budget to Congress "not later than the first Monday after the beginning of the regular session." That budget must contain the following elements: a message making the case for the significance of the proposals, a financial statement including a summary of expenditures and contracts made by the government, revenues, and a summary of changes in law that the budget would require. Furthermore, the budget should contain comparisons of proposals with historical spending and revenue levels. In addition to the budget submission by the president, departments should also submit detailed reports with spending arranged by "classes of work" so that they can be transparently compared to previous estimates.

The report was initially met with hostility from Congress, who saw the executive budget as a power grab by the president. In fact, Congress rejected the proposal and included language as part of an appropriations bill to both restrict funding for the Commission and prohibit any department from complying with the Commission's recommendation to streamline the budget requests through the president before being sent to Congress. Congress believed that they "knew best the character and extent of the information it desired" and stated explicitly that it would not "abdicate, even by implication, its prerogatives in this matter."[75]

Taft replied to the Congress on February 26, 1913, by issuing a report. The report was a sample budget and message, entitled "Message of the President of the United States Submitting for the Consideration of the Congress a Budget with Supporting Memoranda and Reports." His message included the following:

> *Under the Constitution the President is intrusted [*sic*] with the executive power and is responsible for the acts of heads of departments and their subordinates as his agents, and can use them to assist him in his constitutional duties, one of which is to recommend measures to Congress and to advise it as to the existing conditions and their betterment…*
>
> *If the President is to assume any responsibility for either the manner in which the business of the Government is transacted or the results obtained, it is evident that he cannot be limited by Congress to such information as the branch may think sufficient for his purpose. In my opinion, it is entirely competent for the President to submit a budget, and Congress cannot forbid or prevent it. It is quite within his duty and power to have prepared and to submit to Congress and to the country a statement of resources, obligations, revenues, expenditures, and estimates in the form he deems advisable. And this power I propose to exercise.*

Taft had a point. If the Constitution is to provide the president with powers to administer the executive branch, that power should include some influence over the budget process. In the end, this logic would generally make sense to the public whose support for a national budget process would grow over the next decade. This support, along with renewed attention to the debt with the onset of World War I, would convince Congress that fighting a national budget process was a losing effort.

Continued Support for Budget Reform

Edward Fitzpatrick's 1918 book, *Budget Making in a Democracy*, advocated for a decentralized process where administration, including budgeting decisions, were handed over to experts serving on independent boards. Furthermore, Fitzpatrick criticized the concept of an executive budget as a movement toward autocracy or a "one-man government." In a review of the book, Cleveland criticized his claim by responding, "proponents of the executive budget are the only ones who have proposed a method of popular control."[76]

His assertion was largely based on a claim previously published in his 1913 book, *Organized Democracy: An Introduction to the Study of American Politics*, that the president maintained "the right" to refuse the will of Congress and to petition the people directly on matters of disagreement. Cleveland believed that this level of popular control was necessary to a functioning democracy.

Still, his proposition for the public adjudication of disagreements and popular control could only work with a well-informed public. To ensure this, there must be a mechanism by which the citizenry can understand the activities of government. A transparent budget process accomplished this feat. This was an emphasized point in Cleveland's *The Budget and Responsible Government* published in 1920.

In addition to popular control of the government, a secondary priority for a strong democracy was a budget process that supported responsible administration. In fact, Cleveland came very close to supporting a parliamentary government over the American Republic for its more publicized budget process. For example, he wrote explicitly about the benefits of the Canadian government and system of budgeting which created conflict, engaging the public and forcing policy decision-making through budget process. Indeed, upon reviewing *The Budget and Responsible Government*, A. C. Hanford wrote that "although he does not state so in definite terms it appears that Dr. Cleveland's plan would in the last analysis, necessitate a parliamentary system of government."[77] Nevertheless, he did advocate for changes to the Constitution to reorder the budgeting powers from Congress to the executive.

William Willoughby, another member of Taft's Commission, explicitly proposed that Congress play a supporting, if any, role in budgetary decisions. In *The Problem of a National Budget*, published in 1918, Willoughby argued that "the executive alone is in a position to determine in detail the administrative needs of the governed and intelligently to formulate an annual work program."[78] Indeed, administrative changes would be necessary in order to reallocate budgetary powers from the Congress to the presidency.

The Beginning of the Modern Budget Process

I hope that Congress will bring to a conclusion at this session legislation looking to the establishment of a budget system. That there should be one single authority responsible for the making of all appropriations and that appropriations should be made not independently of each other, but with reference to one single comprehensive plan of expenditure properly related to the nation's income, there can be no doubt. I believe the burden of preparing the budget must, in the nature of the case, if the work is to be properly done and responsibility concentrated instead of divided, rest upon the executive. The budget so prepared should be submitted to and approved or amended by a single committee of each House of Congress and no single appropriation should be made by the Congress, except such as may have been included in the budget prepared by the executive or added by the particular committee of Congress charged with the budget legislation

—President Woodrow Wilson, Annual Message to Congress, December 2, 1919

The Constitution requires the support of the Congress for spending and taxes. Congressional affirmation requires deliberation and discussion. Open discussion requires Transparency. Therefore, the main purpose of the budget process should be to provide transparency regarding how and toward what purposes the money is allocated. The voters can then independently verify whether or not the budget is consistent with their values. This was a concept that the early reformers understood.

Taft believed that the budget should focus on the "principal government objectives in which the people of the United States are interested."[79] This included the national defense; the regulation of commerce; the promotion of industry (for instance, agriculture, fisheries, forestry, mining, manufacturing, and banking); the postal service; promotion of education, the arts, science, and recreation; public health; and the education and general care of Native Americans. However, the influence of these topics can evolve over time and the purpose of the budget is to reflect that evolution.

Although Taft had been unsuccessful in achieving a legislative victory by establishing a national budget, its day would soon come. A new budget process was part of the 1916 and 1920 Republican and Democratic platforms.[80] The 1920 Republican platform went so far as to suggest a "universal demand for an executive budget" whereas the Democratic platform recommended that the new budget system should include an audit of the executive, and that Congress should not be able to increase spending over the president's budget without a supermajority in support.[81]

In October 1919, after months of hearings, a Select Committee on Consideration of a National Budget System reported a bill which the House would quickly pass. The Senate proceeded with its own version which was introduced on December 2, 1919 and unanimously passed on May 1, 1920. There were some differences between the two, including who would be responsible for developing the new budget. In conference with the House, the Senators agreed to give the president responsibility over issuing the budget, but the Secretary of the Treasury would be the *ex-officio* director of the new budget bureau.[82]

However, that bill was be vetoed by President Woodrow Wilson on June 4, 1920, based on the belief that it was unconstitutional for Congress to remove the Comptroller, who was selected by the president.[83] Congress would return to a similar bill that contained the elements which Wilson opposed after the Warren Harding was elected to the presidency in 1920.

Finally enacted on June 10, 1921, the Budget and Accounting Act of 1921 cast the president as a central figure of the budget process. The president would both set the legislative agenda and guide policy decisions through the annual budget. The Budget Act also created several institutions that would serve to execute the budget-making process and provide oversight directly to Congress. These two institutions were called the Bureau of the Budget and the General Accounting Office, which would eventually become the Office of Management and Budget and the Government Accountability Office, respectively.

At first, the Bureau of the Budget resided within the Treasury Department under the supervision of a director who would answer to the president. Treasury had, historically, been central to the development of requests used by Congress to inform the annual appropriations. However, the early reformers (Cleveland, for example), believed that the success of the budget process would originate from its proximity to the president. The Bureau of the Budget was given the responsibility of developing a unified fiscal plan for the government, overseeing the fiscal operations of the departments, researching and developing new management techniques, promoting statistical and other budgetary information, and coordinating the administration's approach to new legislation.

The Bureau of the Budget immediately began treating appropriations by Congress as a ceiling for expenditures where fulfillment of executing of the law was a debatable motion.[84] The administration was not held to Congressional spending ceilings as long as they justifiably carried out their mission. The first Director of the Budget, Charles Dawes, instructed each agency to begin a process of distinguishing funds that were necessary to carry out their obligations and the excess.[85] The identified funds would be set aside in a reserve and used to either offset other deficiencies or to retire debt. In practice, this was not all that different than how funds were managed during the previous century. The actual innovation here was a consolidated effort by Treasury, through the new Bureau of the Budget, to coordinate savings efforts while clearly making priorities for the administration.

The General Accounting Office was created as an independent organization, and the comptroller's office within the Treasury Department was abolished. The Budget Act gave the Comptroller the authority to investigate the executive branch on all issues related to public funds and to make recommendations to Congress. However broad this mandate might sound, the General Accounting Office "concentrated primarily on conducting centralized audits and also engaged in such activities as claims settlement and rendering opinions as to the legality of the disbursement of government funds" until after World War II.[86] In other words, the GAO did little more than the Treasury Department's Comptroller prior to 1921.

There is little evidence that the process changes produced more accurate fiscal plans or even eliminated waste.[87] They did, however, create a sustained bureaucracy focused on producing the budget and overseeing the administration of policy. At the same time, the accounting systems slowly adopted administrative improvements.[88]

Summary

The progressive budget reformers sought efficiency through standardization, transparency, and bringing business practices to the government. Balancing the federal budget was seen as a form of efficiency. Their reforms came from the bottom up, beginning in New York City before spreading to the states and the federal government. However, ultimately, the executive budget process that was delivered through the Budget and Accounting Act of 1921 was a difficult fit when compared with the way that congressional budgeting and appropriations had developed until that point. This was lost on neither the Congress nor the reformers themselves.

Congress also continued to trade away their power over controlling the debt by replacing a system where they governed federal debt on a rolling basis with a series of limits. It is impossible to know for sure how the American Founders would have considered the fundamental reforms of this period, however, the control over taxation and debt had been seen as the primary determinant of sovereignty to be vested in the people.[89] The progressive reformers, of course, believed this power was best placed in the hands of the executive.

Notes

1. Kennon and Rogers, *The Committee on Ways and Means: A Bicentennial History.*
2. Jefferson had advocated for both reducing internal taxes and the size of government as president.
3. Advocates did not argue that income was equivalent to personal property. Rather, personal property was not taxed and an income tax was closer to a personal property tax than any other assessment made by the federal government.
4. Adam Smith, *An Inquiry into the Nature and Causes of the Wealth of Nations by Adam Smith*, ed. Edwin Cannan (London: Methuen, 1904).
5. Sandy Brian Hager, *Public Debt, Inequality, and Power: The Making of a Modern Debt State* (Oakland: University of California Press, 2016).
6. John Stuart Mill, *Principles of Political Economy, 7th edition* (London: Longmans, Green, and Company, 1909).
7. Jesse Burkhead, "The Balanced Budget," *The Quarterly Journal of Economics* 68, no. 2 (1954): 191–216.
8. Ibid.
9. Ibid.
10. Ibid.
11. David Levy, "Paradox of the Sinking Fund," in *Deficits*, by James M. Buchanan, Charles K. Rowley, and Robert D. Tollison (New York, NY: Basil Blackwell, Inc., 1987).
12. Ibid.
13. For instance, Alfred Marshall's *Principles of Economics* does not address government debt. (Burkhead 1954).
14. Burkhead, "The Balanced Budget."
15. Ibid.
16. Ibid.
17. H.J. Cooke and M. Katzen, "The Public Debt," *The Journal of Finance* 9. no. 3 (1954): 298–303.
18. Ibid.
19. Douglas A. Irwin, "Higher Tariffs, Lower Revenues? Analyzing the Fiscal Aspects of 'The Great Tariff Debate'," *The Journal of Economic History* 58, no. 1 (1998): 59–72.
20. Barry Eichengreen, Asmaa El-Ganainy, Rui Redro Esteves, and Kris James Mitchener, "Public Debt Through the Ages", *IMF Working Paper* Number WP/19/6 (2019).
21. Ibid.
22. Irwin, "Higher Tariffs, Lower Revenues? Analyzing the Fiscal Aspects of 'The Great Tariff Debate'."
23. Kennon and Rogers, *The Committee on Ways and Means: A Bicentennial History.*

24. Grover Cleveland, "Third Annual Message (first term)," *The American Presidency Project*. John Woolley and Gerhard Peters. December 6, 1887, www.presidency.ucsb.edu/node/204041
25. Irwin, "Higher Tariffs, Lower Revenues? Analyzing the Fiscal Aspects of 'The Great Tariff Debate'."
26. Kennon and Rogers, *The Committee on Ways and Means: A Bicentennial History*.
27. D. A. Irwin (1998) notes that John James in Public Debt Management finds that the government paid as much as 29 percent premiums to chase non-callable debt.
28. Ibid.
29. Ibid.
30. Kennon and Rogers, *The Committee on Ways and Means: A Bicentennial History*.
31. Joanne Reitano, *The Tariff Question in the Gilded Age: The Great Tariff Debate of 1888* (University Park, PA: Pennsylvania State University Press, 1994).
32. Irwin, "Higher Tariffs, Lower Revenues? Analyzing the Fiscal Aspects of 'The Great Tariff Debate'."
33. Marc-William Palen, "Protection, Federation and Union: The Global Impact of the McKinley Tariff upon the British Empire, 1890–94", *Journal of Imperial and Commonwealth History* 38, no. 3 (2010): 395–418.
34. The tariff also gave the sugar industry a subsidy in an attempt to offset any trouble caused by the repeal of the tariff.
35. Kennon and Rogers, *The Committee on Ways and Means: A Bicentennial History*.
36. Speaker of the House Charles Crisp speaking, 53rd Cong., 2nd sess., *Congressional Record* 26, February 1, 1894 (Washington, DC: U.S. Government Printing Office, 1894), 1791.
37. Francis R. Jones, "Pollock v. Farmers' Loan and Trust Company," *Harvard Law Review* 9, no. 3 (1895): 198–211.
38. Oscar Kraines, "The Dockery-Cockrell Commission, 1893–1895," *The Western Political Quarterly* 7, no. 3 (1954): 417–462.
39. Bolles (1969) provides a history of the accounting system prior to this period including the issuance of the appropriations warrant and roles of the US Treasurer and other responsible parties.
40. Kraines, "The Dockery-Cockrell Commission, 1893–1895."
41. Ibid.
42. Gifford Pinchot, *Breaking New Ground* (New York, NY: Harcourt Brace and Co., 1947).
43. Harold T. Pinkett, "The Keep Commission, 1905–1909: A Rooseveltian Effort for Administrative Reform." *The Journal of American History* 52, no. 2 (1965): 297–312.

44. "President Would Cut Out Red Tape: He Tells the Keep Commission That There Is Too Much of It in Departments," *New York Herald*, March 24, 1906.
45. Ibid.
46. "President Stops Contract: Mergenthaler Company Believes Politics Figures in Choice of Machines," *New York Times*, June 25, 1905.
47. "Typesetting Stock Scandal: Printing Office Inquiry as to Holdings of Employees," *The New York Times*, July 4, 1905.
48. "Printer Palmer May Go: Typesetting Investigation at Washington Expected to Cause a Change," *The New York Times*, July 14, 1905.
49. "Against Printer Palmer: Commission Would Remove Him and Cancel Type Machine Contract," *The New York Times*, August 1, 1905.
50. "Palmer Order Upheld; His Method Censured: President Denounces Mergenthaler Co. for False Charge," *The New York Times*, September 11, 1905.
51. "Printer Palmer Ousted: Ignored President's Order—Ricketts Is in His Place," *The New York Times*, September 9, 1905.
52. "Will Not Overrule Palmer: President to Leave Printing Office Removals to Keep Committee," *The New York Times*, September 5, 1905.
53. "New Public Printer In: Ricketts Gets an Ovation—Palmer to Demand Investigation," *The New York Times*, September 10, 1905.
54. "Palmer Order Upheld; His Methods Censured: President Denounces Mergenthaler Co. for False Charge," *The New York Times*, September 11, 1905.
55. "Keep Makes Report on Machine Inquiry: Investigation Into Contract for Typesetting Machines Ends," *The New York Times*, August 17, 1905.
56. Valerie Heitshusen, *The Speaker of the House: House Officer, Party Leader, and Representative*, Report to Congress (Washington, DC: Congressional Research Service, 2017).
57. House Committee on Rules, *A History of the Committee on Rules, 1st to 97th Congress, 1789–1981* (Washington, DC: U.S. Government Printing Office, 1983).
58. United States Senate Committee on Appropriations, *Committee on Appropriations, 1867–2008* (Washington, DC: U.S. Government Printing Office, 2008).
59. R. Penny Marquette and Richard K. Fleischman, "Government/Business Synergy: Early American Innovations in Budgeting and Cost Accounting," *The Accounting Historians Journal* 19, no. 2 (1992): 123–145.
60. *Congressional Record*, 79th Cong., 2nd sess., March 11, 1946.
61. Marquette and Fleischman, "Government/Business Synergy: Early American Innovations in Budgeting and Cost Accounting."
62. Ibid; (Rubin 2008) provides another good history of the NYB and the early progressive budget movement.

63. Marquette and Fleischman, "Government/Business Synergy: Early American Innovations in Budgeting and Cost Accounting."
64. Jonathan Kahn, *Budgeting Democracy: State Building and Citizenship in America* (Ithaca, NY: Cornell University Press, 1997). Kahn offers a good history of the early budget reformers including The New York Bureau of Municipal Research, the campaign for a national budget system, and the early years of the Bureau of the Budget.
65. Augustus Cerillo, *Reform in New York City: A Study of Urban Progressivism* (New York: Routledge, 1991).
66. Ibid.
67. Ibid.
68. Marquette and Fleischman, "Government/Business Synergy: Early American Innovations in Budgeting and Cost Accounting."
69. Ibid.
70. Frederick Cleveland, "Budget Making and the Increased Cost of Government," *The American Economic Review* 6, no. 1 (1916): 50–70.
71. A.E. Buck, "The Development of the Budget Idea in the United States," *The Annals of the American Academy of Political and Social Science* 113 (1924): 31–39.
72. Cleveland, "Budget Making and the Increased Cost of Government."
73. The Commission on Economy and Efficiency, 62nd Cong., 2nd sess. "The Need for a National Budget," *U.S. House of Representatives Document* 854, June 12, 1912.
74. Ibid.
75. Stephen Skowronek, *Building a New American State: The Expansion of National Administrative Capacities, 1877–1920* (Cambridge: Cambridge University Press, 1982).
76. Frederick A. Cleveland, "Review of Budget Making in a Democracy: A New View of Budget Making by Edward A. Fitzpatrick," *Political Science Quarterly* 34, no. 3 (1919): 510–512.
77. A.C. Handford, "Review of The Budget and Responsible Government by Frederick A. Cleveland and Arthur Eugene Buck: Evolution of the Budget of Massachusetts, 1691–1919 by Luther H. Gulick," *The American Political Science Review* 14 (1920): 711–713.
78. William Willoughby, *The Problem of a National Budget* (Berkeley, CA: University of California Libraries, 1918).
79. William Taft, "Message of the President of the United States on Economy and Efficiency in the Government Service", Communication to Congress, April 4, 1912.
80. "Republican Party Platforms: Republican Party Platform of 1916," *The American Presidency Project*, June 7, 1916, https://www.presidency.ucsb.edu/documents/republican-party-platform-1916

81. "Democratic Party Platforms, 1920 Democratic Party Platform," *The American Presidency Project*, June 28, 1920, https://www.presidency.ucsb.edu/documents/1920-democratic-party-platform; "Republican Party Platforms: Republican Party Platform of 1920," *The American Presidency Project*, June 8, 1920, https://www.presidency.ucsb.edu/documents/republican-party-platform-1920
82. G. Granger, "The national budget system," *Editorial research reports 1930* 4 (Washington, DC: CQ Press, 1930).
83. The language allowed Congress to remove the Comptroller by resolution.
84. Louis Fisher, "The Politics of Impounded Funds", *Administrative Science Quarterly* 15, no. 3 (1970): 361–377.
85. Ibid.
86. John T. Rourke, "The GAO: An Evolving Role", *Public Administration Review* 38, no. 5 (1978): 453–457.
87. Hugh Rockoff, "The Origins of the Federal Budget", *The Journal of Economic History* 45, no. 2 (1985): 377–382.
88. John McDiarmid, "Public Administration: Reorganization of the General Accounting Office," *The American Political Science Review* 31, no. 3 (1937): 508–516.
89. Ferguson, *The Power of the Purse: A History of American Public Finance, 1776–1790.*

References

Bolles, Albert S. 1969a. Financial History of the United States from 1774 to 1789. Vol. I. 3 vols. New York, NY: Augustus M. Kelly Publishers.

———. 1969b. Financial History of the United States from 1861 to 1885 Volume III. New York, NY: Augustus M. Kelley Publishers.

Buck, A.E. 1924. "The Development of the Budget Idea in the United States." The Annals of the American Academy of Political and Social Science 113: 31–39.

Burkhead, Jesse. 1954. "The Balanced Budget." The Quarterly Journal of Economics 68 (2): 191–216.

Cerillo, Augustus. 1991. Reform in New York City: A Study of Urban Progressivism. New York: Routledge.

Cleveland, Frederick A. 1919. "Review of Budget Making in a Democracy: A New View of Budget Making by Edward A. Fitzpatrick." Political Science Quarterly 34 (3): 510–512.

Cleveland, Frederick. 1916. "Budget Making and the Increased Cost of Government." The American Economic Review 6 (1): 50–70.

Cleveland, Grover. 1887. "Third Annual Message (first term)." The American Presidency Project. John Woolley and Gerhard Peters. December 6. www.presidency.ucsb.edu/node/204041.

Congressional Record. 79th Cong., 2nd sess. 1946. March 11.

Cooke, H.J., and M. Katzen. 1954. "The Public Debt." The Journal of Finance 9 (3): 298–303.

Crisp, Charles. 1894. Congressional Record. Vol. 26. Washington, DC: Government Printing Office, February 1.

1920. "Democratic Party Platform, 1920 Democratic Party Platform." The American Presidency Project. June 28. https://www.presidency.ucsb.edu/documents/1920-democratic-party-platform.

Ferguson, E. James. 1961. The Power of the Purse: A History of American Public Finance, 1776–1790. Chapel Hill, NC: The University of North Carolina Press.

Fisher, Louis. 1970. "The Politics of Impounded Funds." Administrative Science Quarterly 15 (3): 361–377.

Granger, G. 1930. "The national budget system. Editorial research reports 1930 (Vol. IV)." Congressional Quarterly. Accessed June 21, 2019. http://library.cqpress.com/cqresearcher/cqresrre1930120100.

Hager, Sandy Brian. 2016. Public Debt, Inequality, and Power: The Making of a Modern Debt State. Berkeley, CA: University of California Press.

Handford, A.C. 1920. "Review of The Budget and Responsible Government by Frederick A. Cleveland and Arthur Eugene Buck: Evolution of the Budget of Massachusetts, 1691–1919 by Luther H. Gulick." The American Political Science Review 14: 711–713.

Heitshusen, Valerie. 2017. The Speaker of the House: House Officer, Party Leader, and Representative. Report to Congress, Washington: Congressional Research Service.

Irwin, Douglas A. 1998. "Higher Tariffs, Lower Revenues? Analyzing the Fiscal Aspects of the 'Great Tariff Debate'." The Journal of Economic History 58 (1): 59–72.

Irwin, Douglas. 2010. "Revenue or Reciprocity? Founding Feuds Over Early U.S. Trade Policy." In Founding Choices: American Economic Policy in the 1790s, by Douglas Irwin and Richard Sylla. Chicago, IL: University of Chicago Press.

James, John A. 1984. "Public Debt Management and Nineteenth Century American Economic Growth." Explorations in Economic History 21 (2): 192–217.

Jones, Francis R. 1895. "Pollock v. Farmers' Loan and Trust Company." Harvard Law Review 9 (3): 198–211.

Kahn, Jonathan. 1997. Budgeting Democracy: State Building and Citizenship in America. Ithaca, NY: Cornell University Press.

Kennon, David R., and M. Rebecca Rogers. 1989. The Committee on Ways and Means: A Bicentennial History, 1789–1989. Washington, DC: Government Printing Office.

Kraines, Oscar. 1954. "The Dockery-Cockrell Commission." The Western Political Quarterly 7 (3): 417–462.

Levy, David. 1987. "Paradox of the Sinking Fund." In Deficits, by James M. Buchanan, Charles K. Rowley and Robert D. Tollison. New York, NY: Basil Blackwell, Inc.

Marquette, Penny R., and Richard K. Fleischman. 1992. "Government/Business Synergy: Early American Innovations in Budgeting and Cost Accounting." The Accounting Historians Journal 19 (2): 123–145.

McDiarmid, John. 1937. "Public Administration: Reorganization of the General Accounting Office." The American Political Science Review 31 (3): 508–516.

Mill, John Stuart. 1909. Principles of Political Economy. 7th. London: Longmans, Green, and Company.

New York Herald. 1906. "President Would Cut Out Red Tape: He Tells the Keep Commission That There Is Too Much of It in Departments." March 24.

Palen, Marc-William. 2010. "Protection, Federation and Union: The Global Impact of the McKinley Tariff upon the British Empire, 1890–94." Journal of Imperial and Commonwealth History 38 (3): 395–418.

Pinchot, Gifford. 1947. Breaking New Ground. New York, NY: Harcourt Brace and Co.

Pinkett, Harold T. 1965. "The Keep Commission, 1905–1909: A Rooseveltian Effort for Administrative Reform." The Journal of American History 52 (2): 297–312.

Reitano, Joanne. 1994. The Tariff Question in the Gilded Age: The Great Tariff Debate of 1888. University Park, PA: Pennsylvania State University Press.

1916. "Republican Party Platforms: Republican Party Platform of 1916." The American Presidency Project. June 7. https://www.presidency.ucsb.edu/documents/republican-party-platform-1916.

1920. "Republican Party Platforms: Republican Party Platform of 1920." The American Presidency Project. June 8. https://www.presidency.ucsb.edu/documents/republican-party-platform-1920.

Rockoff, Hugh. 1985. "The Origins of the Federal Budget." The Journal of Economic History 45 (2): 377–382.

Rourke, John T. 1978. "The GAO: An Evolving Role." Public Administration Review 45 (2): 377–382.

Rubin, Irene S. 2008. "Who Invented Budgeting in the United States?" In Public Budgeting: Policy, Process, and Politics, by Irene S. Rubin. Armonk, NY: M.E. Sharpe.

Skowronek, Stephen. 1982. Building a New American State: The Expansion of National Administrative Capacities, 1877–1920. Cambridge: Cambridge University Press.

Smith, Adam. 1904. An Inquiry into the Nature and Causes of the Wealth of Nations. Edited by Edwin Cannan. London: Methuen.

Taft, William. 1912. "Message of the President of the United States on Economy and Efficiency in the Government Service." Communication to Congress. April 4.

The Commission on Economy and Efficiency. 1912. The Need for a National Budget. Document 854, 62nd Congress, 2nd Session, Washington: U.S. House of Representatives.

The New York Times. 1905. "Against Printer Palmer: Commission Would Remove Him and Cancel Type Setting Machine Contract." August 1.

The New York Times. 1905. "Keep Makes Report on Machine Inquiry: Investigation Into Contract for Typesetting Machines Ends." August 17.

The New York Times. 1905. "Palmer Order Upheld: His Method Censured: President Denounces Mergenthaler Co. for False Charge." September 11.

The New York Times. 1905. "Palmer Order Upheld; His Methods Censured: President Denounces Mergenthaler Co. for False Charge." September 11.

The New York Times. 1905. "President Stops Contract: Mergenthaler Company Believes Politics Figures in Choice of Machines." June 25.

The New York Times. 1905. "Printer Palmer May Go: Typesetting Investigation at Washington Expected to Cause a Change." July 14.

The New York Times. 1905. "Printer Palmer Ousted: Ignored President's Order—Ricketts Is in His Place." September 9.

The New York Times. 1905. "Typesetting Stock Scandal: Printing Office Inquiry as to Holdings of Employees." July 4.

The New York Times. 1905. "Will Not Overrule Palmer: President to Leave Printing Office Removals to Keep Committee." September 10.

U.S. House Committee on Rules. 1983. A History of the Committee on Rules, 1st to 97th Congress, 1789–1981. Washington, DC: U.S. Government Printing Office.

U.S. Senate Committee on Appropriations. 2008. Committee on Appropriations, 1867–2008. Washington, DC: U.S. Government Printing Office.

Willoughby, W.F. 1931. Financial Condition and Operations of the National Government, 1921–1930. Washington, DC: The Brookings Institution.

Willoughby, William. 1918. The Problem of a National Budget. Berkeley, CA: University of California Libraries.

CHAPTER 5

The End of Balanced Budgets

During the 1930s it had become commonplace to hear politicians demanding that the budget be balanced immediately for numerous reasons. In January 1940, President Franklin D. Roosevelt responded by suggesting that "it costs nothing to make such statements and they can be decorated to fit into the applause of many audiences."[1] Roosevelt was writing as a leader burdened by the decisions he faced during one of the worst economic recessions in the country's history. He was also speaking to the public, who surely would have judged the president on his track record after running in both the 1932 and 1936 elections on balancing the budget based in large part on reducing spending.

Between 1789 and 1932, the annual budget had been balanced 66 percent of the time (or 87 percent of the time when excluding periods of major wars and economic recessions).[2] Balancing the budget was a common strategy to retire debt and debt retirement was the primary long-run fiscal policy objective until the 1930s. This objective made it desirable to balance the budget during all periods of the business cycle. It was also integral in informing revenue and spending policy. When the budget was in deficit, both Congress and the president debated fiscal reforms to bring the budget back into surplus.

There were periods when debt rollover was entertained as a retirement strategy based on its theoretical benefits. However, this was rarely put into practice, and it eventually fell out of style once Gallatin took over the

P. Winfree, *A History (and Future) of the Budget Process in the United States*, https://doi.org/10.1007/978-3-030-30959-6_5

Treasury under Jefferson. Instead, the sinking fund was applied as a way to manage debt retirement from the 1790s and throughout much of the 1800s and would return as a means of managing debt retirement following World War I.[3] Furthermore, Congress routinely approved new loans when they needed to finance any number of projects, from infrastructure investments to the military, until 1917.

But that all changed during the Great Depression. Prior to the Depression, the federal government did not have a significant role in providing for poor relief or unemployment assistance.[4] It was widely accepted that the best thing the government could do was to provide confidence in the economy by limiting the amount of credit for public use. Jobs were best created by private businesses and poor relief was left to private institutions or state and local governments.[5]

Furthermore, recessions were thought to be caused by either too much money in the economy or overly optimistic views of the future.[6] In other words, when the money supply contracted or when investors realized that the growth projections were too high, there would be a large stock of unprofitable investments.[7] The Depression was believed to be the readjustment of investment to the correct level, hence government spending would only exacerbate the problem.

President Roosevelt, however, would push a series of public works programs, a compulsory social insurance program unattached to financial need, an unemployment insurance program, and grants to states to provide welfare as part of his New Deal. The impetus for these programs was the belief that the government could do more to manage economic cycles through fiscal and monetary policy and should thus help provide relief. Many of these programs would be enacted by 1935 and ruled constitutional by the Supreme Court in United States v. Butler (1936) and Helvering v. Davis (1937) under the "general welfare" clause.[8]

The New Deal period marked two important turning points, both in the legal and fiscal realms off government power. First, the Supreme Court had explicitly expanded Congressional power to tax, spend, and issue debt on behalf of a more expansive view of promoting the "general welfare." Second, the New Deal brought about a fiscal policy outlook where the government assumed responsibility over promoting full employment and providing poor relief through deficit spending. The president's budget would subsequently evolve throughout the Roosevelt administration. At first, the primary fiscal objective remained debt retirement. But over time, the Roosevelt administration presented a plan to manage the business cycle and continually put pressure on Congress to use tax reform to reduce perceived inequities.

This transition in power was not unchallenged. The 1936 Republican Party Platform condemned the New Deal for having "dishonored American traditions and flagrantly betrayed the pledges upon which the Democratic Party sought and received public support."[9] "The powers of Congress," Republicans decried, "have been usurped by the President." In reality, the federal government's powers and expected interventions in the economy would increase drastically because of the New Deal.

In addition to the precedent set by the New Deal, other important changes ripened during this period. Congress attempted to take back some control over the appropriations process but ultimately failed. The income tax came to replace tariffs and other internal taxes as a permanent source of revenue. After the end of World War II, Congress would enact the Employment Act of 1946, which committed the government to the new primary objective of using fiscal policy to reach full employment.[10] Congress also went through a reorganization to cope with the "greatly enlarged and active Executive Branch," that expanded the size of committees and introduced a new legislative budget process.[11]

Appropriating Change

Several important changes to the appropriations process occurred early in the twentieth century. In 1920, the House voted to give the Appropriations Committee jurisdiction over general appropriations bills on a contentious 158 to 154 vote that divided the parties.[12] The new House Rule XXI prohibited authorizing committees from providing appropriations, thus ending a process that had been followed since 1865 but expanded in practice since the 1880s. The Senate followed suit in 1922.

The Antideficiency Act, enacted in 1870, was erected from language originally included as part of an 1868 appropriations bill restricting deficient appropriations. The 1870 Act was intended to curb "coercive deficiencies," which was a common practice within agencies, where money allocated for the entire year would be used up within a few months. Additionally, agencies would enter into contracts under the assumption that Congress would later authorize appropriations for the agency. The 1870 law, however, was largely a failure. In a well-known example from

1879, the Post Office spent all of its appropriation and asked Congress for an additional $2 million, including $1.7 million to fulfill contractual agreements made after running out of spending authority.[13]

By 1905, the deficiency appropriations process had been abused so frequently that Congress amended the 1870 law in an attempt to enhance its enforcement powers. The 1905 changes required that the annual budget authority be apportioned throughout the year and that Congress be notified when a deficiency appropriation was anticipated. The changes also carried criminal penalties including "fines, imprisonment, and removal from office for violations."[14] However, these revisions still failed to curb deficiency appropriations. In fact, it was less than a year before the executive branch requested another deficiency appropriation in 1906.

The 1905 amendments also included provisions intended to ban "moral obligation" deficiencies. These were deficient appropriations incurred when employees volunteered their time or when federal employees routinely worked overtime hours not authorized by Congress.[15] In 1868, Congress had imposed an eight-hour work restriction for federal employees, and overtime pay had become a relevant issue by 1900.

In 1920, the General Accounting Office was created with jurisdiction of the oversight of appropriations to ensure compliance with the Antideficiency Act's requirements, while the Bureau of the Budget would soon come to oversee the execution of the budget and apportionment process. However, the General Accounting Office, "which conceptually should provide the policing talent to Congress [within regards to Antideficiency Act compliance], has not functioned effectively in this area."[16] To this day, no one has ever been convicted under the criminal terms of the Antideficiency Act. This has led observers to refer to the Act as "more of a matter of folklore than law."[17]

Rise of the Income Tax

The United States entered a recession in January 1913.[18] Later that year, Congress passed the Federal Reserve Act, establishing a central banking system with twelve semi-autonomous regional banks that would "furnish a national currency." The authors of the Federal Reserve Act believed that the new law would prevent future bank panics altogether which were endemic throughout the rural US. [19] An earlier bill, the Aldrich-Vreeland Act, had also provided a method to issue emergency currency as a response to the 1907 panic, but was surpassed by the Federal Reserve system.[20]

The 16th Amendment to the Constitution was also ratified in 1913, resolving the legal issues posed by an establishment of the income tax discussed in Chap. 3. Congress was quick to seize its new-found Constitutional authority. The Revenue Act of 1913 lowered tariffs and replaced the lost revenue with an income tax of 1 percent on income between $0 and $20,000, and then six additional brackets with a marginal tax rate of 7 percent on income above $500,000.

When the World War broke during the summer of 1914, a small banking panic was triggered but ultimately put to rest as the emergency cash from Aldrich-Vreeland became available.[21] The war, however, brought recovery as the demand for goods produced in the United States increased in Europe. The later stages of the recovery would also be fueled by an increase in the money supply, as the Federal Reserve monetized a significant portion of the debt during 1917 and 1918.[22]

Between 1914 and 1919, the federal government began to grow in response to the war effort. Civilian employment alone increased from 401,900 to 794,300 with employees at the War and Navy Departments accounting for only half of the increase. The nonfarm workforce grew by 12 percent (3.3 million workers) between 1914 and 1918.[23] Nominal manufacturing wages grew 20 percent faster than the cost of living between 1916 and 1918.[24]

The wartime recovery came with a hefty price tag. Annual spending increased from $726 million in 1914 to $18.5 billion by 1919. In 1917, spending was 0.6 percent of the economy, and by 1919, it was 11.4 percent. The usual methods were used to pay for the war: public debt, taxes, and money creation.

President Wilson wanted taxes, rather than debt, to fund the war. He thought that the cost of war should, to the greatest extent possible, be "borne by taxation of the present generation."[25] Likewise, Wilson's Treasury Secretary William Gibbs McAdoo thought debt would be too inflationary and that the government should be financed by progressive income and wealth taxes even in times of peace.[26] The Chairman of the House Ways and Means Committee, Claude Kitchen of North Carolina, professed that "It would be unjust and cruel and cowardly to shift upon them the burden [of the war]."[27] Congress backed the administration early in 1917, passing a special appropriation for the military using money from estate and excess profits taxes.[28]

The Department of Treasury initially estimated that about half of all war spending would be funded through taxes.[29] However, at the war's conclusion, only 22 percent was financed through taxes.[30] Public borrowing amounted to about 58 percent of the total financing.[31] Meanwhile, debt increased from 5 to 32 percent of the economy between 1917 and 1919. Money creation accounted for the remainder (20 percent) of the war financing.[32] The reliance on public borrowing was consistent with present-day theories of optimal tax smoothing, which state that the economy optimizes when tax rates stay relatively steady over periods of time.[33] Thus public borrowing during war was seen as a better alternative to drastically increasing taxes to finance it.

Secretary McAdoo believed that there had to be popular support for the war reflected in both the sales of bonds and taxes. McAdoo wrote that war "is a kind of crusade; and like all crusades, it sweeps along with powerful romanticism."[34] The Treasury hired movie stars to market government bonds and artists to produce now famous posters exhorting the public with messages like "Your Forefathers Died for Liberty in 1776 – What Will You do for it in 1917?" and "Let's End It – Quick with Liberty Bonds."[35]

McAdoo believed the tax burden would need to fall predominately on the rich and those most likely to benefit from war profiteers, as there was still a popular conception of business having benefited from earlier wars. McAdoo even told Kitchen that the Congress should distinguish between profits from war-related industries and all other businesses as the former would have fewer political adversaries.[36] Other revenue would be raised through excise taxes on "unproductive behavior" such as tobacco, chewing gum, liquor, and soft drinks. This was, in part, a pivot from the government's response to funding the Spanish American War twenty years earlier which had put a larger burden of taxation on the working classes.

In order to meet Wilson's demand for additional tax revenue to fund the war, Congress passed the Revenue Act of 1916 and War Revenue Act of 1917. Both laws significantly increased the number of tax brackets and the top rates. The 1916 law increased the top rate from 7 to 15 percent while the 1917 tax law increased the top rate to 67 percent. For tax year 1918, Congress would again increase the top rate to 77 percent and change the bottom rate from 2 to 6 percent in a bill enacted in February 1919.

Internal revenue collected would increase from $380 million in 1914 to $3.2 billion by 1918. Excise taxes were also raised on spirits, freight and passenger transportation, electric lights, telephone services, insurance, automobiles, musical instruments, motion pictures, jewelry, sports equipment, perfume, medicine, tobacco, chewing gum, cameras, club dues, and a number of other items.[37] The authors of the tax laws intended to have two groups pay for the war: the rich and those engaged in unapproved behavior. The tax garnered public support, for many business leaders did not want to be seen as profiteering from the war.[38]

Congress also enacted an estate tax that went into effect for those who died after September 9, 1916. The tax started at 1 percent on the net value of inheritances over $50,000 and rose to 10 percent on inheritances over $5 million. Congress would later raise the minimum rate to 2 percent and the maximum rate to 25 percent for those with inheritances over $10 million. This remained in place until 1926 when the top rate was dropped to 20 percent.

The main objective of the wartime taxes was to bring in additional revenue paid for by those with higher incomes who were more likely to benefit from the war. As examined in Chap. 2, the public was concerned that the financing of war may unevenly enrich the businessmen profiting directly from the war, as well as the wealthy citizens with the means to purchase government bonds. The excess profits tax and progressive income tax were at the heart of an attempt to make war economically neutral. However, with the conclusion of World War I at the end of 1918, the outlook of future tax policies was uncertain.

In 1921, newly elected President Warren G. Harding appointed Andrew W. Mellon to become Secretary of the Treasury. When Mellon was appointed, he was already a sixty-five-year-old financier who was well known amongst bankers but not yet a household name. Mellon came to the Treasury with a distrust of the progressives and a commitment to reduce tax rates. Similar to Thaddeus Stevens, Mellon believed that high tax rates encouraged evasion and other poor behavior, thus reducing revenues.

Mellon also believed that taxes on wages should be lower than taxes on income generated from capital. He argued that wages were earned income, whereas capital returns were merely unearned income from investments, so wages should be treated more favorably. At the same time, he was supportive of maintaining the corporate income tax.[39]

Meanwhile, prohibition under the 18th Amendment to the Constitution was ratified in 1920. Revenues fell because of the many internal taxes that had been assessed against alcoholic beverages.[40] The Fordney-McCumber Tariff Act of 1922 doubled tariff rates in an attempt to make up for the lost revenue. However, this was merely a veil for protectionist actions that had taken off once again after Joseph Fordney, a Republican from

Michigan, had become Ways and Means Chairman in 1919. Fordney had earlier pushed the Fordney Emergency Tariff Act in response to falling farm prices, which was vetoed by Wilson but later resurrected by Harding. Revenues ultimately fell in response to the Fordney-McCumber tariffs. Congress again attempted to increase revenues in 1930 by passing the Smoot-Hawley Tariff, which reduced revenues even further by cutting off trade.

While tariffs continued to increase, Mellon began efforts to lower income taxes. In 1923, Mellon proposed reducing all income taxes including the surtax on higher incomes to 25 percent. He also proposed a new Board of Tax Appeals to resolve tax disputes within the Bureau of Internal Revenue. However, he was ultimately unsuccessful. Two years later, Mellon again argued that the surtax should be reduced as well as for the repeal of estate and gift taxes. Congress responded by reducing tax rates in 1926 and 1928 on both individual and corporate income. The top rate on individual income fell from 56 percent in 1922 to 24 percent by 1929, whereas the rate on corporate income fell from 13.5 to 12 percent.

The 1926 Act also established the Joint Committee on Internal Revenue Taxation, which later became the Joint Committee on Taxation.[41] The new committee was created in an attempt to provide Congress with additional autonomy over revenue policy without having to rely as much on the Treasury. The committee would also be responsible for providing oversight of the Bureau of Internal Revenue. This may have been a response to a dispute between Senator Couzens, a Republican from Michigan, who was interested in investigating an accusation that Treasury had overlooked the tax compliance of large corporations, and Mellon, who charged Couzens with being delinquent for a large amount of unpaid taxes.

Until the 1930s, three things had driven fiscal policy throughout the period: debt retirement, tariffs, and income tax policy. Debt fell from 27 percent of the economy in 1920 to 18 percent by 1930. The continuation of a debate from the late 1800s over tariff policy and protectionism. Finally, the debate over tax policy as a substitute for tariffs heightened, however, this pot had been boiling since the 1890s.

The country was on the precipice of the Great Depression, where economic crisis would overtake international conflict in the attention of fiscal policy. Furthermore, debt retirement would soon fall out of fashion as the incoming Franklin D. Roosevelt administration would adopt the suggestions of British economist Lord Keynes that deficits were preferable even in peacetime until reaching full employment.

The Evolution of Budget Doctrine Under Hoover and Roosevelt

Share prices on the New York Stock Exchange collapsed in October 1929, precipitating the Great Depression, which spread throughout the world economy. Public debt in advanced economies would rise 24 percentage points because of the events associated with the Depression, while median unemployment rose to 25 percent in the United States by 1932.[42] For the most part, the rise in debt levels was driven by lost revenue within the economy.[43] However, important fiscal policies were enacted during the period, including in the emergency relief appropriations that funded many of the New Deal era programs, such as the Public Works Administration, as well as the Social Security Acts of 1935 and 1939.

The period also marked important evolutions in budgeting and public finance. The president's budget became the primary document for transmitting messages about economic and fiscal policy to the Congress. The Bureau on the Budget was moved to the Executive Office of the President in 1939 and its institutional powers strengthened. Regarding fiscal policy, in the beginning of Roosevelt's tenure, his administration prioritized balanced budgets to ensure that the government was not removing productive resources from the economy. As a result, jobs would be created by allowing the economy to be most efficient. However, as his tenure continued, his administration began to view the government as having a central role in promoting work more directly through deficit spending.

In fact, when Franklin D. Roosevelt began his campaign for the presidency in 1932, he advocated for balanced budgets at a time when the unemployment during the Depression was at its height. The Democratic Party Platform that year espoused the "maintenance of the national credit by a federal budget annually balanced on the basis of accurate executive estimates within revenues, raised by a system of taxation levied on the principle of ability to pay."[44] Roosevelt himself called for dramatic reductions in spending to bring the budget into balance—something that Hoover was reluctant to do, as Roosevelt pointed out.

As a presidential candidate, Roosevelt believed that balancing the budget was critical to economic recovery because it would inspire confidence in the markets. This was also the policy of his adversary and then President Herbert Hoover. Hoover continually maintained that balanced budgets were good for economic recovery but was reluctant to reduce spending. Therefore, the budget would have to be balanced with increased revenues. Hoover's budget for the fiscal year 1931, sent to Congress just six weeks after the stock market crash, included $500 million for debt retirement along with a small tax cut to account for an anticipated surplus.[45] Congress acquiesced by cutting taxes, but did not extend the tax cuts (to the next year, as the budget surplus never arrived).

Hoover responded to the reduction in revenues with a new proposal to increase taxes in order to balance the budget. Congress passed the proposal, but Hoover's plan did not work.[46] Between 1930 and 1932, total revenues fell from $4 billion to $1.9 billion. Meanwhile, the Depression caused a fall in the demand for foreign goods, which in turn caused a reduction in customs revenues by 44 percent over the same period. The Hoover administration, still focused on the budget deficit, shifted money around to the newly created Reconstruction Finance Corporation, but held aggregate spending relatively steady. They continued their strategy of debt retirement, which reduced potential interest costs by 9 percent.

Roosevelt capitalized on Hoover's failure to balance the budget, which was widely considered to be the correct fiscal policy objective of the time. Hoover was blamed for not bring himself to do what was needed–to reduce spending by "not less than twenty-five percent" in order to balance the budget in order to get the economy out of a tailspin.[47] However, Roosevelt would do no such thing after being elected in 1932. Rather, he introduced an unprecedented emergency spending program with spending dispersed throughout the many New Deal initiatives, including new public works programs. Roosevelt would also implement other economic initiatives intended to address the Depression directly or reduce its effects; such initiatives include taking the United States off the gold standard in an attempt to stop falling prices (leading to a devaluation of the dollar by 50 percent), banking insurance, and additional economic regulation.[48] However, targeted economic stimuli were relatively modest in comparison with later fiscal stimuli.[49]

Roosevelt also made steps to better control agency decision-making over the new emergency programs by consolidating power with his budget office. In President Roosevelt's first budget, he wrote, "Up to now there has been no coordinated control over emergency expenditures. Today, by Executive order, I have imposed that necessary control in the Bureau of the Budget." Roosevelt's actions provided the Bureau of the Budget with additional control over virtually all New Deal expenditures.[50] Specifically, Executive Order 6548 prohibited agencies from making any emergency appropriations until the Director of the Bureau of the Budget had given approval.

President Hoover had requested reorganization authority from Congress to reduce government employee pay and to consolidate agencies.[51] Under Hoover's plan, funds previously appropriated by Congress for these activities would be returned to the Treasury. Congress had provided Hoover with authority, but a little more than a month before he left office, they disapproved of his plan.[52]

Roosevelt also received reorganization authority from Congress in the Economy Act of 1933 which he used to reduce payments to veterans by $460 million in 1933. Congress would end up restoring about one-quarter of the benefit reduction with the blessing of the President who admitted that the executive branch(?) had gone too far during the Depression.[53]

Roosevelt also issued Executive Order 6166 on June 10, 1933, which consolidated agencies associated with the maintenance of the national parks, federal law enforcement, administrative courts, and a variety of other functions into various other agencies. The order also bestowed all "functions of making, waiving, and modifying apportionments" upon the Bureau of the Budget. All unobligated balances from the reorganization effort were sent to the Treasury.

Between 1933 and 1938, nominal spending increased by about 47 percent, but as a percentage of the economy, it remained relatively steady over the period. However, primary deficits increased by $12.5 billion (or about 3 percent of the economy) as Roosevelt decided against the policy of new taxes to offset the budget shortfall. In a 1936 speech delivered on the campaign trail, Roosevelt argued that "to balance our budget in 1933 or 1934 or 1935 would have been a crime against the American people." He continued by arguing that "to do so we should either have had to make a capital levy that would have been confiscatory, or we should have had to set our face against human suffering with callous indifference." In other words, the spending cuts and tax increases would have been the wrong policy prescription. "Humanity came first," Roosevelt said.[54]

As the economy improved, Roosevelt's 1937 budget promised "a balanced Budget that will also include a provision for reduction of public debt." The President recommended cutting back on the temporary relief programs, but he soon changed his tune as another recession struck in 1937 and extended into 1938. In the first six months of 1937, Congress increased spending on existing relief programs and enacted the Work Relief and Public Works Appropriation Act, including additional funding for the Works Progress Administration and National Youth Administration.

Roosevelt ultimately blamed the 1937 recession on over-optimism, a reduction in emergency spending (including public works programs), and an increase in the price level of goods, leading to an increase in the supply of goods and a fall in demand.

Roosevelt's Treasury Secretary, Henry Morgenthau Jr., maintained that balanced budgets were the correct fiscal policy pursuit during economic recessions. This was a fairly orthodox perspective at the time. Friedrich Hayek, Lionel Robbins, Joseph Schumpeter, and many others believed that alleviating recessions by increasing government spending would only prolong them, as the economy would not be able to fully adjust.

However, among Roosevelt's Cabinet members, Morgenthau was alone in his economic policy prescription. Harry Hopkins and Henry Wallace, the Secretaries of Commerce and Agriculture, respectively, had both subscribed to the idea that deficit spending was a policy to ensure reaching full employment. They both had the support of large teams of economists inspired by the British economist John Maynard Keynes, who argued that increasing aggregate demand was the key to economic recovery in his 1936 magnum opus *The General Theory of Employment, Interest and Money*. Additionally, his book suggested that government borrowing and monetary policy (including lower interest rates) would help combat periods of recession until the economy reached full employment.

In the end, Roosevelt was persuaded by his secretaries under the influence of Keynes' ideas on their new approach to fiscal policy during economic recessions, writing in his 1940 budget that "the deliberate use of Government funds and of Government credit to energize private enterprise – to put purchasing power in the hands of those who urgently needed it and to create a demand for the products of factory and farm – had a profound effect both on Government and private incomes."

Roosevelt also used his 1940 budget, issued just before the US became directly involved in World War II, to characterize himself as a savior and distinguish his policy from that of the Hoover administration:

> In the early thirties – prior to 1933 – fiscal policy was exceedingly simple in theory and extraordinarily disastrous in practice. It consisted in trying to keep expenditures as low as possible in the face of shrinking national income. Persistence in this attempt came near to bankrupting both our people and our Government.

This was, however, very different from the promises that Roosevelt delivered on the campaign trail. After inauguration, he claimed to have held a certain "wisdom to use its credit to sustain economic activity in periods of economic recession and the courage to withhold it and retire debt in periods of economic prosperity." But Roosevelt was never presented with the opportunity to display such courage. He continued in his 1940 budget:

> Following 1933 the fiscal policy of the Government was more realistically adapted to the needs of the people. All about were idle men, idle factories, and idle funds, and yet the people were in desperate need of more goods than they had the purchasing power to acquire. The Government deliberately set itself to correct these conditions by borrowing idle funds to put idle men and idle factories to work.

The 1940 budget also called on Congress to levy a special war tax. Details were left to Congress, but Roosevelt asked them to "follow the accepted principle of good taxation of taxing according to ability to pay and will avoid taxes which decrease consumer buying power." In other words, Roosevelt was calling for a progressive income tax. This was a distinction from previous wars which had raised money through taxes on consumption goods. Roosevelt, however, did not want to tax consumption in an economy where there were already fears about weak aggregate demand.

Though gains had been made to employment (the unemployment rate had fallen from 20 percent in June 1938 to 15 percent by January 1940), Roosevelt still worried about unemployment for the young and those "displaced by machines." He called for additional support for farm programs, which were redistributionist in their very nature based on the premise that agriculture was not "receiving the proper share of the national income." As political reassurance for those worried about the national debt, which had increased by 82 percent under his administration, Roosevelt claimed that:

> When the increase in the national debt is viewed against the background of what was accomplished by the growth of useful physical assets, and of effective national earning power, and by the strengthening of the Nation's credit and morale, there is no economic ground for anxiety, so far as the national debt is concerned, as to the Nation's future.

Roosevelt was fairly sensitive to the political pressures regarding balanced budgets and rising debt. However, he used the presidential budgets, and especially the 1940 budget, to show a clear pivot in fiscal policy. Balanced budgets during economic crises were a policy of the past. Economic experts, inspired by Mr. Keynes, had promoted a program intended to increase aggregate demand and full employment during recessions, when the economy was thought to be below its potential. The reduction in unemployment and the growth in the economy following the recession were pointed at as successes of his new vision. This pivot would become even more profound during World War II.

The Social Security Act

On June 8, 1934, President Roosevelt issued a special message to Congress making an appeal to finish the work of the New Deal. The "hazards and vicissitudes of life" had created "fear and worry based on un-known danger" which "contribut[ed] to social unrest and economic demoralization."[55] Economic security was paramount. It was central to sustained recovery and, in Roosevelt's own words, important to "rebuilding many of the structures of our economic life and for reorganizing it in order to prevent a recurrence of collapse."

Roosevelt drew upon the works of Henry Seagar, a professor of Columbia, and other economists, sociologists, and social reformers who had made a similar point since the late-1800s. William Howells, a writer and editor of the Atlantic Monthly wrote in 1896 that "economic equality is the month of all other equalities." Without economic equality, social, and political equality were out of reach.[56]

An important part of his statement to Congress was conveying that his actions in response to the Depression were not unique. He noted that other countries had success in creating their own systems of social insurance. Germany had enacted the Sickness Insurance Law in 1883, the Accident Insurance Law in 1884, and the Old Age and Disability Insurance Law of 1889. The United Kingdom had adopted their own old-age pension in 1908 and national insurance in 1911. Of course, these reforms did not prevent the Great Depression from having considerable effects on their respective countries(?).

In January 1935, Roosevelt sent to Congress his new plan for what would become the Social Security Act. Eight months later, Congress passed the Social Security Act of 1935. The law created four benefit programs: a public pension for older people with work experience; a federal-state unemployment insurance program; grants to states to provide aid to dependent children, as well as for the blind; and additional grants to states to provide health care for mothers and children.

One of the primary political disagreements surrounding the bill was whether the social insurance system should be compulsory.[57] However, its compulsory nature is what ultimately helped with its popularity.[58] The old-age program (and now the disability program) was funded through a payroll tax that was linked to the benefit. The payroll tax imitated a contribution where wage earners pay into a federal trust fund that invests the incoming receipts in US Treasury securities.

From a budgeting perspective, the use of the trust fund was simply an accounting exercise. Through the investment of payroll taxes collected in Treasury securities, the government was simultaneously collecting money through the tax, putting it into an account, and borrowing the money to spend it on other programs. The entitlement benefit was tied to a formula rather than the earnings on investment plus the principal. At the same time, this accounting exercise was critical to the program's success. As Roosevelt noted, "We put those pay roll contributions there so as to give the contributors a legal, moral, and political right to collect their pensions and unemployment benefits."[59]

The primary legacy of the Social Security Act was that it fundamentally changed the notion of the federal government's responsibility in providing for welfare and insurance against foreseeable and unforeseeable events. Furthermore, it instilled in government programs for the first time the idea that the government should address economic inequalities, rather than just inequality before the law. There had previously been tax policies which had attempted to remove what were seen as unfair advantages for certain groups. However, for the first time, the Social Security Act compelled workers to participate in a new federal entitlement program and inserted the federal government into the provision of income security, all to promote public welfare.

Fiscal Policy Behind Another World War

Roosevelt's economic advisers considered the war in Europe an opportunity for economic expansion.[60] Furthermore, they viewed full employment as the primary solution to social problems. Around the same time Roosevelt issued his budget in January 1940, he also received a paper by Harry

Hopkins, Secretary of Commerce, noting that the war was a tremendous opportunity to boost national defense spending along with military goods as the basis for expansion. Hopkins wrote that "once full employment is attained, the task of fiscal policy is twofold: (1) to maintain full employment; (2) to secure as rapidly as possible that orientation of production which our defense demands."[61] For President Roosevelt, who had been worried about both youth unemployment and technological unemployment, this was an opportunity.

Around the same time as the Hopkins paper was published, Roosevelt's Agriculture Secretary, Henry Wallace, reported that only if America committed itself directly to war would the budget deficits be high enough to increase output.[62] However, enduring deficit spending was not part of the plan. Roosevelt discussed both public and privately the need for progressive taxation to pay for additional public works projects and domestic infrastructure.[63]

John Maynard Keynes, in his 1940 book How to Pay for the War, argued that to combat inflation the government must raise taxes on those with higher incomes and compel those with lower and middle incomes to save their money.[64] However, in America, fiscal policy would initially resemble something closer to that of World War I, in which taxes were raised under the intention of offsetting some of the costs of the war. Rather than attempting to alter individuals' economic behavior, it paid attention to those with the opportunity to profit from the conflict, ensuring that their taxes would offset any profits. United States government economists argued for controls on civilian consumption and taxes on excess profits from the war production.[65] Still others, like Richard Gilbert, the director of Division of Industrial Economics at the Department of Commerce and later director of the Defense Economics Section of the Office of Price Administration, advocated for delaying taxes and using price controls to limit deflation brought on by budget deficits.[66] John Kenneth Galbraith also favored price controls and rationing.[67]

As the war began to wind down, a fear came over the economists back home that unemployment may spike when the war ended. This led economists at the War Production Board to begin thinking about the transition to civilian industries, but not until the collapse of Germany.[68] Specifically, the New Deal economists advocated for a combined policy of deficit spending on infrastructure and public works projects, as well as continued rationing in order to constrain inflationary pressures.

Intentions to manage the economy would continue after the war. The initial conception of what became the Employment Act of 1946, or what was then called the Full Employment Act, included the creation of a National Production and Employment Budget (NPEB). Each fiscal year, the president would be required to submit a proposal to attain full employment composed by a new institution established within the Bureau of the Budget or an independent entity not unlike the Federal Reserve.[69] Eventually, the NPEB was watered down, and in the final bill, it became the Economic Report of the President issued by Council of Economic Advisors (also created by the Employment Act of 1946) from within the Executive Office of the Presidency.[70]

The Economic Report was a far cry from the NPEB. Alvin Hansen, a Harvard economist who helped spread Keynes' ideas in America, said that the economic philosophy outlined in the first Economic Report "could not pass muster as a serious economic document and its journalistic flavor indicates that it was perhaps not so intended."[71] Hansen went on to say that "if the Economic Report becomes, year by year, a mere resume of proposed legislation which the President has urged upon Congress, it is not likely to serve any very useful purpose, and it will certainly not preform the function intended in the Employment Act of 1946."[72] That is, however, essentially what the Economic Report continues to be.

The most significant policy change after the war was allowing automatic stabilizers to adjust to the business cycle.[73] This recommendation was captured in the first Economic Report and may be thought of as a lasting impact of the Employment Act of 1946.[74] To illustrate this, the economist J. Bradford DeLong found that a 5 percentage point increase in the unemployment rate was associated with a 0.28 increase in the federal deficit as a share of the national product prior to World War I.[75] After World War II, the same increase in unemployment was associated with an increase in the deficit by 4.5 percentage points.

Success in managing the economy proved to be another challenge altogether. The Federal Reserve has been able to move relatively quickly in order to counterbalance the onset of new economic conditions. However, for the most part, fiscal policy is based on changes to existing law, which is an arduous process riddled with politics even under the best circumstances. The American Recovery and Reinvestment Act of 2009 was perhaps the most significant fiscal stimulus during a recession since World War II and estimates have suggested very large costs for each additional job added and a relatively low multiplier.[76]

There are also political problems associated with deficit spending. The political economists James Buchanan and Richard Wagner pointed out in Democracy in Deficit (1977) that economic management through deficit financing induces structural deficits, rather than just cyclical deficits, unless there are some constraints on debt accumulation. A moral constraint on debt works well, but when morality changes (which it has, historically) a constitutional balanced budget amendment might be needed.[77] More attention will be paid to the rise of structural deficits later in this book.

Out with Tariffs, in with Income Taxes

Roosevelt's Secretary of State, Cordell Hull, helped write the first income tax bill two decades earlier. He was also a strong advocate for replacing tariffs with income taxes. Hull's support of income taxes over tariffs was as much about foreign policy as domestic. As Secretary, Hull declared it to be "virtually impossible to develop friendly relations with other nations in the political sphere so long as we provoked their animosity in the economic sphere" by imposing restrictions on trade.[78]

In February 1934, the Roosevelt administration produced a draft for a tariff revision that proposed a reduction in rates by giving the president the authority to negotiate bilateral trade agreements. The Congress processed the bill in just three months, which was a relatively quick amount of time, and it delegated tariff policy to the administration for the first time. The only catch was that the authority would expire after three years. To this day, Congress has never taken back their power over regulating trade, which now largely exists under Trade Promotion Authority.

Congress took up tax reform following the enactment of the Reciprocal Trade Agreements Act. In 1934, Congress passed the Revenue Act, establishing a single rate of 4 percent with graduated surtaxes on higher income going up to 59 percent on income above $1 million for a combined rate of 63 percent as well as a corporate income tax rate of 13.5 percent. In addition, the Revenue Act of 1934 established a 35 percent tax on undistributed profits of holding companies that had been established to avoid the higher surtaxes. Taxes were decreased on consumption goods such as soft drinks, candy, furs, and jewelry.

However, Roosevelt fired back at Congress, claiming that they had "done little to prevent an unjust concentration of wealth and economic power" through the implementation of the New Deal programs and the 1934 tax law.[79] His solution was a wealth tax which increased surtaxes on higher incomes to a combined rate of 75 percent and(?) a new tax on estates valued at over $40,000. These proposals were carried in the Revenue Act of 1935, which also added a tax on profits exceeding 10 percent of the company's value/revenue(?) in addition to the corporate income tax. Funds were earmarked for the purpose of debt reduction under Roosevelt's proposal. Republicans, however, would criticize the President for using the tax system for "punitive or political purposes" rather than to generate revenue.[80]

Roosevelt again requested comprehensive changes to the tax code in June 1936. These occurred in two main waves. In 1936, the President called on Congress to "stop the leaks in the tax code" which resulted in more significant changes to the corporate tax. Due to the high proposed rates on businesses, his proposal received some pushback in Congress.[81] Congress raised taxes on dividends, the sale of oil and gas properties, undistributed profits, and windfall profits. A number of businesses went from having no tax burden to a significant tax bill including American Telephone and Telegraph, General Electric, Goodyear Tire and Rubber, and National Dairy Products.[82]

In 1937, Congress began to finalize the changes requested in 1936 including several provisions intended to reduce tax evasion by the creation of personal wealth holding companies, trusts, partnerships, and the incorporation of estates, yachts, and other forms of personal property.[83] In 1938, Congress would attempt to reduce the undistributed profits tax after blowback from the 1937 reforms.[84] Roosevelt refused to sign the bill, however, defending his position for higher taxes on undistributed corporate earnings and capital gains. Bolstered by continued resentment from the business community and the ongoing recession, the undistributed profits tax was finally ended in 1939. However, this was only after Roosevelt received a commitment from Congress to strengthen the corporate excess profits tax and not to reduce the corporate rate.

As World War II began, it also brought the impetus for new taxes. Between 1940 and 1945, five different revenue bills were enacted. The Revenue Acts of 1940 and 1941 increased taxes on individuals and corporations and also imposed excise taxes on playing cards, safe deposit boxes, tires, tire tubes, sparkling wine, club dues, matches, luggage, washing machines, light bulbs, toilets, bowling alleys, and slot machines. In addition, new use taxes were assessed on automobiles ($5 each) and boats (between $5 and $200). The 1941 tax bill also created a Congressional committee to study nonessential federal expenditures.

There was also discussion of using Social Security taxes to fund the war effort, but that idea was ultimately rejected.[85] Increasing the payroll tax, which was imposed to fund Social Security, was seen as a way to combat inflation that would have otherwise been driven by high government spending on the war.[86] However, the various excise taxes were believed to function in a similar way.

Like Wilson, Roosevelt believed that at least a portion of the war should not be funded through debt. In 1942 Congress/Roosevelt's administration(?) assessed a new "victory tax" on all annual incomes over $624 and levied a flat excess profits tax was at 90 percent. The excess profits rate was increased to 95 percent in 1943. The 1942 bill, known as "the greatest tax bill in American history" at the time of its enactment, also included the first deduction for medical expenses.[87] Beginning in 1943, individuals were required to file a tax return in order to claim any tax refunds. Meanwhile, tax withholding and the concept of "adjusted gross income" were introduced as part of the Individual Income Tax Act of 1944.

In 1945, the individual and corporate income rates were reduced. The top rate on individuals fell from 94 percent during the end of the war to 86 percent whereas the top corporate rates fell from 40 to 38 percent. However, the general structure of the tax system had gone through an incredible evolution from 1934 until 1945. In 1935, only about 15 percent of total revenues came from individual income taxes and another 15 percent came from corporate income taxes. Excise taxes accounted for 40 percent of total revenues. By 1945, total revenues had increased by 1150 percent. Individual income taxes accounted for 41 percent of total revenues and corporate income taxes accounted for 35 percent. Excise taxes had decreased to 14 percent of the total although the nominal amount collected had increased by four times since 1935.

Reorganizing the Government

As the government grew out of the Depression and World War II, there became a renewed earnestness to modernize the executive branch and Congress. Roosevelt began taking advice from outside practitioners on what exactly would be his legacy on the functioning of the federal government. In March 1936, Roosevelt established the Committee on Administrative Management to study what exactly needed to be adapted. The Committee, also known as the Brownlow Committee, comprised three members: Louis Brownlow (director of the Public Administrative

Clearing House of Chicago), Charles Merriam (professor of political science at the University of Chicago), and Luther Gulick (professor of public administration at Columbia University). Merriam had been offered a seat on the Commission on Economy and Efficiency by Taft twenty-five years earlier but declined. In many ways, the Brownlow Committee resembled the Taft Commission in that it assembled outside academic experts with experience in local administration to help reform the functions of government at the federal level.

However, the Brownlow Committee's work was much less extensive than the Taft Commission. The Taft Commission issued around twenty-four reports, and one report The Need for a National Budget alone was 568 pages. The Brownlow Committee issued one fifty-three-page report in total. However, it made several important recommendations that were later adopted.

The Brownlow Committee famously suggested:

> *In this broad program of administrative reorganization the White House itself is involved. The President needs help. His immediate staff assistance is entirely inadequate. He should be given a small number of executive assistants who would be his direct aides in dealing with the managerial agencies and administrative departments of the Government .... These aides would have no power to make decisions or issue instructions in their own right. They would not be interposed between the President and the heads of his departments .... Their function would be, when any matter was presented to the President for action affecting any art of the administrative work of the Government, to assist him in obtaining quickly and without delay all pertinent information possessed by any of the executive departments so as to guide him in making his responsible decisions; and then when decisions have been made, to assist him in seeing it that every administrative department and agency affected is promptly informed.*[88]

The Brownlow Committee also recommended moving the Bureau of the Budget to the Executive Office, along with the Civil Service Administration and the National Resource Board. These three were seen as the central managerial agencies of the executive branch. The Committee convinced Roosevelt to propose that the president should continually be reorganizing the government based on its evolving needs.[89]

Around the same time the Brownlow Committee was assembled by Roosevelt, the House of Representatives established a select committee to investigate reorganization and management under the chairmanship of James P. Buchanan, a Democrat from Texas. Brownlow and Gulick also advised a similar select committee established by the Senate. During its investigation, the Brookings Institution was put under contract by the Senate to provide a "survey of government" to all three committees.

During this period, a number of important ideas were discussed, many of which would develop even further in the decades to follow. One of these ideas was the question of impoundment or the withholding of money appropriated by Congress. Clifton Woodrum, a Democratic Congressman from Virginia and political ally of Roosevelt, proposed extending executive authority to impound funds, possibly by use of a line item veto, as long as it would either reduce the debt or benefit public welfare.[90]

However, many other members in Congress were skeptical of providing the president with this level of power, suggesting that the president could potentially use this authority as a political tool rather than to promote the general welfare. As deficits mounted, Congress provided Roosevelt with reorganization authority in 1939 to consolidate and abolish unnecessary agencies. Roosevelt used this authority to adopt several of the Brownlow Committee recommendations, including creating an Executive Office of the Presidency and moving the Bureau of the Budget from the Treasury to the Executive Office.[91]

Congress would also reorganize themselves during the 1940s as a response to the growing size of government. This reorganization would bring about several important reforms of government. However, they were not always lasting changes. The Legislative Reorganization Act of 1946 increased the size of committee staff and increased the budget for the Legislative Reference Service, created in 1912 to provide expert advice and research to Congress.[92] Each standing committee was allowed to hire four professional staff and six clerical staff to help prepare legislation and provide oversight.[93]

The 1946 Legislative Reorganization Act also attempted to reinsert Congress into the forefront of the budget making process. Most of the Congressional debate following the enactment of the 1921 Budget and Accounting Act centered around amending the process surrounding the presidents' budgets. Many in Congress believed that it was their own responsibility to adjust the presidents' requests to reflect Congressional priorities. However, the presidents' budgets shaped not only the budgeting process but also the outcome of appropriations. They were, in every way, the point from which Congress began their work developing appropriations bills and other legislation.

In 1946, Congress established a joint budget committee to prepare a legislative budget that included a limit on spending based on estimates of revenues and expenditures.[94] The joint committee was made up of 102 members from the House Ways and Means Committee, the Senate Finance Committee, and the Appropriations Committees. A great deal of the new joint committee's work coincided in content/timing with the production of appropriations bills and the review of the president's budget by the appropriations subcommittees of both houses. This overlap caused some friction.

The joint committee was instructed to provide its report to Congress, along with a concurrent resolution establishing appropriations and budget spending limits by the 15th of February each year. Mike Monroney, a Democratic Congressman from Oklahoma, said that the new congressional budget process was intended to "induce Congress to chart a financial course for the year and to follow it as closely as possible rather than continue the practice of unrelated action by spending and taxing committees, with the total expenditures still in doubt until the last appropriation bill is passed."[95] After adoption by Congress, the legislative budget would go to the president, a concept which garnered strong bipartisan support.[96]

The new procedure was a clear attempt by Congress to get back in the driver's seat over the budget process. Congress would review the presidents' requests, assemble their own budgets, and offer the president their own fiscal policy, which the president would sign or veto. In theory, this process made a lot of sense. In practice, however, the legislative budget was a colossal failure.

The first legislative budget, released in 1947, was criticized for arbitrarily setting expenditure limits and recommending spending cuts.[97] Rather than reflecting a more intermediate position, the legislative budget attempted to provide everyone with a little bit of what they had wanted. For instance, it allowed the estimated surplus to be used for both debt retirement and tax cuts, which was aimed at appeasing those who were concerned about the growing debt and also providing a politically popular position. Supporters of the legislative budget told the skeptics that the budget would not commit Congress to anything but would rather establish a target for future action in an attempt to gain the support of the legislative budget.[98] Meanwhile, as Congress attempted to conclude its work on the first legislative budget, the Truman administration began notifying Congress that deficiency appropriations would need to be made that year, an action which undermined the entire process.

Monroney conceded that the 1947 legislative budget was an "outstanding failure," blaming the Republican leadership for using the new process for political purposes.[99] Congress attempted to pass the legislative budget three more times before abandoning and ultimately repealing it in 1970. However, the legislative budget would inform the direction of process changes to the nation's budget over the next thirty years, culminating with the enactment of the Congressional Budget Act in 1974.

Summary

The federal government had been comparatively small prior to the Great Depression. During this period, it grew in size, scope, and responsibility. By the end of World War II, the dominate position of public policy was that the government had a formal role in promoting economic outcomes.

As the government grew to take on new roles a reorganization became necessary. The budgeting institutions established in 1921, in particular the Bureau of the Budget, took on additional responsibilities and ultimately moved from the Treasury to the White House. This move and the additional responsibilities assumed by the Bureau during this time were indicative the level of importance the presidential budget had come to reflect.

Congress and the White House also formerly engaged in a comprehensive policy to replace tariff revenues with taxes to finance federal spending but also to manage individual behavior. At the same time, the federal government came to be seen as having an active role in managing the economy. This was exemplified by the New Deal programs and the Employment Act of 1946.

Notes

1. U.S. Bureau of the Budget, *The Budget of the United States Government For the Fiscal year Ending June 30, 1941* (Washington, DC: U.S. Government Printing Office, 1940).
2. Major wars include the War of 1812, the Mexican–American War, the American Civil War, the Spanish–American War, and World War I. Recessions include periods of significant decline in economic activity equivalent to the National Bureau of Economic Research definition.
3. The Victory Liberty Loan Act of 1919 established a sinking fund. For details, see: Willoughby (1931).
4. John. F. Cogan, *The High Cost of Good Intentions: A History of U.S. Federal Entitlement Programs* (Stanford, CA: Stanford University Press, 2017).

5. Ibid.
6. J. Bradford De Long, "Keynesianism, Pennsylvania Avenue Style: Some Economic Consequences of the Employment Act of 1946," *The Journal of Economic Perspectives* 10, no. 3 (1996): 41–53.
7. Ibid.
8. Cogan, *The High Cost of Good Intentions: A History of U.S. Federal Entitlement Programs.*
9. "Republican Party Platforms: Republican Party Platform of 1936," *The American Presidency Project*, June 9, 1936, https://www.presidency.ucsb.edu/documents/republican-party-platform-1936
10. Dennis S. Ippolito, *Congressional Spending* (Ithaca, NY: Cornell University Press, 1981).
11. Kennon and Rogers, *The Committee on Ways and Means: A Bicentennial History.*
12. Dennis Ippolito, *Why Budgets Matter: Budget Policy and American Politics* (University Park, PA: Pennsylvania State University Press, 2003).
13. Herbert L. Fenster and Christian Volz, "The Antideficiency Act: Constitutional Control Gone Astray", *Public Contract Law Journal* 11, no. 1 (1979): 155–231.
14. Ibid.
15. Ibid.
16. Ibid.
17. Ibid.
18. Business Cycle Dating Committee of the National Bureau of Economic Research, "US Business Cycle Expansions and Contractions," *The National Bureau of Economic Research*, September 20, 2010, https://www.nber.org/cycles.html
19. Michael D. Bordo, and David C. Wheelock, "Chapter Two – The Promise and Performance of the Federal Reserve as Lender of Last Resort 1914–1933" in *The Origins, History, and Future of the Federal Reserve: A Return to Jekyll Island*, ed. Michael D. Bordo and William Roberds (Cambridge: Cambridge University Press, 2013): 59–98.
20. Ibid; Hugh Rockoff, "Until it's Over, Over There: The U.S. Economy in World War I," *NBER Working Paper*, no. w10580 (2004); Margaret G. Myers, *A Financial History of the United States* (New York: Columbia University Press, 1970).
21. Rockoff, "Until it's Over, Over There: The U.S. Economy in World War I."
22. Ibid.
23. Ibid.
24. Ibid.
25. Ippolito, *Why Budgets Matter: Budget Policy and American Politics.*

26. Rockoff, "Until it's Over, Over There: The U.S. Economy in World War I."
27. Kennon and Rogers, *The Committee on Ways and Means: A Bicentennial History.*
28. Ippolito, *Why Budgets Matter: Budget Policy and American Politics.*
29. Ibid.
30. Rockoff, "Until it's Over, Over There: The U.S. Economy in World War I."
31. Ibid.
32. Ibid.
33. Robert Barro, "Government Spending, Interest Rates, Prices, and Budget Deficits in the United Kingdom, 1701–1918", *Journal of Monetary Economics* 20, no. 2 (1987): 221–247.
34. Kennon and Rogers, *The Committee on Ways and Means: A Bicentennial History.*
35. Rockoff, "Until it's Over, Over There: The U.S. Economy in World War I"; Library of Congress, World War I Poster Collection.
36. Kennon and Rogers, *The Committee on Ways and Means: A Bicentennial History.*
37. Roy G. Blakey, "The War Revenue Act of 1917", *The American Economic Review* 7, no. 4 (1917): 791–815.
38. Rockoff, "Until it's Over, Over There: The U.S. Economy in World War I."
39. Kennon and Rogers, *The Committee on Ways and Means: A Bicentennial History.*
40. Ippolito, *Why Budgets Matter: Budget Policy and American Politics.*
41. Kennon and Rogers, *The Committee on Ways and Means: A Bicentennial History.*
42. Eichengreen et al., "Public Debt Through the Ages."
43. Ibid.
44. "Democratic Party Platforms, 1932 Democratic Party Platform," *The American Presidency Project*, June 27, 1932, https://www.presidency.ucsb.edu/documents/1932-democratic-party-platform
45. Ippolito, *Why Budgets Matter: Budget Policy and American Politics.*
46. Ibid.
47. Ibid.
48. Ibid; Eichengreen et al., "Public Debt Through the Ages."
49. Eichengreen et al., "Public Debt Through the Ages."
50. In 1936, Roosevelt would also issue Executive Order Number 7298 empowering the Director of the Bureau of the Budget as the first line of approval, above the Attorney General, on all Executive Orders or Presidential Proclamations.

51. Beard and Smith (1933).
52. Fisher, "The Politics of Impounded Fund."
53. Ibid.
54. "FDR: From Budget Balancer to Keynesian," *Franklin D. Roosevelt Library and Museum*, https://www.fdrlibrary.org/budget
55. "President Franklin D. Roosevelt's Message to Congress Announcing a Program for Social Security, June 8, 1934," *U.S. Senate, National Archives and Record Administration.*
56. Paul Winfree, "Bringing Proverbs to Policy: Classical Economics, Proverbial Wisdom, and Applications for Welfare Policy," *Social Science Research Network Working Paper* (2018).
57. Cogan, *The High Cost of Good Intentions: A History of U.S. Federal Entitlement Programs.*
58. Ibid.
59. Ibid.
60. Byrd L. Jones, "The Role of Keynesians in Wartime Policy and Postwar Planning, 1940–1946," *The American Economic Review* 62, no. 1/2 (1972): 125–133.
61. Ibid.
62. Ibid.
63. Ibid.
64. Ibid.
65. Ibid.
66. Ibid.
67. Ibid.
68. Ibid.
69. J. Bradford De Long, "Keynesianism, Pennsylvania Avenue Style: Some Economic Consequences of the Employment Act of 1946," *The Journal of Economic Perspectives* 10, no. 3 (1996): 41–53.
70. Ibid.
71. Alvin Hansen and Jacob Viner, "Two Discussions of the Employment Act of 1946 and Its Early Operation," *The Review of Economics and Statistics* 29, no. 2 (1947): 69–79. On general background regarding Hansen's views on fiscal policy, see: (A. H. Hansen 1968).
72. Ibid.
73. De Long, "Keynesianism, Pennsylvania Avenue Style: Some Economic Consequences of the Employment Act of 1946."
74. Ibid.
75. Ibid.
76. James Feyrer and Bruce Sacerdote, "Did the Stimulus Stimulate? Real Time Estimates of the Effects of the American Recovery and Reinvestment

Act," *NBER Working Paper*, no. 16759 (2011). Feyrer and Sacerdote (2011) find that the cost of each additional job was between $100,000 and $400,000 implying a multiplier between 0.5 and 1.0.

77. James Buchanan, "Clarifying Confusion About the Balanced Budget Amendment," *National Tax Journal* 48, no. 3 (1995): 347–355.
78. Kennon and Rogers, *The Committee on Ways and Means: A Bicentennial History.*
79. Ibid.
80. "Republican Party Platforms, Republican Party Platform of 1936," *The American Presidency Project*, June 9, 1936, https://www.presidency.ucsb.edu/documents/republican-party-platform-1936
81. Roy G. Blakey and Gladys C. Blakey, "The Revenue Act of 1936," *The American Economic Review* 26, no. 3 (1936): 466–482.
82. Ibid.
83. Roy G. Blakey and Gladys C. Blakey, "The Revenue Act of 1937," *The American Economic Review* 28, no. 3 (1938): 447–458.
84. Ibid.
85. Ward Macy, "Social Security Taxes in the War Finance Program," *Journal of Political Economy* 51, no. 2 (1943): 135–147.
86. Ibid.
87. Paul G. Kauper, "Significant Developments in the Law of Federal Taxation, 1941–1947: I," *Michigan Law Review* 45, no. 6 (1947): 659–678.
88. The President's Committee on Administrative Management, "The Report of the Committee with Studies of Administrative Management in the Federal Government" (Washington, DC: U.S. Government Printing Office, 1937).

    Note: Commonly known as "The Brownlow Committee Report."
89. Fisher, "The Politics of Impounded Funds."
90. Ibid.
91. Ibid.
92. Brooke W. Graves, "Legislative Reference Service for the Congress of the United States." *The American Political Science Review* 41, no. 2 (1947): 289–293.
93. Kennon and Rogers, *The Committee on Ways and Means: A Bicentennial History.*
94. Ibid.
95. L. B. Wheildon, "Legislative budget-making," *Editorial Research Reports 1948* 1 (Washington, DC: CQ Press, 1948).
96. Ibid.
97. Ibid.
98. Ibid.
99. Ibid.

References

Barro, Robert. 1987. "Government Spending, Interest Rates, Prices, and Budget Deficits in the United Kingdom, 1701–1918." Journal of Monetary Economics 20 (2): 221–247.

Beard, Charles A., and George H.E. Smith. 1933. The Future Comes: A Study of the New Deal. New York, NY: The MacMillan Company.

Blakey, Roy G. 1917. "The War Revenue Act of 1917." The American Economic Review 7 (4): 791–815.

Blakey, Roy G., and Gladys C. Blakey. 1936. "The Revenue Act of 1936." The American Economic Review 26 (3): 466–482.

Blakey, Roy G., and Gladys C. Blakey. 1938. "The Revenue Act of 1937." The American Economic Review 28 (3): 447–458.

Bordo, Michael D., and David C. Wheelock. 2013. "Chapter Two – The Promise and Performance of the Federal Reserve as Lender of Last Resort 1914–1933." In The Origins, History, and Future of the Federal Reserve: A Return to Jekyll Island, edited by Michael D. Bordo and William Roberds, 59–98. Cambridge, England: Cambridge University Press.

Buchanan, James M. 1995. "Clarifying Confusion About the Balanced Budget Amendment." National Tax Journal 48 (3): 347–355.

Cogan, John F. 2017. The High Cost of Good Intentions: A History of U.S. Federal Entitlement Programs. Stanford, CA: Stanford University Press.

Congressional Record. 76th Cong., 1st sess. 1939. July 27–28.

De Long, J. Bradford. 1996. "Keynesianism, Pennsylvania Avenue Style: Some Economic Consequences of the Employment Act of 1946." The Journal of Economic Perspectives 10 (3): 41–53.

1932. "Democratic Party Platforms, 1932 Democratic Party Platform." The American Presidency Project. June 27. https://www.presidency.ucsb.edu/documents/1932-democratic-party-platform.

Eichengreen, Barry, Asmaa El-Ganainy, Rui Redro Esteves, and Kris James Mitchener. 2019. Public Debt Through the Ages. Working Paper WP/19/6, Washington: IMF.

2016. FDR: From Budget Balancer to Keynesian. https://www.fdrlibrary.org/budget.

Fenster, Herbert L., and Christian Volz. 1979. "The Antideficiency Act: Constitutional Control Gone Astray." Public Contract Law Journal 11 (1): 155–231.

Feyrer, James, and Bruce Sacerdote. 2011. Did the Stimulus Stimulate? Real Time Estimates of the Effects of the American Recovery and Reinvestment Act. Working Paper Number 16759, Cambridge: National Bureau of Economic Research.

Graves, Brooke W. 1947. "Legislative Reference Service for the Congress of the United States." The American Political Science Review 41 (2): 289–293.

Hansen, Alvin, and Jacob Viner. 1947. "Two Discussions of the Employment Act of 1946 and Its Early Operation." The Review of Economics and Statistics 29 (2): 69–79.

Ippolito, Dennis S. 1981. Congressional Spending. Ithaca, NY: Cornell University Press.

———. 2012. Deficits, Debt, and The New Politics of Tax Policy. New York, NY: Cambridge University Press.

———. 1990. Uncertain Legacies: Federal Budget Policy from Roosevelt through Reagan. Charlottesville, VA: University of Virginia Press.

———. 2003. Why Budgets Matter: Budget Policy and American Politics. University Park, PA: Pennsylvania State University Press.

Jones, Byrd L. 1972. "The Role of Keynesians in Wartime Policy and Postwar Planning." The American Economic Review 62 (1/2): 125–133.

Kauper, Paul G. 1947. "Significant Developments in the Law of Federal Taxation, 1941–1947." Michigan Law Review 45 (6): 659–678.

Kennon, David R., and M. Rebecca Rogers. 1989. The Committee on Ways and Means: A Bicentennial History, 1789–1989. Washington, DC: Government Printing Office.

Macy, Ward. 1943. "Social Security Taxes in the War Finance Program." Journal of Political Economy 51 (2): 135–147.

Myers, Margaret G. 1970. A Financial History of the United States. New York, NY: Columbia University Press.

1936. "Republican Party Platforms, Republican Party Platform of 1936." The American Presidency Project. June 9. https://www.presidency.ucsb.edu/documents/republican-party-platform-1936.

1936. "Republican Party Platforms: Republican Party Platform of 1936." The American Presidency Project. June 9. https://www.presidency.ucsb.edu/documents/republican-party-platform-1936.

Rockoff, Hugh. 2004. "Until it's Over, Over There: The U.S. Economy in World War I." NBER Working Paper (w10580).

The President's Committee on Administrative Management. 1937. The Report of the Committee with Studies of Administrative Management in the Federal Government. Washington, DC: U.S. Government Printing Office.

U.S. Bureau of the Budget. 1940. The Budget of the United States for the Fiscal Year Ending June 20, 1941. Washington, DC: Government Printing Office.

———. 1947. An Act for the establishment of the Commission on Organization of the Executive Branch of the Government. Public Law 80–162, July 7.

Wheildon, L.B. 1948. Legislative budget-making. Editorial Research Reports 1948, Vol. 1, Washington: CQ Press.

Willoughby, W.F. 1931. Financial Condition and Operations of the National Government, 1921–1930. Washington, DC: The Brookings Institution.

Winfree, Paul. 2018. Bringing Proverbs to Policy: Classical Economics, Proverbial Wisdom, and Applications for Welfare Policy. Working Paper, Social Science Research Network.

CHAPTER 6

In Pursuit of Full Employment

Franklin D. Roosevelt died on April 12, 1945. During his twelve years in the White House, President Roosevelt oversaw a number of significant changes. Roosevelt confronted the Great Depression with an aggressive domestic agenda based on a new approach of financing state-based income support programs by the federal government, a new social insurance program to provide income in old age, and public works programs. He took the country off of the gold standard to increase the supply of money when his predecessors believed that loose money had been a root cause of economic recessions. Finally, Roosevelt began to change the public narrative on using government spending and deficits to pull the economy out of recession.

Roosevelt reorganized the executive branch and consolidated decision-making within the White House through the creation of the Executive Office of the President. Like his predecessors, Roosevelt used the presidential budget (a process that was still in its adolescence) to develop a cohesive policy agenda that was used to put political pressure on Congress to execute the administration's priorities. President Roosevelt further empowered the Bureau of the Budget by putting the Director in charge of overseeing many of the New Deal programs and then moving the Bureau out of the Treasury Department and under the White House. After the National Emergency Council was disbanded, the Bureau of the Budget was also given the authority to review all nonfinancial legislation for the purposes of maintaining policy conformity with the president's agenda.[1]

P. Winfree, *A History (and Future) of the Budget Process in the United States*, https://doi.org/10.1007/978-3-030-30959-6_6

The Great Depression had, in many ways, fundamentally changed the landscape of fiscal policy in America. The United States was behind many of the European countries in terms of establishing national social insurance programs. Under systems of social insurance individuals pay premiums, usually through a tax on wages or a tax that employers pay on behalf of workers, in exchange for the provision of income protection by the government should some event occur that prevents an individual from working. Covered events could include general health, disability, old age, or unemployment.

The Great Depression had also fundamentally changed the pursuit of fiscal policy. Policymakers began to view unemployment and high inflation as two problems that the government could actively manage. No longer was retiring the federal debt the primary long-run objective for fiscal policy. Both the Truman and Eisenhower Administrations still subscribed to the premise that debt retirement was beneficial to the long-run health of the country. However, both sought to expand the provision of domestic services and maintain low-unemployment through their fiscal policy programs. Truman was also driven to use tax policy to combat the threat of inflation while monetizing the debt following World War II. He battled Congress on tax policy to combat inflation throughout his entire administration.

The need for reorganization became even more apparent as the government continued to grow. Congress created the Commission on the Organization of the Executive Branch of Government in 1947, which was chaired by former President Hoover, to consider fundamental institutional reforms that covered a number of areas such as the restructuring of agencies, the privatization of federal power installations, as well as accounting and budgeting process changes. Truman would submit thirty-seven reorganization plans for Congressional consideration while Eisenhower would submit fourteen plans. Accompanying the reorganizations was the process of "impoundment," or the withholding of Congressional appropriations, which became more important during the period.

Following the Eisenhower administration, the pursuit of fiscal policy would continue to evolve in the direction of full employment through sustained economic growth. John F. Kennedy criticized Eisenhower for failing the embrace the concept of federal government's central involvement in promoting economic growth through deficit-financed tax cuts as well as investments in science, technology, and education. Lyndon B. Johnson dramatically increased the government's involvement in the provision of domestic services and poverty alleviation. Meanwhile, the wars in Korea and Vietnam continued to commit a majority of federal spending to national defense from 1951 through 1961.[2] All of these things would serve to increase debt as policymakers moved balanced budgets.

The New Debt Limit

Congress continued to differentiate between long-term and short-term debt obligations during the twenty years following the enactment of aggregate limits on public debt beginning with the First Liberty Loan Act of 1917. However, by the 1930s, the restriction on long-term debt was eliminated.

In 1935, the limit on all new issues of Treasury notes was combined into a single revolving ceiling.[3] Bonds were limited by their own ceiling and restrictions were placed on individuals for the amount of bonds they could purchase.[4] This was changed in 1938 in two important ways. First, an overall limit was applied to bonds, notes, certificates of indebtedness, and other forms of government debt. However, within the overall limit, a second limit was placed on bonds in order to restrict the long-run liabilities.

A year later, in July 1939, the second limit on bonds was eliminated, in part, to allow the administration to rollover more short-term debt into long-term debt. This left the first overall limit on public debt and eliminated any secondary restriction on long-term debt. However, many Republican Members of Congress decried the policy suggesting that Roosevelt had abandoned his stance that debt was harmful to the economy. They blamed Federal Reserve Chairman Eccles for suggesting that the positive aspects of government debt to the economy and monetary policy.[5]

Congress failed to raise the debt limit to $50 billion per Roosevelt's request in 1939. However, that would soon change as the war increased demand for resources. At the beginning of World War II, the single debt limit was raised from $45 to $65 billion under the Second Liberty Loan Act of 1941. The debt limit was raised as the war continued to $125, $210, $260, and finally $300 billion in 1945. Debt incurred by government-sponsored entities, such as mortgage guarantees, was also included in the overall ceiling.

In 1946, the debt ceiling was reduced to $275 billion and the value of the bonds assessed against the ceiling was changed from the maturity value to the current redemption value. By 1953, the Treasury requested a new debt limit of $290 which was passed by the House relatively quickly (the House passed the new debt limit by a vote of 239 to 158 the day after President Eisenhower's message was transmitted to Congress). However, legislative progress on the debt limit slowed in the Senate as the debt limit was seen as a way to force action to reduce the deficit during a relatively good economy.

The Senate Finance Committee, to whom the House bill was referred, simply did not take up the House-passed debt limit bill. The Senate wanted to increase their leverage on both a tax bill and appropriations for that year. In particular, the Senate had made more than 500 amendments to the House-passed bill cutting individual and corporate income taxes.

The Eisenhower administration was eager to get the tax bill across the finish line but the government's debt subject to the statutory limit was already at $266 billion during the summer of 1953. After the tax bill was finished, the Senate acquiesced to a portion of the president's request by allowing a temporary increase in the debt ceiling of $6 billion until June 30, 1955. However, the debt limit had already become a tool for political bargaining.

"Voodoo Economics"? Truman's Fiscal Policy

The end of World War II fostered an environment able to support budget surpluses once again. Defense spending was falling and revenues increased as the economy improved. Normally, such a condition could have led to an attempt by Congress or perhaps an administration to reduce revenues and spending while balancing the budget and retiring the national debt. This time was no different. Congressional Republicans advocated for lower income taxes and would make tax cuts a central campaign narrative during the 1948 presidential election.

However, returning to that pre-war status quo has never been particularly easy.[6] For instance, after the Civil War, Republicans successfully justified a continuation of high protective tariffs to support new programs for veterans. By the end of World War II, tariff policy was no longer a significant source of revenue. Specifically, the income tax had become much more important as it was used to systematically replace the reduction in tariff revenues (and tariff rates) during the interwar period.

President Truman did not support the Republican position to reduce income taxes. His justification was based on two doctrines. First, Truman believed that Americans had come to expect more from the government.

This included providing a larger array of domestic services but also providing programs aimed at economic security. Truman acknowledged the beginning of what would become a shift from defense spending to newer domestic priorities in advance of the Cold War buildup. This was based, in part, on the principle of maintaining full employment through fiscal policy.

Second, Truman believed that high tax rates were central to controlling inflation while monetizing the national debt. Truman articulated this point in a statement issued on April 11, 1946:

> *It is the aim of our fiscal policy to balance the budget for 1947 and to retire the national debt in boom times such as these. In our present fight against inflation, fiscal policy has a vital role to play. A continuation of our present policy, which is to maintain the existing tax structure for the present, and to avoid nonessential expenditures, is the best contribution we can make to economic stability.*

At first, Truman's policy of maintaining wartime taxes had Congressional support. In a speech delivered on the House floor in March 1946, John McCormack, an influential Democrat from Massachusetts, advocated to keep taxes "as low as is consistent with" balancing the budget while also providing for "natural human needs of food, clothing, and shelter."[7] The President and Democrats in Congress were attempting to establish a new baseline for what the federal government was responsible for providing and that required additional revenue from the income tax.

Truman laid out his own vision for building upon the New Deal in a speech to Congress five months after ascending to the presidency. In a twenty-one-point plan, Truman offered a number of new domestic reforms in what is known as the "Fair Deal." These included universal healthcare, an increased minimum wage, a federal agency focused on research, public employment for military veterans, a permanent Fair Employment Practices Committee, and an extension of unemployment insurance among other new policies. It also included additional price controls as the Truman administration was concerned about inflation. Truman's request was that "there is much that Congress can do to help this process and to tide over the period between now and the time when reconversion is completed and civilian jobs are plentiful in a stable economy that provides full production, full employment, and a high standard of living."[8]

Furthermore, the central role of the government in promoting full employment tied together Truman's fiscal policy. "Full employment" was mentioned fifteen times during the Fair Deal address. Truman's course was consistent with the direction of the Employment Act of 1946 which in many ways helped to establish full employment as a primary objective of fiscal policy and was the biggest legislative success of the Fair Deal. The government's role in promoting full employment through fiscal policy was articulated by many economists of the time, including Jacob Mosak an economist at the Office of Price Administration and former student of Henry Schultz at the University of Chicago. Mosak argued that it would have been unreasonable to believe that a reduction of government spending consistent with the war effort would have been made up by the private sector even if taxes were reduced. In a paper published by the *American Economic Review* in March 1946, Mosak wrote that "Unless… the federal government adjusted its revenues and outlays so as to raise the annual aggregate volume of expenditures… to the level required for full-employment production… it is evident that mass unemployment and depression will follow."[9]

President Truman had less success with the other parts of his domestic agenda. When the 80th Congress came into session in January 1947, Republicans were elected to the majority in both the House and Senate for the first time in two decades. The first major piece of legislation in the House that year, H.R. 1, was a bill to reduce taxes. Republicans introduced that tax cuts on the premise that cutting marginal tax rates at all incomes, but more for lower income brackets, would both stimulate the economy and contain Truman's domestic programs.[10] That bill was vetoed in June 1947 by Truman. The President believed the tax cuts would increase the threat of inflation. After failing to override the veto, Congress again passed a bill to delay the enactment of the tax cuts until 1948. Truman again vetoed the bill which was sustained by the Senate.

At the beginning of 1948, Congress attempted once more to reduce taxes across all brackets. The bill also created a $600 deduction for the blind as well as those over the age of sixty-five and created a deduction on the estate tax for the spouse. The bill required married couples filing jointly to split their incomes and thus receive a lower tax rate. Prior to the 1948 bill, only single filing had been permitted.[11] Truman again disapproved of the bill but this time Congress was able to successfully override the President's veto.

The economy entered what would become an eleven-month recession in November 1948. Democrats took back control of the House in the beginning of 1949 and President Truman encouraged Congress to reverse that tax cuts in order to provide adequate defense funding and certain domestic initiates that were part of the Fair Deal, such as public housing and health care. However, Congress made only technical changes to the existing tax system.[12]

Truman would return with his request to Congress by asking for more revenue in 1951, including additional excise taxes and a higher corporate income tax rate. A deficit was expected as the United States entered the Korean War. Meanwhile, the President continued to be concerned with threats of inflation as debt was retired. Between 1946 and 1951 debt as a percentage of the economy declined from 118 to 74 percent. Joseph Martin, the Republican Minority Leader in the House, called Truman's plan to use taxes to combat inflation "economic voodoo talk."[13]

Business groups came forward with a recommended sales tax as a replacement for the corporate income tax; however, this was strongly opposed by Democrats on the Ways and Means Committee.[14] The Congress would largely enact the reforms asked for by Truman, including excise taxes on alcohol and automobiles, but would also create a number of special tax deductions. These included a new deduction for medical expenses, earnings of dependents, and special carve outs for particular industries.[15] The 1951 tax bill also allowed taxpayers to elect whether they filed joint or separate returns and took the standard deduction.

Hoover Commissions

President Truman signed the act establishing the Commission on Organization of the Executive Branch of the Government on July 7, 1947. This became known as the first Hoover Commission and was a creation of the Congress. Congress was controlled by Republicans and the Commission's governing statute largely reflected the party's priorities. However, the Commission was bipartisan, comprising equally of Democrats and Republicans. It also included private citizens, members of the executive branch, and members of Congress. The primary objective of the first Hoover Commission was to "promote economy, efficiency, and improved services in the transaction of public business" within the executive branch.[16]

To address its primary objective, Congress instructed the first Hoover Commission to find ways to cut government spending to the lowest amount possible while still preforming essential services. This could include identifying areas of duplication, or where consolidation and elimination of certain programs might be recommended. Finally, the Commission was instructed to identify areas where the executive branch's power should be limited. Congress also provided the Commission with staff and a budget in order to conduct its work.

Former President Hoover was one of four appointees by the Republican Speaker of the House, Joseph Martin of Massachusetts, and he went on to become elected chairman. The scope of the Commission prior to beginning its work was, as Hoover stated, not to "say whether [the functions of government] should exist or not," but rather "if we cannot make it work better."[17] Many of the proposals of this first Commission were absent of major policy decisions and focused on the organization of government.

The Commission also solicited ideas from private industry and other experts. For instance, Hoover asked the National Bureau of Economic Research to conduct a study of the government's statistical agencies and to make recommendations.[18] By 1949, the Commission began sending its task force reports to Congress with what ultimately amounted to 273 recommendations. A quarter of the recommendations fell under reorganization proposals that could be submitted by the Truman administration as part of the Reorganization Act of 1949; another third could be adopted through executive action; and the remainder required Congress to amend the law.[19]

The first Commission's key budget recommendation was to adopt what they called a performance budget. The performance budget would classify programs based on functions or activities. The Commission also recommended getting rid of itemized appropriations which they believed hid the true costs of programs. This was critical, the Commission maintained, to providing the public with transparency required to show what the "taxpayers get" for their money:

> *Budgeting and accounting go hand in hand. Sums budgeted in advance are subsequently accounted for as obligated and spent. The activities are the same and the accounts themselves must be the same. Only by making comparisons between similar activities, and between the same activity in one year against another year, can efficiency be tested. Only by making the head of each activity financially responsible for all the costs of his program, can he be held to account. Only be modernizing the Federal system of budgeting and accounting will it be possible to tell exactly how much any single program or project is costing. The Federal Government must be able to assess results intelligently.*

Most of the recommendations to change the budget system were adopted as part of the Budget and Accounting Procedures Act of 1950. Conforming amendments to various parts of the government were also included in the Post Office Financial Control Act of 1950, a 1950 bill to finance the Bureau of Engraving and Printing Fund, and the National Security Act Amendments of 1949. The two significant recommendations rejected were to separate current and capital expenditures in the budget as well as to create an Accountant General within the Treasury to standardize accounting methods.[20]

The Budget and Accounting Procedures Act contained three main sections that were intended to implement both the performance budget and bring changes to the appropriations process. Title I of the act also directed the President, through the Bureau of the Budget, to continually develop proposals to reorganize the executive branch and promote new management techniques. These plans would be submitted to Congress as part of the presidential budget within the first fifteen days of each session. This section also further empowered the General Accounting Office to audit the executive agencies as part of the legislative branch. Title II of the act allowed agencies to transfer funds pursuant a reorganization. Title III repealed obsolete sections of the Budget and Accounting Act of 1921.

Overall, the first Hoover Commission was highly successful. More than 70 percent of the Commission's recommendations were at least partly adopted including the performance budget.[21] By 1954, 15 percent of the remaining recommendations that had not been acted upon were obsolete while about half those remaining were not significant. The first Hoover Commission had set a new standard for successfully developing and executing a plan to reorganize the government. It was so successful, in fact, that Congress established a second Hoover Commission in July 1953.

President Eisenhower appointed Hoover to the Second Commission on Organization of the Executive Branch. Hoover was subsequently elected chairman to serve with six other Republicans and five Democrats. The six Republicans included Herbert Brownell (Eisenhower's Attorney General), Arthur Flemming (Director of the Office of Defense Mobilization), Homer Ferguson (a former Senator from Michigan), Solomon Hollister (Dean of Engineering at Cornell University), Clarence Brown (a member of the House from Ohio), and Sidney Mitchell (executive director of the first Hoover Commission). Democrats on the Committee included Joseph Kennedy (former ambassador to Great Britain and the father of freshman Senator John F. Kennedy of Massachusetts),

Chet Holifield (a member of the House from California), John McClellan (a Senator from Arkansas), Robert Storey (Dean of the Law school at Southern Methodist University), and James Farley (former Postmaster General).

Similar to the first Commission, the second Hoover Commission was given two years to conduct its work. The Commission was divided into seventeen task forces covering government personnel, federal medical services, lending services, transportation infrastructure, legal services, surplus and real property management, food and clothing, research and development, and budgeting and accounting. However, the second Hoover Commission was less successful and significant disagreement overwhelmed many of the group's findings. Holifield, for instance, filed eleven minority reports objecting many of the task forces' recommendations.

When it came to budgeting, the second Hoover Commission was, in many ways, a response to the executive budget process in that it intended to give "full control of the national purse to the Congress." Similar to the first Commission, the second Hoover Commission began by focusing on transparency. They pointed out that broad, multi-year budget authority had hidden the true long-term costs of programs. The use of cash budgeting had resulted in an inattention paid to controlling growing costs. Furthermore, the growing use of capital funds meant that agency spending had escaped Congressional review.

"Unexpended balances" had become a problem as agencies were receiving appropriations and then failing to spend both obligated and unobligated resources. In other words, there was a growing disconnect between what the Congress was appropriating and how the executive branch was using the funds. The concept of whether an obligation had actually been made was, as the Commission put it, "fluid." This made it difficult for Congress to regain control over unspent resources. The agencies, on the other hand, had a strong incentive to "obligate" the appropriations before they expired in order to control their use.

The Commission recommended the use of accrual accounting for budgeting purposes which they believed would put Congress back in control over spending decisions. Specifically, they recommended that Congressional appropriations be based on expenditures associated with the period of authorization and also the goods and services received by an agency in any given year.[22] Rather than providing budget authority, the Commission recommended that Congress provide accrued expenditure authority to the agencies which would be apportioned by the Bureau of the Budget.

However, Congressional appropriations based on accrued expenditures rather than accrued costs may have led to less Congressional control.[23] This is because any degree of cost control would have been entirely dependent on whether the agencies could control the aggregate spending over the programs. At the same time, Congress would be giving up additional control they have over the scope of appropriations. This recommendation would ultimately not be adopted.

The Commission also recommended three important, though smaller in scale, budget process changes. The first was a periodic review of programs whose long-term costs were likely to grow making it difficult for Congress to control, such as veterans' programs and farm supports. The second recommendation was to empower the Bureau of the Budget through the oversight of agency budget preparation. In essence, the Bureau of the Budget would oversee and audit the agency budgets. Third, that cost-based operating budgets be established by each agency. The Commission also recommended that agencies use comptrollers, or essentially Inspector Generals, to oversee spending decisions as well as a new Office of Accounting to standardize practices from the Bureau of the Budget.

A number of the budget and accounting recommendations were adopted. In July 1956, Congress passed a bill consolidating all unobligated balances into a general-purpose account that could be used to pay claims from previously expired appropriations. A month later, Congress provided for the use of cost-based operating budgets. Finally, in 1958, Congress authorized the development of the presidential budget based on accrued expenditure limits, but the limits would only be effective if approved by Congress.[24] Congress also created the new position of Assistant Director of the Bureau of the Budget based on the Commission's recommendations.

Fiscal Policy, from Eisenhower to Johnson

Eisenhower ascended to the presidency after having campaigned on ending the Korean War, balancing the budget, and tax reform. The Korean War had largely been financed with taxes during the Truman administration. After the armistice was signed six months into the new administration, President Eisenhower ordered the preparation of a new defense budget 10 percent lower than Truman's last request.[25] Actual defense spending would be reduced by 7 percent between 1953 and 1954 and by another 13 percent by 1955. However, defense spending was still 225 percent higher in 1955 compared to before the beginning of the Korean War and it would begin increasing on an annual basis starting in 1956 due to pressures imposed by the onset of the Cold War. As a share of the economy, defense spending would remain high and would not fall to the pre-Korean War level until after the conclusion of the Vietnam War.

Taxes to pay for the Korean War had been imposed in 1950 and 1951. Three major tax bills were enacted during that time raising the corporate tax rate from 45 to 52 percent, the top excess profits tax from 30 to 53 percent, the top individual income tax rate to 92, and excise taxes on a number of consumer items. Revenues as a share of the economy rose from 14.2 percent in 1950 to 18.5 percent in 1952. The increases in the individual income taxes alone accounted for half of the increased revenue and corporate income taxes accounted for most of the remaining increase. Meanwhile, defense spending increased from 4.8 to 12.9 percent of the economy over that same period.

The final tax bill of the war, the Revenue Act of 1951, had included an expiration of the higher wartime tax rates. The higher individual income rates were scheduled to expire by January 1954, whereas the corporate and excise taxes would expire four months later. Contrary to his campaign promises, Eisenhower argued for extending the excess profits tax which was eventually approved with support from Congressional Democrats.[26] However, other tax rates were allowed to expire. When Eisenhower delivered his 1954 annual message to Congress he had already pivoted from his campaign rhetoric eliminating the Korean War taxes to declaring a need for tax reform.[27]

Later that spring, Eisenhower's budget offered twenty-five changes to the tax law. These changes included an expanded deduction for children with earnings, the inclusion of children under foster care as dependents, the ability to deduct childcare, a new head of household tax filing status, an expanded medical care deduction, the exclusion of health insurance paid by the employer as income, new methods of deducting capital depreciation, research and development tax deductions, and advanced payment of the corporate income tax. These changes, and a number of other important proposals, have shaped the tax policy landscape that the United States still has today. Many of these proposals were authorized by Congress in the Internal Revenue Act of 1954.

President Eisenhower also sought to expand domestic programs. These included an extension of Social Security, a federal reinsurance program to promote private health insurance, grants to build health facilities including hospitals and nursing homes, and housing subsidies. At the same time, Eisenhower proposed a "New Look" military strategy based on force reductions, a larger Air Force, and deterrence through nuclear capabilities.[28] Broad based and permanent tax cuts were not in the picture.

Senator John F. Kennedy criticized Eisenhower for making tradeoffs between fiscal control, including the rejection of large tax cuts, and defense spending. During his 1960 presidential campaign against Eisenhower's Vice President Richard Nixon, Kennedy ran on the platform of "getting America moving again." As President, Kennedy's platform took the form of planned deficits, lower taxes, and additional spending—especially on national defense.[29] As Dennis Ippolito depicts in his book *Why Budgets Matter*, "his departure from conventional fiscal policy was the call for major tax cuts when budget deficits were already quite large."[30] To put this into perspective, Kennedy's 1963 proposal for an across the board tax cut was projected to increase the deficit by 50 percent (though the actual deficit impact was much lower). The Kennedy Administration had doubled down on deficits in the pursuit of full employment.

There is an additional factor that separates Kennedy's tax policy from the rest of the period in that there was a relatively low level of concern with inflation during his presidency. It was inflation that inspired Truman as well as Eisenhower and later Johnson to propose tax increases. However, inflation immediately preceding and during the Kennedy administration had been relatively low. This likely provided additional shelter from political pressures which allowed Kennedy to advocate for lower taxes during a period of budget deficits.

After Kennedy's assassination his successor, Lyndon B. Johnson, was reelected to the presidency in 1964 along with large Democratic majorities in both the House and Senate. The reelection occurred during an economic expansion. The deficit as a share of the economy fell from 1.2 percent in 1962 to 0.2 percent in 1965. This was even after the Kennedy tax cuts had been enacted in 1963. However, the Vietnam War was heating up which put additional pressure on Johnson to maintain high levels of defense spending rather than substituting his aggressive domestic reforms for reductions in the military.

Johnson's Great Society initiative contributed to the large increases in health, welfare, and education programs beginning in 1965. The human resources portion of the federal budget grew from 5.2 percent of the economy in 1965 to 7.2 percent by 1970. These programs—including

Medicare, Medicaid, and food assistance—largely comprise the United States income support system that we have today. Between 1971 and 2018, human resources spending averaged about 12 percent on the economy.

The Great Society initiatives were the next iteration of the pursuit of full employment. It was not simply an assortment of individual initiatives including civil rights, public welfare, and federal job training intended to eradicate poverty in both rural and urban areas. Rather it was intended to fulfill the pursuit that Roosevelt has initiated resulting in the transformation of fiscal policy as it related to the economy. As Johnson's domestic policy adviser Joseph Califano said: "The cornerstone of the Great Society was a robust economy. With that, the overwhelming majority of the people could get their fair share of America's prosperity."[31] President Johnson's message from the 1965 Economic Report of the President reiterated the connection, "Economic policy can more than ever become the servant of our quest to make American society not only prosperous but progressive, not only affluent but humane, offering not only higher incomes but wider opportunities, its people enjoying not only full employment but fuller lives."

At first, Johnson was reluctant to increase taxes believing that he could fund domestic priorities by ending the war in Vietnam quickly. However, he did recommend the extension of expiring excise tax increases as well as the suspension of the investment tax credit and the deduction related to depreciation.[32] By 1967, Johnson was calling for higher taxes based on the premise of combating inflation. Inflation had increased somewhat in 1966 and 1967 but a skeptical Congress believed that Johnson was unwilling to make necessary tradeoffs between revenues, domestic priorities, and national defense.[33]

Congress would force Johnson to accept limits on spending in exchange for a tax increase.[34] The Revenue and Expenditure Control Act of 1968 was the first serious attempt by Congress to impose some level of external control over annual spending apart from the appropriations process. The four main parts of the act dealing with spending were a freeze on federal hiring and a process of reducing overhead costs through attrition, an overall limit on federal expenditures, a reduction in the statutory debt limit, and a requirement for a proposal from the President to rescind $8 billion in unobligated spending authority. The expenditure limit, however, was not absolutely encompassing. Spending on the Vietnam War, Social Security, veterans' benefits, and debt services were all excluded from the limit.[35]

The Budget Concepts Commission

Beginning in 1951, the presidential budget had been a "performance budget" which had been a development based on a recommendation from the Hoover Commission. Performance budgets attempt to justify the allocation of resources based on different goals so as to provide some assessment to analyze if the budget is working as intended. However, by the 1960s, the federal government had a more complex set of goals than when the 1921 act had initially established the presidential budget process. These multiple goals were captured in multiple budget concepts.

The three competing budgets concepts included an administrative budget, a consolidated cash budget, and a national income accounts budget. The administrative budget included the costs and taxes, as well as seigniorage, associated with running the government absent trust funds on a cash basis. The consolidated cash budget was similar to the administrative budget but excluded seigniorage and included trust funds. The national income accounts budget included trust funds, excluded seigniorage and loans made on behalf of the federal government, and used a combination of cash and accrual accounting methods.

Furthermore, both the administrative and consolidated cash budgets included participation certificates as negative expenditures. Participation certificates are interest-bearing debt securities that represent shares in a pool of assets held by the federal government which are sold to private investors.[36] The sale of the security was treated as revenue because it reflected the sale of an asset.

In 1967, President Johnson assembled a commission to reconcile these competing concepts. The Budget Concepts Commission reflected quite the composition. It included the politically well-connected, stake holders in the current system, professional economists, businessmen, and even an influential journalist. The Budget Concepts Commission was chaired by David Kennedy. Kennedy was the President and CEO of Continental Illinois Bank and a member of the board of trustees at Brookings. He would later become the Secretary of Treasury and Ambassador to NATO under President Nixon.

Other members of the Budget Concepts Commission included Robert B. Anderson (Eisenhower's Secretary of the Treasury and Defense), Frank Bow (a Republican member of Congress from Ohio and ranking member of the Ways and Means Committee), Henry Fowler (Johnson's Secretary of the Treasury), Carl Hayden (a Democratic Senator from Arizona and chairman of the Senate Appropriations Committee), Winthrop Lenz (executive vice president of Merrill, Lynch, Pierce, Fenner, and Smith), George H. Mahon (a Democratic member of Congress from Ohio and Chairman of the Appropriations Committee), Paul W. McCracken (professor of economics at the University of Michigan and former member of the Council of Economic Advisers), Charles Schultze (director of the Bureau of the Budget), Carl Shoup (professor of finance at Columbia University), Leonard Silk (vice chairman of the editorial board at Business Week), Elmer Staats (Comptroller General at the General Accounting Office), Robert Trueblood (partner at Touche, Ross, Bailey, and Smart in Chicago), Robert Turner (professor of business and government at Indiana University), Theodore O. Yntema (professor of economics at Oakland University), and Milton Young (a Republican Senator from North Dakota and ranking member of the Appropriations Committee).

Budgetary presentation was almost as important to the Commission as reconciling the different budgetary concepts. In their only report to President Johnson, the Commission noted their attempt "to recommend an approach to budgetary presentation that will advance both the public and congressional understanding of this vital document." This goes back to the original intent of the executive budget which had been to promote budget transparency. In fact, the Budget Concepts Commission is best identified as an iteration or update of the executive budget process started in 1921.

There were relatively few disagreements on the Commission. The main recommendation, which was adopted, was that a unified budget statement replace the three competing budgets. They recommended that accrual accounting be used to record expenditures and receipts, like the Hoover Commission before them, rather than the system of cash accounting which had been used. They also recommended that Congressional priorities be given "more prominence" in the presentation of the budget so as compare the president's requests with that of the legislature. There was also reconciliation on a number of other accounting issues, such as how to treat loans, trust funds, and financing the debt based on a common definition of deficits and surpluses. The Commission also recommended against the use of a capital budget, which can be helpful when assessing the value of investments, as they believed that it would impair the transparency of the presentation.

Many of the recommendations could be adopted without Congressional approval given the president's wide latitude in establishing the presentation of the budget under the Budget and Accounting Act of 1921. However, the government predominantly continued to use cash accounting (outside parts of the Department of Defense) and it still does to this day.

The treatment of participation certificates turned into a fairly controversial matter dealt with by the Budget Concepts Commission. Ultimately, the Commission recommended excluding participation certificates from the final recommendation of what should be included in a budget. However, Fowler, Schultze, and Turner all maintained that this was the incorrect decision as the money raised from the sales reduced the amount of federal borrowing.[37]

The Commission recommended that the new unified budget also be "part of a broad fiscal plan," which is nearly identical to the original intention of the presidential budget. However, the budget would reflect additional goals. In addition to establishing new programs, requests for appropriations and new tax policy, the budget was also to embody "the fiscal policy of the Government for promoting high employment, price stability, healthy growth of the national economy, and equilibrium in the Nation's balance of payments."[38] Fiscal policy was a tool of full employment and price stability.

Full employment and price stability had been critical drivers of fiscal policy since the Great Depression. The architects of the Employment Act of 1946 had envisioned their own budget toward the promotion of full employment; just like the administrative budget might promote a balancing of expenditures and receipts. This adoption by the Budget Concepts Commission reflects two important changes in the budgetary process. First, that the presidential budget process was no longer about reaching balance of payments with revenues, but rather managing debt while promoting other objectives. Second, in the end, the Keynesians behind the 1946 act had ultimately been successful. They did not need a new budget. The presidents' budgets were now explicitly acknowledged as a mechanism for attempts to manage the economy.

Reorganizations of 1970

On March 12, 1970, President Nixon proposed to eliminate the Bureau of the Budget and then resurrect it as an even more empowered Office of Management and Budget.[39] In addition, he proposed consolidating decisions on domestic policy within the White House. The proposal, known as Reorganization Plan No. 2 of 1970, was filed under the authority of the

Reorganization Act of 1949 which gave Congress sixty days to reject the plan before it went into effect. After failing to disapprove, the plan went into effect on May 16, 1970.[40]

The plan was originally a part of several suggestions that were made by the President's Advisory Council on Executive Organization chaired by Roy Ash. Ash would go on to become the Director of the Office of Management and Budget (OMB) under both Presidents Nixon and Ford. The Ash Commission, the usual reference to the President's Council, and was made up entirely of members from the business community and academia. Under Reorganization Plan No. 2, the newly created OMB was responsible for additional oversight of the departments and agencies including their management agendas. OMB would help by "providing the tools that are needed to reduce duplication, to monitor performance, and to promote greater efficiency throughout the Executive Branch."[41]

"The new office did not downgrade the budgeting function but amplified it," *Congressional Quarterly* reported.[42] The Bureau of the Budget, which had been created as an arm of Treasury back in 1921, was continuing to amass power and rise in influence as each new president found that control and oversight of spending decisions from within their own executive office was useful. The Director of the Bureau of the Budget was, in many ways, nothing more than an Assistant Secretary or a mid-level political appointment. The Director of the Office of Management and Budget, on the other hand, would eventually become a member of the Cabinet under President Carter and was responsible for executing the president's agenda.

The Reorganization Proposal No. 2 also created a Domestic Policy Council, chaired by the President, to coordinate domestic policy from the White House. As the Reorganization Plan No. 2 put it, "The Domestic Policy Council will primarily be concerned with what we do; the Office of Management and Budget will be primarily concerned with how we do it, and how well we do it."

Congress was also in the reorganization mood. Enacted on October 26, 1970, the Legislative Reorganization Act made a few important changes to the budget process. First, the General Accounting Office was empowered to review administration policy which expanded its scope beyond financial audits. Second, the act required the president to submit follow-up to the presidential budget in the form of a summary of finances partly through the year, called the mid-session review, before July 15.[43]

Budget Reform Heats up Congress

Nixon attacked the congressional budget process as a "hoary and traditional procedure" and swore to limit spending "with or without the cooperation of Congress" during the 1972 presidential election.[44] On July 26, 1972, Nixon demanded that Congress enact a $250 billion limit on spending, or $3 billion more than the budget he had submitted earlier that year, to help control inflation.[45] The spending limit was not particularly controversial and, in fact, an expenditure limit had been imposed each year from 1968 to 1970. However, Nixon also wanted flexibility to reduce spending on certain programs while "an Administration spokesmen refused to specify in advance which programs would be cut."[46]

In October 1972, the House passed a bill enacting Nixon's requested limit and provided the President with near-unlimited flexibility to withhold expenditures in order to meet the target.[47] The Senate then amended the President's impoundment authority with the instruction to make proportional cuts in programs up to 10 percent.[48] The requirement to produce proportional cuts was removed in conference but a requirement was imposed to limit the cuts on any single program to 20 percent. On October 27th, the President signed the bill providing for impoundment authority in order to meet the new statutory spending limit. However, the bill also allowed for the spending limit to expire immediately thus deeming it void.

Following Nixon's reelection, presidential impoundments reached a new level. The exact levels of impoundment by the Nixon administration depend on the definitions used. However, it was widely reported that around $15 billion was impounded including $6 billion in contract authority for the Environmental Protection Agency.[49] Impoundment had been used by previous administrations as it was typically associated with government reorganizations. However, the use of impoundment had been increasing. According to the Office of Management and Budget, $53 billion had been impounded by Nixon's administration between 1969 and 1973 compared to $39 billion during the Johnson administration.[50]

The October bill establishing the spending limit also provided for the establishment of the Joint Study Committee on Budget Control. The Joint Study Committee was instructed to look into limits on spending and obligation authority, allocating budget authority to congressional committees for budgeting, and a congressional procedure to determine fiscal policy. The Committee had until February 1973 to produce a report.

The Joint Study Committee blamed Congress for the growing budget deficits. Between the end of World War II and 1961, the budget had been in deficit during nine of the years or 60 percent of the time. Though, since 1962, the budget had been in deficit every year. The Committee believed that if tax rates had not been reduced in 1962, during the Kennedy administration many of the budget deficits during this period would have turned to surpluses.[51] It is, however, unclear whether this would have been true as receipts as share of the economy had stayed at the same level between 1962 and 1972. Rather, federal spending had grown by 0.8 percent of the economy due to the Vietnam War and the Great Society programs.

Meanwhile, the federal budget had become seen as a central component of macroeconomic policy. The budget analyst Allen Schick wrote in 1975 that unlike earlier periods, "Nowadays, taxes and expenditures are volatile factors, sensitive to policy determinations and to economic conditions. The budget has become a main determinant of the economy and it impacts (though not always in an understood way) on employment, prices, and economic growth."[52] Arthur Burns, Chairman of the Federal Reserve, told the Joint Study Committee, "You have the opportunity to enable Congress to turn its powers of the purse into a truly effective instrument for stabilizing our economy."[53]

The pursuits of monetary and fiscal policy were one and the same. Burns went on in his testimony saying, "In addition to its implications for employment, price stability, and our international payments position, the budget is bound to leave its mark on interest rates." The Federal Reserve Chairman feared that if deficits continued to grow then the government's demand for credit would push interest rates higher while putting strain on credit markets. Burns advocated for a limit on spending or additional taxes, but favored an expenditure limit because "As government assumes wider responsibilities, it becomes increasingly apparent that we must have a better system of controls to screen out low-priority programs and to ensure that high-priority programs operate efficiently."[54]

However, Congress's recent attempts at imposing expenditure limits had been unsuccessful. This was not lost on the Joint Study Committee and was a point made by their interim report issued on February 7, 1973.[55] The Joint Study Committee also acknowledged the federal budget's growing role in the economy and suggested "that when a deficit or surplus occurs, it should, to the extent possible, be the result of a planned rather than an unplanned congressional policy."[56] The budget was as much a tool of economic management as it was a reflection of the government's priorities.

Hubert Humphrey, a Democratic Senator from Minnesota and former Vice President under Lyndon Johnson, made this point directly when arguing before the Joint Study Committee in March 1973 that congressional budgeting should be in the jurisdiction of the Joint Economic Committee that had been established by the Employment Act of 1946. Humphrey testified that, "Clearly with government spending at more than ¼ of the GNP, these government programs are a major instrument of government economic policy. Moreover, many of them are major instruments for allowing people to become employable, health, education and manpower training programs are clearly essential to a fully productive society."[57] Congress was not simply abdicating their constitutional responsibilities by failing to execute on a budget process. The breakdown in the congressional process was actually detrimental to the economy.

The Joint Study Committee identified a number of areas that needed additional congressional oversight. These included areas of "backdoor spending" or agency spending that was not subject to the annual appropriations process.[58] Forms of backdoor spending included contract authority and mandatory entitlements. The Committee also believed that the fiscal year, which ran from July 1st to June 30th, did not provide enough time for congressional consideration of program authorizations in advance of providing appropriations.[59] Historically this had not been a problem because most programs and agencies were permanently authorized and existed in perpetuity or until Congress repealed the authorization.[60] However, since 1950, Congress had provided more limited-term authorizations which had become difficult to review on an annual basis under the existing time schedule.[61]

The Joint Study Committee recommended that a permanent budget committee be created in both the House and the Senate with the intention of coordinating fiscal policy. The budget committees would be responsible for producing a budget resolution by May 1st of each year that could not be freely amended on the floor of either the House or Senate. Besides spending through trust funds (such as the Social Security program), all new forms of backdoor spending including mandatory entitlements would need to be funded through the annual appropriations bills. Finally, the Committee recommended that all programs would need to be authorized by Congress in advance of the beginning of the fiscal year on July 1.

The idea of having a budget committee with jurisdiction over the entire budget process was not a new concept. During the consideration of the Budget and Accounting Act of 1921, Senator Medill McCormick, a Republican from Illinois, recommended the creation of a budget committee.[62] The committee would have authority to reduce spending relative to the president's budget with a simple majority. Two-thirds majority or presidential approval would have been needed to increase spending relative to the request. Wilson's Treasury Department supported the idea.[63] However, the 1921 act had left the budget committee idea out of its final form.

The Joint Study Committee recommendations were included in two bills, H.R. 7130 and S. 1641, introduced in April 1973. The Committee's proposal immediately came under criticism. The House Democratic Study Committee was particularly vocal suggesting that the proposal would "lock the congressional budget process into a conservative mold for generations to come," for including members from the Appropriations as well as the Ways and Means Committees on the new budget committees who were viewed as more conservative.[64] They feared that Republicans would form an alliance with Southern Democrats to control budgeting decisions.[65]

Albert Ullman, a Democratic Member of the House from Oregon and co-chair of the Joint Study Committee, offered several amendments to the Committee's proposal when the House Rules Committee began their consideration in July.[66] These included dropping the requirement that the chairman of the new House budget committee be selected from Appropriations or Ways and Means Committees.[67] Ullman also recommended additional flexibility to the amendment process to give Members of Congress that were not on the budget committees more input into the process.

Nevertheless, budget process reform was moving through Congress. Both 1973 and 1974 would be pivotal years marking a reintroduction of Congress back into the budgeting process. However, there were two differences compared to the bygone eras when Congress had more control over the decision-making process. First, the executive budget still reigned. Therefore, Congressional reformers were looking to increase engagement with the administration over budgeting decisions rather than taking over the process entirely. The Presidential priorities reflected in the unified budget would continue to dominate the process even under a new process where Congress would offer their own budget resolution. Second, as Ullman noted, "For the first time, we will debate economic policy," before setting fiscal objectives.[68] The new age of congressional budgeting was intended to be as much about managing the economy as fiscal management of the government.

Summary

The government and the economy were now seen as inseparable by many policymakers. This was exemplified by the different responsibilities of the budget listed in the Budget Concepts Commission's report. Full employment and stable prices were the principal economic objectives of the period and acted as a driving force behind new legislation, including the Great Society programs.

The Office of Management and Budget had become central to not only executing financial plans but also overseeing the management of agencies. Nixon would push the powers amassed during the last fifty years too far. Congress's response would result in a significant reform to the budget process. However, economic policy would not fundamentally change and the reforms would only place Congress in a formal role within the executive budget process still driven by the presidency.

Notes

1. Percival Flack Brundage, *The Bureau of the Budget* (New York, NY: Praeger Publishers, 1970).
2. Between 1951 and 1961, outlays for national defense averaged 59.4 percent of total outlays. Office of Management and Budget, Historical Table 3.1.
3. Cooke and Katzen, "The Public Debt."
4. Ibid.
5. Mr. George, Mr. Maloney, Mr. Townsend, Mr. Barkley, Mr. Mead speaking, 76th Cong., 1st sess., *Congressional Record*, July 27–28, 31, 1939.
6. Charles L. Schultze, "Is There a Bias Toward Excess in U.S. Government Budgets or Deficits?" *The Journal of Economic Perspectives* 6, no. 2 (1992): 25–43. (Schultze 1992) observed that "Voters are very loathe to support a general tax increase to raise federal civilian spending; but they will forgo a tax cut when defense spending declines as a way of reallocating the resources to civilian programs."
7. *Congressional Record*, 79th Cong., 2nd sess., March 11, 1946.
8. Harry S. Truman, "Special Message to the Congress Presenting a 21-Point Program for the Reconversion Period" (1945), *The American Presidency Project*, https://www.presidency.ucsb.edu/documents/special-message-the-congress-presenting-21-point-program-for-the-reconversion-period

9. Jacob L. Mosak, "National Budgets and National Policy," *The American Economic Review* 36, no. 1 (1946): 20–43.
10. Kennon and Rogers, *The Committee on Ways and Means: A Bicentennial History.*
11. Wesley A. Dierberger, "Revenue Act of 1948," ed. Paul A. Walkin and Marcus Manoff, *Indiana Law Journal* 25, no. 3 (1950): 416–419.
12. Kennon and Rogers, *The Committee on Ways and Means: A Bicentennial History.*
13. Ibid.
14. Ibid.
15. George D. Webster, "Taxpayer Relief: The Revenue Act of 1951," *Virginia Law Review* 37, no. 8 (1951): 1039–1081.
16. U.S. Congress, *An Act for the establishment of the Commission on Organization of the Executive Branch of the Government*, July 7, 1947, Public Law 80–1.
17. Congressional Quarterly, "Hoover Commission Reports" *CQ Almanac 1955, 11th edition* (Washington DC: Congressional Quarterly, 1956).
18. Frederick C. Mills and Clarence D. Long, *The Statistical Agencies of the Federal Government: A Report to the Commission on Organization of the Executive Branch of the Government*, Research Staff of the National Bureau of Economic Research (New York, NY: National Bureau of Economic Research, Inc., 1949).
19. Ferrel Heady, "The Reports of the Hoover Commission," *The Review of Politics* 11, no. 3 (Cambridge: Cambridge University Press, 1949).
20. U.S. Congress Senate Committee on Government Operations, *Organizing for national Security. Hearings before the Subcommittee on National Policy Machinery of the Committee on Government Operations, United States Senate* (Washington, DC: U.S. Government Printing Office, 1961).
21. Ferrel Heady, "The Reports of the Hoover Commission."
22. Erle Cato, "Accrued Cost, not 'Accrued Expenditures' is the Answer for Government," *The Accounting Review* 34, no. 3 (1959): 392–398.
23. Ibid.
24. U.S. Congress Senate Committee on Government Operations, "Financial Management in the Federal Government: A Comprehensive Analysis of Existing and Proposed Legislation Including Financial Management Improvements Made on a Government-Wide Basis," US Senate, 87th Cong., 1st sess., Document 11 (1961).
25. Ippolito, *Why Budgets Matter: Budget Policy and American Politics.*
26. Ibid.
27. Herbert Stein, *The Fiscal Revolution in America: Policy in Pursuit of Reality* (Washington, DC: The AEI Press, 1996). Stein discusses the Eisenhower economic agenda, including its moderation, which was a point noticed at the time by economist John Kenneth Galbraith.

28. Ippolito, *Why Budgets Matter: Budget Policy and American Politics.*
29. Ronald J. King, *Money, Time, and Politics: Investment, Tax Subsidies, and American Democracy* (New Haven, CT: Yale University Press, 1993).
30. Ippolito, *Why Budgets Matter: Budget Policy and American Politics.*
31. Joseph C. Corey and Jason E. Taylor, "'Oversell and Underperform': The Impact of the Great Society Economic Programs Upon the City of Detroit, 1964–1968," *Essays in Economic & Business History* XXVIII (2010): 73–90.
32. Ippolito, *Why Budgets Matter: Budget Policy and American Politics.*
33. Ibid.
34. Ibid.
35. U.S. Congress, "Revenue and Expenditure Control Act of 1968: Explanation of the Bill H.R. 15,414 As Agreed to in Conference," 90th Cong., 2nd sess. (Washington, DC: U.S. Government Printing Office, 1968).
36. Paul E. Junk and Lonnie Nickles, "Federal Participation Certificates," *Nebraska Journal of Economics and Business* 9, no. 2 (1970): 21–29.
37. Joseph Scherer, "The Report of the President's Commission on Budget Concepts: A Review," *Federal Reserve Bank of New York Monthly Review* (December 1967): 231–238.
38. President's Commission on Budget Concepts, *Report of the President's Commission on Budget Concepts* (Washington, DC: U.S. Government Printing Office, 1967).
39. Shelley Lynne Tomkin, *Inside OMB: Politics and Process in the President's Budget Office* (New York, NY: Routledge, 1998). Tomkin provides a history of OMB and its functionality within the executive branch.
40. "Congress Accepts Four Executive Reorganization Plans," *CQ Almanac, 1970, 26th ed.* (Washington, DC: Congressional Quarterly, 1971).
41. Richard Nixon, "Reorganization Plan No. 2 of 1970," *Public Administration Review* 30, no. 6 (1970), 611–619.
42. *CQ Almanac, 1970, 26th ed.*, "Congress Accepts Four Executive Reorganization Plans."
43. Michelle D. Christensen, "The Executive Budget Process Timetable," *CRS Report for Congress* RS20152 (Congressional Research Service, December 5, 2012).
44. Allen Schick, "The Congressional Budget Act of 1974 (P.L. 93–344): Legislative History and Analysis," *Congressional Research Service Report* 75–94 (Washington, DC: Library of Congress, 1975).
45. Ibid.
46. Ibid.
47. Ibid.
48. Ibid.

49. Richard D. Lyonscot, "Nixon's Impounding of Billion in Federal Money is Complicated Issue, Abounding in Misconceptions," *The New York Times*, October 7, 1973.
50. Ibid.
51. Schick, "The Congressional Budget Act of 1974 (P.L. 93–344): Legislative History and Analysis."
52. Ibid.
53. Arthur Burns, "Statement by Arthur F. Burns before the Joint Study Committee on Budget Control," March 6, 1973.
54. Ibid.
55. U.S. Congress Joint Study Committee on Budget Control, *Improving Congressional Control Over Budgetary Outlay and Receipt* Totals, Interim Report (Washington: U.S. Government Printing Office, 1973).
56. Schick, "The Congressional Budget Act of 1974 (P.L. 93–344): Legislative History and Analysis."
57. Hubert H. Humphrey, "Testimony by Senator Hubert H. Humphrey Before the Joint Study Committee on Budget Control," March 6, 1973.
58. Schick, "The Congressional Budget Act of 1974 (P.L. 93–344): Legislative History and Analysis."
59. Ibid.
60. Ibid.
61. Ibid.
62. Fisher, "The Politics of Impounded Funds."
63. Ibid.
64. "House Voted to Reform Federal Budget Oversight," *CQ Almanac 1973, 29th ed.* (Washington DC: Congressional Quarterly, 1974): 243–252.
65. Ibid.
66. Ibid.
67. Ibid.
68. Ibid.

References

Brundage, Percival Flack. 1970. The Bureau of the Budget. New York, NY: Praeger Publishers.

Burns, Arthur. 1973. "Statement by Arthur F. Burns before the Joint Study Committee on Budget Control." Washington, DC: U.S. Congress, March 6.

Cato, Erle. 1959. "Accrued Cost, not 'Accrued Expenditures' is the Answer for Government." The Accounting Review 34 (3): 392–398.

Christensen, Michelle C. 2012. The Executive Budget Process Timetable. Report to Congress, Washington: Congressional Research Service.

Congressional Quarterly. 1971. “Congress Accepts Four Executive Reorganization Plans.” In CQ Almanac, 1970, by Congressional Quarterly. Washington: Congressional Quarterly.

Congressional Quarterly. 1956. Hoover Commission Reports. CQ Almanac 1955, 11th edition, Washington, DC: Congressional Quarterly.

Congressional Record. 76th Cong., 1st sess. 1939. July 27–28.

Congressional Record. 79th Cong., 2nd sess. 1946. March 11.

Cooke, H.J., and M. Katzen. 1954. “The Public Debt.” The Journal of Finance 9 (3): 298–303.

Corey, Joseph C., and Jason E. Taylor. 2010. ‘Oversell and Underpreform’: The Impact of the Great Society Economic Programs Upon the City of Detroit, 1964–1968. Vol. XXVIII. Essays in Economic & Business History.

Dierberger, Wesley A. 1950. “Revenue Act of 1948, edited by Paul A. Walkin and Marcus Manoff.” Indiana Law Journal 25 (3): 416–419.

Fisher, Louis. 1970. “The Politics of Impounded Funds.” Administrative Science Quarterly 15 (3): 361–377.

Heady, Ferrel. 1949. “The Reports of the Hoover Commission.” The Review of Politics 11 (3).

Humphrey, Herbert H. 1973. “Testimony by Senator Hubert H. Humphrey Before the Joint Study Committee on Budget Control.” Washington, DC: U.S. Congress, March 6.

Ippolito, Dennis S. 2003. Why Budgets Matter: Budget Policy and American Politics. University Park, PA: Pennsylvania State University Press.

Kennon, David R., and M. Rebecca Rogers. 1989. The Committee on Ways and Means: A Bicentennial History, 1789–1989. Washington, DC: Government Printing Office.

King, Ronald J. 1993. Money, Time, and Politics: Investment, Tax Subsidies, and American Democracy. New Haven, CT: Yale University Press.

Lyonscot, Richard D. 1973. “Nixon’s Impounding of Billions in Federal Money is Complicated Issue, Abounding in Misconceptions.” The New York Times. October 7. Accessed June 22, 2019. https://www.nytimes.com/1973/10/07/archives/nixons-impounding-of-billions-in-federal-money-is-complicated-issue.html.

Mills, Frederick C., and Clarence D. Long. 1949. The Statistical Agencies of the Federal Government: A Report to the Commission on Organization of the Executive Branch of the Government. Research Staff of the National Bureau of Economic Research, New York: National Bureau of Economic Research, Inc.

Mosak, Jacob L. 1946. “National Budgets and National Policy.” The American Economic Review 36 (1): 20–43.

Nixon, Richard. 1970. “Reorganization Plan No. 2 of 1970.” Public Administration Review 30 (6): 611–619.

President's Commission on Budget Concepts. 1967. Report of the President's Commission on Budget Concepts. Final Report, U.S. Government Printing Office.

Schick, Allen. 1975. The Congressional Budget Act of 1974: Legislative History and Analysis. Report to Congress, Washington: Congressional Research Service.

Schultze, Charles L. 1992. "Is There a Bias Towards Excess in U.S. Government Budgets or Deficits?" The Journal of Economic Perspectives 6 (2): 25–43.

Stein, Herbert. 1996. The Fiscal Revolution in America: Policy in Pursuit of Reality. Washington, DC: The AEI Press.

Tomkin, Shelley Lynne. 1998. Inside OMB: Politics and Process in the President's Budget Office. New York, NY: Routledge.

Truman, Harry S. 1945. "Special Message to the Congress Presenting a 21-Point Program for the Reconversion Period." The American Presidency Project. September 6. https://www.presidency.ucsb.edu/documents/special-message-the-congress-presenting-21-point-program-for-the-reconversion-period.

U.S. Congress. 1947. An Act for the establishment of the Commission on Organization of the Executive Branch of the Government. Public Law 80–162, July 7.

U.S. Congress. 1968. Revenue and Expenditure Control Act of 1968: Explanation of the Bill H.R. 15414 As Agreed to in Conference. 90th Congress, 2nd Session, Washington: U.S. Government Printing Office.

U.S. Senate Committee on Government Operation. 1961. Financial Management in the Federal Government: A Comprehensive Analysis of Existing and Proposed Legislation Including Financial Management Improvements Made on a Government-Wide Basis. Committee Report, Washington: U.S. Senate, 87th Congress, 1st Session.

Webster, George D. 1951. "Taxpayer Relief: The Revenue Act of 1951." Virginia Law Review 37 (8): 1039–1081.

CHAPTER 7

A New Era of Congressional Budgeting

The summer of 1974 was sweltering. Washington, D.C., is a town known to be humid in the summer months. However, that summer was hot and dry. A. James Wagner, a meteorologist at the National Oceanic and Atmospheric Administration, wrote that for many places around the United States, "it was the worst July heat wave since the disastrous 'Dust Bowl' period of 1934 through 1936, with most days having maxima about 90 degrees Fahrenheit and several above 100 degrees Fahrenheit."[1]

That summer must have been especially uncomfortable for President Nixon. His disapproval rating had risen from 49 to 63 percent since July 1973. Facing impeachment, he would resign a month later. Just a month early, Congress had passed the most significant budget process reforms since 1921 in direct response to Nixon's attacks and activities. Congress had sought to limit the power of the executive by playing a larger role in developing the federal budget.

The budget process had come a long way since 1921 when the executive budget had been implemented in order to give some focus to policy decision-making. The executive budget, it was thought, would help to eliminate waste by creating more transparency around how the government allocated resources. It had also been believed that the executive budget would create additional certainty around spending and revenue policy.

In 1921, however, tariffs were still responsible for a significant portion of total receipts collected. The national income tax was less than a decade old. Government spending as a percent of the economy was modest. The

P. Winfree, *A History (and Future) of the Budget Process in the United States*, https://doi.org/10.1007/978-3-030-30959-6_7

primary objective of fiscal policy was to develop a plan for how to spend government receipts or how to correct for deficiencies. In other words, balanced budgets were a normality. Furthermore, debt management drove fiscal policy during war or economic downturns while debt retirement took over as the principle objective during other times.

There were, of course, innovations over the next fifty-three years. Congress experimented with the legislative budget in the 1940s. The Bureau of the Budget grew in size and influence to become the Office of Management and Budget by 1970. The Government Accountability Office was expanded to preform policy audits and to help Congress review the presidential budgets. The presidential budget itself began to take on new demands reflecting new theories for how to manage economic policy. The evolution of competing budget concepts led to the Presidential Commission on Budget Concepts during the Johnson Administration. As the federal government grew in scope so too did the need for modernization and reorganization. The combination of this experience, along with the growth in centralized power within the executive, resulted in abuses within the budget process that reflected both political and institutional divisions.

The perception of Congress's abdication of many budgeting decisions to the president was coming to an end. When the Congressional Budget and Impoundment Control Act was signed into law twenty-eight days before Nixon's resignation it was done so with overwhelming congressional support. The law itself reflected a mistrust in the existing institutions. However, it was conservative in the sense that it was not an upending the existing executive budget process. At the time, it was widely perceived to be a move by Congress to grab the purse strings back from the presidency.

The new budgeting rules would, however, provide presidents with additional opportunities to implement their own agendas. The budget reconciliation process established by the 1974 Budget Act would soon be used to carry out sweeping reforms that were perceived as undermining the Senate's minority party. Additional rules governing the process were adopted in the 1980s along with another experiment with statutory budget limits, but this time taking the form of deficit targets. This was a slight departure from the automatic stabilization policy widely subscribed to during the post-war period.[2]

By the early 1990s, attempts at deficit targeting were abandoned to experiment with limits on annual appropriations and additional mandatory spending. The end of the decade would also be marked by the return of balanced budgets (if almost by accident) and the beginning of a shift in the use of budget reconciliation for specific policy initiatives rather than to conform current law with the entire budget plan. Modern budgeting was beginning to take shape while new challenges ascended, such as growing entitlement spending relative to annual operating budgets and a renewed attention to deficits.

The Congressional Budget Act

The Congressional Budget and Impoundment Control Act became law on July 12, 1974.[3] The final version of the bill overwhelmingly passed both chambers of Congress. Only six members of the House defected and the Senate unanimously passed the bill just weeks before. The culmination of a process that had begun twenty months earlier had initiated a new era in the history of the federal budget.

The final version of the Congressional Budget Act (CBA) was reflective of the deficiencies widely regarded of the existing process. As Allen Schick pointed out in an analysis following the CBA's enactment:

> *Virtually every component of the 1974 Act is traceable to a perceived shortcoming in the existing process. Thus: impoundment control derives from the large-scale withholding of funds by the Nixon Administration; the Budget Committees from the lack of a congressional mechanism to coordinate tax and spending policies; the Congressional Budget Office from the dependence of Congress on executive agencies for essential budget information; the budget resolutions from the lack of a procedure to determine budget totals and priorities.*[4]

The CBA should be viewed as a significant iteration to a continuing process in the struggle between the executive and legislative branches over the budgeting decisions. But the CBA was not as seismic in scale as the Budget and Accounting Act of 1921 which had created a new centralized process around the presidency and unseated a period of congressional domination over spending decisions.[5]

In fact, the CBA is best interpreted as inserting Congress into a process that is not their own but rather one still dominated by the executive branch. Therefore, if the CBA intended to "assure effective congressional control over the budgetary process," as it purports to do in its own declaration of purpose, then it largely failed from its very inception. The CBA did, however, create the mechanisms to give Congress a larger role in determining fiscal and economic priorities.

As many analysts have noted, the CBA is fairly reactionary and tells us something about the period in which it was enacted. It also reflects a compromise between different factions who believed in strengthening Congress' power over the purse. This makes the law similar to other budget process changes throughout history that were responding to challenges of the day. However, the institutions and processes developed from the CBA have shaped policymaking at the margin over the last forty years. Therefore, it is worth considering a brief legislative history of the law and exploring where we have come since its enactment.

The legislative history begins with the Joint Study Committee on Budget Control. Chapter 5 recalls the history of the Joint Study Committee that had originally carried a catchier title: Joint Committee to Review Operation of Budget Ceiling and to Recommend Procedures for Improving Congressional Control Over Budgetary Outlay and Receipt Totals. The Committee's initial designation reflected Congress's frustration over its inability to control spending. However, therein lie the problem. Congress does not control spending because it does not execute federal programs. It controls the authorization associated with an agency's ability to spend money. The Joint Study Committee's name was most likely shortened during their meeting on January 18th as it was reflected in the *Congressional Record* by January 20, 1973.

On April 18, 1973, the Joint Study Committee issued its final report which supplemented two identical bills—one for the Senate and the other for the House.[6] However, because the Joint Study Committee did not have formal jurisdiction over any particular matter the bills were immediately referred to the House Rules Committee and the Senate Committee on Government Operations.

The House Rules Committee amended the bill, primarily on the grounds of changing the Budget Committee makeup.[7] In the past, a joint budget committee had been conceptualized as early as the 1910s and adopted as part of the legislative budget process during the 1940s. However, according to the Senate's Government Operations report, "The House had never gone along with the formation of a joint budget committee, for it is concerned that its asserted prerogative to initiate appropriations would be diluted."[8]

The Joint Study Committee also recommended that a legislative staff be shared between the separate House and Senate Budget Committees.[9]

This would become the Congressional Budget Office (CBO) which was established by Title II of the CBA. However, once the bills came under consideration, it became clear that the establishment of the CBO did not prohibit the individual Budget Committees from hiring their own staff as was the prerogative of every standing committee.[10]

There were some differences worked out regarding the independence of the CBO. The Joint Study Committee had envisioned a very close working relationship between the two Budget Committees and the legislative budget office. This relationship would have been akin to that of the Joint Committee on Taxation (JCT) who works directly for the Chairs of the Senate Finance and House Ways and Means Committees. The House Rules Committee had maintained this relationship but expanded the scope of the budget office to include the provision of budgetary information to other congressional offices as well.[11]

The Senate Government Operations Committee went in a slight different direction by allowing the budget office to function as an independent agency but with oversight from the Budget Committees. The Senate Rules Committee further amended this relationship by allowing the Budget Committees to choose the CBO director and prioritized the CBO's work for the Budget Committees.[12] The Senate Rules Committee also recommended a six-year fixed appointment. In the end, the conference committee's legislation closely reflected the product of the Senate Rules Committee by creating a separate agency led by a director chosen with input from the Budget Committees for a fixed four-year term.[13]

The House Rules Committee moved the beginning of the fiscal year from July to October 1 in order to build additional time into the process relative to the beginning of each session of Congress. A major point that had been made by the Joint Study Committee was that Congress neither had a timeline for considering the presidential budgets nor authorization bills in advance of providing appropriations. This had resulted in an ad hoc process with little coordination between the different standing committees with jurisdiction over the individual executive branch requests.[14] They also adopted two budget resolutions: a target produced in the spring and then a second budget resolution reconciling the aggregate limits with what Congress had done in the intervening period.

The Subcommittee on Budgeting, Management, and Expenditures within the Committee on Government Operations debated early in the process whether to establish budget targets or hard limits on spending within the budget resolution. They ultimately recommended targets as well.[15]

However, the bill reported by the Senate Government Operations Committee had a mix of soft targets and a process for establishing budget limits. The budget resolution would establish spending targets which governed the consideration of any legislation. This allowed appropriations bills to move forward but only if the bills met the targets in the budget resolution. If the appropriations bills did not meet the targets, the budget authority would not become available to the agencies until triggering legislation passed based on the targets.[16] This would leave Congress with two options: a second budget resolution that would revise the targets or make across the board cuts to bring appropriations into compliance with the targets established by the first budget resolution.[17]

The Senate Rules Committee converted the first budget resolution to targets and a reconciliation process was added. Rather than revising targets the new reconciliation process provided for a privileged bill that would amend authorizations for spending programs to bring them into compliance with the budget resolution. In other words, if the appropriation and budget resolution were out of sync, Congress would have a new procedure to change the law. This differed from the previous forms of the bill because it did not require Congress to adjust the budget resolution or adopt across the board cuts. The Rules Committee also removed outlay limitations, a three-year limit that had been placed on authorizations, and additional restrictions were placed on apportionment under the Antideficiency Act.[18]

In the end, the Senate Rules Committee produced a bill that was much closer to the version produced by the House's Rules Committee. These bills would go on to pass both chambers and when the conference committee met they focused on the issue of impoundment. The conferees created a distinction between two types of impoundment: rescissions and deferrals. A rescission is the cancelling of budget authority previously authorized by Congress. A deferral is the withholding of budget authority previously authorized. The final bill put an end to rescissions which would cease unless approved by Congress. Deferrals would cease if disapproved by Congress within forty-five days.[19]

The final bill also created two congressional budget resolutions that would not need the support of the president. The first was a nonbinding resolution that would provide guidance to the committees on spending and tax matters which would be adopted in the spring. The second budget resolution would be adopted in the fall and provide for binding budget limits after Congress was given the opportunity to work on other spending and tax bills based on the guidance provided in the first resolution. Ultimately, the fiscal year was changed to October 1 in order to provide Congress with enough time to enact appropriations and additional authorizations bills.

The Congressional Budget Office

The Congressional Budget Act created a new agency to provide independent assessments of budgetary information to Congress. This new agency, the Congressional Budget Office (CBO), was specifically charged with delivering "information with respect to the budget, appropriations bills, and other bills authorizing or providing budget authority or tax expenditures," as well as revenues and receipts. The CBO was and remains a congressional support agency—similar to the General Accounting Office or the Congressional Research Service. However, a central reason for the creation of CBO was to give Congress additional leverage in budget debates rather than having to rely on the Office of Management and Budget.[20]

The government's budget had become a much larger part of the economy as discussed in previous chapters. At the same time, the budget was seen as a primary way to present a message about the type of economic policy that would be used to achieve certain macroeconomic outcomes. In fact, the first report issued by CBO acknowledges that "[l]ow unemployment and stable prices are the twin goals of economic policy," and presents alternative fiscal and monetary policies that would influence both as well as their estimated effects on the federal budget.[21]

A critical component of deriving independent budgetary information was the production of an independent economic forecast. But coming up with an independent economic forecast by the Congressional Budget Office was not automatic. In fact, it was questioned by many in Congress at time including Edmund Muskie, a Democratic Senator from Maine and Chair of the Senate Budget Committee, who reportedly told CBO Director Alice Rivlin, "We don't need a forecast… the administration does the forecast."[22] As Rivlin wrote after she was director of CBO:

> *No one argues much about the noneconomic assumptions. It is implicitly agreed that the weather will be average, and that the level of international tension will*

> *not rise enough to matter. The arguments relate to assumptions about economic growth, inflation, and interest rates. Even small differences in the assumptions make big differences in budget magnitudes especially in several years.*[23]

She was speaking about the differences in economic assumptions between the Office of Management and Budget and the CBO.

The economic forecast, along with many other decisions made about the institutional role of the Congressional Budget Office in the budget process, were not initially legislated. They were developed by the people who were part of the institution in the early years, especially Alice Rivlin who served as its first director through August 1983.[24] This included its emphasis on political independence which was developed out of its analysis of the Carter and Reagan budgets.[25]

CBO forecasts of major spending and revenue changes would become critical for enacting policy over the next forty years. Chuck Grassley, a Republican Senator from Iowa, would opine in 2006, "I say all the time that CBO is God around here because policy lives and dies by CBO's word."[26] At the same time, CBO estimates of the budgetary effects of legislation would also become objects of political gamesmanship.[27] Nevertheless, CBO remains an important institution that provides assessments of legislation relative to a budgetary baseline. Both the baseline itself and the time period covered by the baseline are both regulated by Congress.

The Beginning of Government Shutdowns

The Antideficiency Act (ADA) prohibits government officials from incurring obligations without an appropriation from Congress. In other words, agency officials must have received explicit spending authority from Congress before they can go about committing resources for various programs or activities. This had been a part of permanent federal law since 1870.

However, the success of the Antideficiency Act at preventing obligations without appropriations was inconsistent. The usual routine of agencies was to go about their business as usual when there was a partial lapse in spending authority. Congress would eventually provide spending authority in addition to occasionally blessing executive branch activities during the interim period.[28]

The General Accounting Office's Comptroller General and Office of Management and Budget had held that during a lapse in appropriations it was permissible to make "controllable obligations" but not to engage in any new activities such as hiring.[29] The idea behind this justification was that Congress had previously authorized an activity and therefore expected that the executive branch carry it out. Eventually Congress would get around to providing money and a break in service was antithetical to congressional intent. Agency obligations would be limited "to only those essential to maintain day-to-day operations."[30]

That all changed during the Carter Administration. President Carter's Attorney General viewed this policy as inconsistent with the Antideficiency Act which included no exceptions to the prohibition on obligations. Specifically, it was impossible for obligations to be both unlawful under the ADA and authorized by Congress. If continuation of a program or activity was the congressional intent, then Congress would provide the program or activity with the requisite budget authority. This makes a great deal of sense especially if Congress is going to attempt to restrict the potential for runaway spending by the executive branch. In 1980, the Department of Justice's Office of Legal Counsel issued a legal opinion stating that "federal agencies may incur no obligations that cannot lawfully be funded from prior appropriations unless such obligations are otherwise authorized by law."[31]

The consequence of the new policy outlined in the opinion was that "government shutdowns" would be mandated during appropriations lapses. When Congress failed to provide an appropriation for agency activities, the agency must begin an "orderly shutdown" process under the assumption that additional spending authority will not be provided. The OLC concluded that "authority may be inferred from the Antideficiency Act itself for federal officers to incur those minimal obligations necessary to closing their agencies."[32] There have been fifteen significant lapses in appropriations although only five have resulted in a significant shutdown resulting in a furlough of government employees since 1980.[33] There has yet to be a government shutdown that resulted in a reduction in the workforce or the actual closing of a federal agency.

The Reagan Budgets

There was a slight shift away from the "full employment budgets" after the Nixon administration in the 1970s.[34] During the 1960s and early 1970s, a great deal of attention had been paid to setting macroeconomic policy based on the Phillips Curve or the relationship between unemployment and inflation over the business cycle. This neo-Keynesian idea was that you could trade higher inflation for lower unemployment. At a very basic level, higher levels of inflation would raise wages and encourage more people to work.

The economists Milton Friedman and Edmund Phelps argued you cannot permanently trade higher inflation for lower unemployment. The root of their observation is that only nominal wages will increase when the government increases the money supply. This will cause some workers to accept jobs because they have not taken into account the real purchasing power of their wages. However, in the long run, it is real wages that matter. Once inflationary policies become predictable they lose any power over unemployment and no longer become simulative.[35] Furthermore, the economist Robert Lucas observed that you cannot make policy based on the assumption that certain parameters remain fixed relative to their historical behavior. This includes the relationship between inflation and unemployment presented by the Phillips Curve.[36] In other words, the Phillips Curve breaks down entirely when would-be workers can't be tricked into accepting a higher nominal wage because they know it won't make them any better off.

However, during the early 1970s the Phillips Curve failed guide policymakers in a predictable way as nominal wages rose relative to increases in unemployment. This led the Nixon administration to use both wage and price controls in an attempt to limit inflation. At the same time, exogenous shocks in both the food supply and oil resulted in sharp increases in commodity and energy prices. The initial result was shortages followed by very high inflation as the price controls were lifted in 1974.[37] Between 1976 and 1979, inflation as measured by the consumer price index rose from 5 to nearly 13 percent while the unemployment rate only fell from 7.7 to 5.8 percent.

President Carter was not particularly interested in macroeconomic policy setting along traditional lines early in his presidency but he did believe in fiscal responsibility.[38] To the extent that he did consider economic policy it was within regards to reducing unemployment and a reluctance to increase the deficit. As a candidate, the Carter economic plan stated that "we should strive toward balance, within an environment of full employment, over the long term.... I therefore call for balanced budgets over the business cycle."[39] Carter also called for a set of policies that would target the unemployment rate at 4 percent and inflation by 4 percent while balancing the budget by 1980. Carter also broke with other post-war

Democratic presidents by failing to fully embrace deficit spending under Keynesianism while advocating for the adoption of a zero-based budget.[40] Ultimately, Carter was unable to tame inflation while joblessness remained a serious problem.

In 1980, Ronald Reagan challenged Carter for the presidency based on a four-part economic plan: (1) to reduce inflation by controlling the growth in the money supply which had begun under Volker's lead at the Federal Reserve; (2) to reduce marginal tax rates in order to encourage work and investment; (3) the reduce regulation; and (4) to reduce the growth in government spending.[41] Reagan had campaigned on the idea that deficits produced inflation and high interest rates.[42] Early on in his presidency, Reagan was able to garner political support for his unconventional economic agenda (at least for the period) because of the relatively high tax burdens that individuals had experienced in the 1970s and the concern for the economy.[43]

The political scientist James Savage has suggested that balanced budgets have, historically, carried a symbolism that is reflected of the political and not only the economic environment of the time. For Reagan, this symbolism reflected a view on federalism. A smaller government relegated to the "proper sphere" of responsibilities with less taxation meant that states could take on more of the responsibility for the provisions of government. However, Reagan also believed that government spending increased inflation.

The president's Council of Economic Advisors (CEA) was not so sure. An outspoken member of the CEA from 1981 to 1985, William Niskanen, for instance, suggested that deficits by themselves do not cause inflation or have any effect on real interest rates but do distort the time distribution of taxes as future taxpayers would pay for today's debt. This theory was supported in a Treasury paper issued in 1984 and in subsequent empirical analysis.[44] However, the *Economic Report of the President* and the view supported by chairman Martin Feldstein was that higher deficits contributed to higher interest rates. In other words, the cause of inflationary monetary policy can be fiscal in nature.[45]

In the end, Reagan supported both balancing the budget by reducing spending through the belief that raising taxes would stimulate more spending. Reagan also believed that cutting taxes would help to curtail spending in the future.[46] This was reflected in Reagan's budgets but also in the establishment of the President's Private Sector Survey on Cost Control, also known as the Grace Commission, which concluded that more than $420 billion could be saved over three years by implementing almost 2500 different recommendations.[47]

There is little evidence to support Reagan's assumption that there is a clear relationship between taxes and spending after about 1960.[48] In the 1980s, both the economist Robert Lucas and political scientist Aaron Wildavsky independently observed that something had happened during the period from 1960 to 1980 where deficit financing had become more important while revenues and expenditures changed independently from one another. Lucas blamed this on both the rules for conducting monetary and fiscal policy.[49] Wildavsky suggests that a breakdown in agreement over the fundamental policy consensus resulted in additional tendencies for deficit finance.[50] This might explain the positive relationship found between tax cuts and spending increases in the post-World War II period.[51]

Democrats in Congress challenged Reagan's willingness to support higher deficits by cutting taxes through their support of policies that also would have reduced the deficit with revenues as well. This included Walter Mondale who, in his 1984 acceptance speech for Democratic nominee for resident, claimed that the Reagan deficits increase "interest rates, clobber exports, stunt investment, kill jobs, undermine growth, cheat our kids, and shrink our future."[52] As Savage suggests, "By the end of Ronald Reagan's first term, the Democrats had helped to create a political climate that could produce the constitutional or statutory limitations on deficit spending that they had long opposed."

Between 1981 and 1985, the deficit as a percent of the economy doubled from 2.5 to 5 percent while the nominal annual deficit had gone from $79 to $212 billion.[53] Revenues fell from 19.1 to 17.2 percent of the economy while spending increased from 21.6 to 22.2 percent. The increase in spending was a derivative of additional resources for defense as all other spending remained relatively constant. The 1981 tax cuts which lowered the top marginal rate from 70 to 50 percent reduced revenues as a percent of the economy by 4.5 percent.[54] However, certain provisions were undone by the Tax Equity and Fiscal Responsibility reconciliation bill in 1982 which increased revenues by 0.8 percent of the economy according to CBO.

President Reagan also used the budget process to curtail regulation.[55] This included explicitly reducing regulation as part of the early reconciliation bills enacted before the Senate's adoption of the Byrd Rule. However, it also included using the budget infrastructure to curtail new regulation. This included reducing the budget requests for regulatory agencies (such as the Consumer Product Safety Commission) but also included empowering the Office of Management and Budget to formally review draft regulations produced by the agencies.

Attempts to Control the Deficit

The mid-1980s brought a renewed focus on the deficit following a recession, high levels of unemployment and inflation, and the early budgets under President Reagan that increased spending on defense. Between 1981 and 1985, the annual deficit averaged 4.2 percent of the economy. Over the same period, revenues had fallen by 1.9 percent of the economy and spending had increased by 0.6 percent of the economy. Meanwhile, public debt as a percent of the economy had increased from 26 to 35 percent.

The Balanced Budget and Emergency Control Act of 1985 (BBEDCA), also known as Gramm-Rudman Hollings, imposed deficit targets for fiscal years 1986 through 1991. Beginning in 1986, the target would be $171.9 billion (3.7 percent of the economy) and would decline to zero (or balance) in 1991. The deficit targets were enforced by across the board reductions of budget authority (called "sequestration") divided equally between defense and non-defense programs. However, certain programs were either exempt or special rules applied to the amount of spending authority that could be reduced under the sequester. Sequestration would be suspended in the event of war or low levels of economic growth.

Under BBEDCA, the Comptroller General of the General Accounting Office would act as an adjudicator between the Office of Management and Budget and the Congressional Budget Office over the extent to which the target was missed. The president would thereby be required to follow the direction of the Comptroller General. However, the General Accounting Office was part of legislative branch. Soon after the law was enacted, the Supreme Court held in Bowsher v. Synar (1986) that BBEDCA provides the Comptroller General with executive power. Therefore, due to the inability of Congress to control how the laws are executed that power was determined to be unconstitutional. Congress responded to the Court's decision by passing the Balanced Budget and Emergency Deficit Control Reaffirmation Act of 1987 to correct for the BBEDCA shortcomings.

The targets were soon amended as part of the debt limit increase in 1987. Failure to meet the $108 billion deficit target in fiscal year 1987 led Congress to amend both the targets with extending them by two years through 1993. The actual deficit targets for 1988 and 1989 were increased by $23 and $36 billion. One of BBEDCA's architects, Warren Rudman, a Republican Senator from New Hampshire, advocated against raising the targets. In a speech delivered on the Senate floor in August 1987 he claimed that by getting the deficit on a path to zero "We will have declining interest rates; we will have more employment and less unemployment; we will have inflation stabilized, and the trade deficit will come down dramatically."[56] He went on, "[I]f you think that the Farm Belt has had problems the last 2 years, you wait and see what the problems will be in the agricultural sector of this economy if Congress walks away from deficit reduction in this year. It will be devastating."[57] The Democratic Senator from North Dakota, Kent Conrad, later acknowledged his agreement with Rudman.[58]

But not all Members of Congress agreed with Rudman or Conrad's assessment of the economic benefits of maintaining the targets. The "Black Monday" stock market crash was still a couple of months away and the economy had been doing well up to this point. The unemployment rate was just over 5 percent and real economic growth exceeded 3 percent. However, Ronald Coleman, a Democratic Congressman from Texas, suggested that across the board spending reductions would harm the economy.[59] Rather, Coleman advocated for an increase in taxes along with spending reductions to achieve the targeted deficit reduction called for under BBEDCA.

In the end, the deficit targets imposed by BBEDCA were not successful in reducing the deficit over any sustainable period of time.[60] In 1990, the Congressional Budget Office Director Robert Reischauer estimated that about half of the deficit reduction from BBEDCA was derived from either one-time savings (for example, asset sales) or by moving agencies off of the budget (for example, the Postal Service was moved off-budget).[61] Even the sequester was ineffective because "its lagged effect did not reflect any change in behavior during 1987 that could be attributed to the new process."[62]

However, BBEDCA did influence the next iteration of the Congressional budget process. The enforceable deficit targets were abandoned in 1990. However, rather than going back to a pre-BBEDCA policy, Congress imposed two types of spending limits as part of the Budget Enforcement Act (BEA). The first spending limit was a set of caps on discretionary spending. The second was a limit on legislation that increased the deficit through changes to revenues or mandatory spending programs (e.g. entitlements such as Medicare or Medicaid). A sequester, ordered by OMB, was used to enforce breaches in either spending limit. Furthermore, under BBEDCA, the sequester order by CBO would need to be voted on by Congress. Under the BEA, no additional vote was necessary.

Along with the BEA, Congress also passed the Federal Credit Reform Act (FCRA) to govern the budgetary accounting for federal credit programs such as those that support loans and loan guarantees. FCRA required credit programs to report the subsidy costs of the loan at the time it was provided rather than the net cash flow of the program.

The BEA was originally intended to help enforce the budget agreement made by President Bush and Congressional Democrats on Andrews Airforce Base that reduced spending by about $500 billion over five years;[63] however, the spending limits were extended in 1993 and again in 1997 before finally expiring in September 2002.[64] Similar to BBEDCA, the set of rules established by the BEA governing spending limits and revenue levels did not make it any easier for Congress to consider tax increases or mandatory spending reductions.[65] In fact, the changes likely pushed decisions regarding tradeoffs on spending toward discretionary programs while inherently blessing all new non-legislative spending on mandatory programs and revenues.

The BEA also moved some of the focus of the budget process to scorekeeping on a continuous basis by the Congressional Budget Office. This likely empowered both Congress and the CBO within the larger budget process as their assessments of individual pieces of legislation became more important relative to OMB for the purposes of budget enforcement.[66] In other words, CBO's analysis was used to determine whether a bill was in compliance with the new spending limits.

The Byrd Rule's Beginning

On April 7, 1986, President Reagan signed the Consolidated Omnibus Budget Reconciliation Act of 1985 (COBRA). The law was a product of the budget reconciliation process that had been established under the 1974 Congressional Budget Act. It was also the fifth reconciliation bill that had been enacted under President Reagan whose Director of OMB, David Stockman, had been a member of Congress and knew how to use the budget process to the administration's advantage.

In total, only six reconciliation bills had been enacted since 1974 with one under Carter and the rest with Reagan. Budget reconciliation had been created as a fast-tracked process to amend the law to bring it into compliance with the congressional budget. In the Senate, where the filibuster can slowdown or threaten the consideration of legislation, budget reconciliation is particularly convenient because it is both privileged and debate is limited by the Congressional Budget Act. In other words, only a simple majority of Senators are needed to both proceed to debating the bill and for final passage.

Prior to 1986, budget reconciliation had been used to enact a number of reforms. These included, tax cuts under and changes in federal pay under Reagan as well as reforming child nutrition and federal health programs under Carter and Reagan, among many other proposals. The first five reconciliation bills had reduced the deficit by about $276 billion over the five-year budget window beginning in the year of enactment.[67]

In 1985, Congress turned its attention to another reconciliation bill after implementing the first round of deficit reduction under BBEDCA. In 1981, Republicans had taken control of the Senate for the first time since 1955. However, Democrats continued to control the House. This political environment along with workings of budget reconciliation had created a dynamic where the President and Senate Republicans could work with House Democrats without the help of Senate Democrats in order to pass legislation.

However, that is not what happened in practice. Besides the Tax Equity and Fiscal Responsibility Act of 1982, which reduced marginal tax rates and spending on low-income assistance programs, the other budget reconciliation bills passed with strong bipartisan majorities (more than two-thirds of Senators voting in the affirmative). That said, the reconciliation bills had also come to include many non-budgetary provisions. For instance, regulatory reforms and other provisions that did not change spending or revenues were fairly common in the early budget reconciliation bills.

This resulted in what became seen by many Senators as a misapplication within the budget process in general and budget reconciliation more specifically.[68] Robert Byrd, a Democratic Senator from West Virginia, suggested:

> *[T]he Pandora's box which has been opened to the abuse of the reconciliation process. That process was never meant to be used as it is being used. There are 122 items in the reconciliation bill that are extraneous .... It was never foreseen that the Budget Reform Act would be used in that way. So if the budget reform process is going to be preserved, and more importantly if we are going to pre-*

> *serve the deliberative process in this U.S. Senate – which is the outstanding, unique element with respect to the U.S. Senate, action must be taken now to stop this abuse of the budget process.*[69]

The reconciliation bill to which Senator Byrd was referring was COBRA which passed the Senate nearly unanimously. However, this led to the Senate adopting a set of rules restricting the application of reconciliation bills in order to preserve the use of the process for only budgetary changes. The "Byrd Rule" includes six definitions for what the Senate agreed to was extraneous and prohibited in their own consideration of reconciliation. This includes provisions that do not produce outlays or revenues and provisions that would increase the deficit over the long-run.

The Byrd Rule is not "self-enforceable" meaning that concerned Senators have an opportunity to use the Byrd Rule prohibitions on extraneous provisions to remove offending language from the reconciliation bill once it is being considered by the full Senate. However, if there are no concerned Senators, the provisions will remain in the bill. The Byrd Rule was made a Senate rule in 1985 before being codified as part of the 1990 budget agreement.

The Byrd Rule has had a tremendous influence in determining the content of reconciliation bills since 1985. However, the political gamesmanship that has been used to avoid Byrd's prohibitions has resulted in the reconciliation process being used more to enact specific, partisan reforms than sweeping budgetary changes in recent years. For instance, the tax cuts of 2001, 2003, and 2017 using budget reconciliation. The 2009–2010 health care reform was also partly enacted using budget reconciliation. Furthermore, even though the Byrd Rule attempts to limit reconciliation for deficit reduction, Congress has found ways to get around those prohibitions. Since the Byrd Rule was first adopted by the Senate, enacted reconciliation bills have been estimated to have increased the deficit by $2.1 trillion over the five- to ten-year budget window beginning with the year of enactment.[70] This is driven entirely by bills imposing revenue reductions. In essence, reconciliation has been incredibly successful at reducing mandatory spending and revenues but not at reducing the deficit.

Budget Reconciliation in the 1990s

The period from 1990 to 1998 has been referred to as the "golden era" of deficit reduction.[71] During that period five reconciliation bills were enacted including two that reduced the deficit by nearly $500 billion apiece according to the Congressional Budget Office. At the same time, the economy grew considerably. Between 1992 and 1999, the economy grew by 4 percent per year while the unemployment rate was cut in half.

In practice, Keynesian macroeconomic policy has never been especially strong even after the enactments of the Employment Act of 1946 and the Humphrey-Hawkins Full Employment and Balanced Growth Act of 1978. However, it was at its strongest in the 1990s.[72] But that may have been driven by politics rather than economic planning.

President Clinton's first budget proposed a large infrastructure proposal that would have exceeded the BEA spending limits imposed in 1990. It would have also reduced the deficit by 22 percent between 1993 and 1998 by imposing additional taxes on higher income individuals. A middle-class tax cut, which Clinton had campaigned on, was absent from his budget. The budget would have also increased government spending by about 20 percent. This was during a time when inflation had gotten back under control and while the unemployment rate had been falling.

Responding to political pressure, Clinton abandoned his stimulus to pursue deficit reduction. The Omnibus Reconciliation Act of 1993 reduced the deficit over the five-year period by $496 billion according to CBO at the time of enactment split almost equally between spending reductions (including debt service) and tax increases. The bill added two new brackets at 36 and 39.6 percent for those with incomes above $115,000 and $25,000 while the alternative minimum tax (AMT) was increased. The bill also raised the tax on Social Security income, it lifted the cap on the Medicare payroll tax, increased the gas tax, and expanded the Earned Income Tax Credit for working parents. Corporate tax revenue was also increased by adding new brackets. Spending reductions included payments to hospitals and physicians under Medicare, the cost of living adjustments for the military, and repealing certain requirements imposed on states for Medicaid. Meanwhile, contrary to breaking the BEA discretionary spending limits as the Clinton budget would have done, the bill established new limits for 1996 through 1998.

The 1993 tax increase ultimately led to Democrats losing control of the House and Senate during the 1994 midterm elections. Republicans picked up ten seats in the Senate and fifty-four seats in the House. The President and Congress eventually turned to welfare reform which had been a common agenda item reflected in the Clinton campaign and the Republicans' "Contract with America." Pursuing the path of budget reconciliation, reforms included converting the federal cash assistance program that had existed since the original Social Security Act, Aid for Families with Dependent Children (AFDC) into fixed block grants to states. Other changes included limiting low-income assistance for certain immigrant populations, increasing child support enforcement, placing a time limit on benefits for those not working, and a number of reforms to Supplemental Security Income (SSI) including new standards to childhood disability.

The 1996 election sent Clinton back to the White House and Republicans back into the majorities in Congress. The results were generally interpreted as a desire by the electorate for bipartisanship. Furthermore, the earlier reconciliation bills as well as the growing economy had put a balanced budget once again in sight as revenues had grown to their highest level since 1981 and spending was at its lowest level since 1975. In an attempt to claim a political victory over deficits while cutting taxes, the Balanced Budget and Taxpayer Relief Acts of 1997 together reduced the deficit over the five-year period from 1998 to 2002 by about $18 billion according to CBO.

The objective of the Balanced Budget Act was specifically to balance the budget within five years. However, only one year was needed thus further demonstrating the external factors that were relevant. The Balanced Budget Act also introduced the Medicare Sustainable Growth Rate (SGR) which would have implemented reductions in Medicare provider payments. However, the threat of the payment cuts was too great for Congress who would override them for many years before replacing the Medicare SGR altogether in 2015. The Medicare SGR is a good example of how budget discipline is often not sustainable in the long-run, especially when the effects are seen as too politically costly.

The Real End to Balanced Budgets

The annual budget deficits during World War II averaged about 18 percent of the economy. The federal government has not approached those levels in the post-war period. Even during the early years of the Reagan administration when deficits were significant they only averaged 4.4 percent of the economy. Debt held by the public fell after the war until the mid-1970s after which point it grew by an average of 3.8 percent (measured as a percent of the economy) until 1993. From 1993 until 2001, debt as a percent of the economy was reduced by about 5 percent per year.

Debt then increased by about 1.9 percent per year between 2002 and the beginning of the global financial crisis in 2007. During this period deficits averaged about 2.5 percent of the economy and the unemployment rate fell from a high 6.3 percent in June 2003 to 4.4 percent by May 2007. The economy was in recession for eight months having experienced the bust of the "Dot-com bubble" after a long period of growth. However, the recession was not enough to take the federal government out of balance. Rather, there were a number of things that happened during the George W. Bush administration that drove the increase in debt.

First, nominal spending on entitlement programs grew 5.2 percent per year (or about 2.5 percent more than inflation), while discretionary spending grew by about 7 percent per year (4.3 percent more than inflation) driven primarily by a buildup in base defense and spending on the wars in Afghanistan and Iraq following the 9/11 attacks. Real spending on defense increased by 36 percent during Bush's first term whereas non-defense spending increased by 20 percent over the same period.[73]

The budget limits imposed by the Budget Enforcement Act expired in September 2002. The budget had been in balance since 1998 and the economy was recovering from recession. CBO Director Dan Crippen testified in 2001 that the surpluses produced by the budget constraint under the BEA limits and the economy had "put increasing pressure on lawmakers to circumvent the discretionary spending caps and the PAYGO requirement."[74] Of course, the budget process simply focuses the attention rather than guaranteeing significant action on policies. It is, therefore, critical for the budget process to reflect the challenges of the day or else lawmakers will just change or ignore the self-imposed rules.

The BEA period had come and gone. Republicans had majorities in both the House and Senate. They also controlled the White House under George W. Bush. In 2000, Bush had run for president on using the surplus to provide for tax cuts, the creation of private accounts within Social Security, and building up the military. Deficits were no longer a central focus but rather, as the *New York Times* put it, "up for grabs in political terms."[75] In many ways, the economic policy of Bush in 2000 reflected that of Reagan twenty years earlier.[76] Bush did, in fact, also subscribe to the idea of using a portion of the surplus to retire the federal debt in his first address to Congress in February 2001:

> *Many of you have talked about the need to pay down our national debt. I listened, and I agree. We owe it to our children and grandchildren to act now, and I hope you will join me to pay down $2 trillion in debt during the next 10 years. At the end of those 10 years, we will have paid down all the debt that*

> *is available to retire. That is more debt, repaid more quickly than has ever been repaid by any nation at any time in history.*[77]

Bush, like Reagan, also pursued tax cuts immediately for their simulative effects even though the 1981 recession was much worse than the Dot-com bust and marginal tax rates were initially much higher. However, after the tax cuts and while in economic recovery neither the White House nor Congress pursued deficit reduction in any meaningful way.

Gross real spending on Medicare increased by an average of 7 percent per year between 2002 and 2007. In 2003, the Medicare Modernization Act (MMA) added a new prescription drug benefit (Part D) and revised the payment system for Medicare managed care (Medicare Advantage), among other changes. At the time of enactment, CBO estimated that MMA would increase spending by about $395 billion over ten years or about a tenth of the programs total cost.[78] Along with Medicare, real spending on food and nutrition assistance grew by an average of 6 percent per year following the enactment of the 2002 Farm Bill which, according to the Congressional Research Service, "substantially expanded food stamp eligibility for legally resident noncitizens (the single largest change), liberalized food stamp benefits and eligibility rules, provided new options for states to vary from regular Food Stamp program rules, greatly changed the system for penalizing states with high rates of erroneous benefit and eligibility determinations," and increased funding for various other programs.[79] CBO estimated that the bill would increase mandatory spending by $87.3 billion over the eleven-year period from 2002 to 2011.

Two reconciliation bills were enacted in 2006 there were related to the budget resolution passed by Congress in 2005. The Deficit Reduction and the Tax Increase Prevention and Reconciliation Acts of 2005 together increased the deficit by $32 billion over five years but by reducing both mandatory spending and taxes. The bills were, in a way, Reaganesque by providing states with additional flexibility under the Medicaid program, reauthorizing welfare grants, trimming back federal spending, and reducing taxes relative to current law. They obviously did not, however, do anything to significantly change the trajectory of federal deficits or retire the debt.

In 2007, Democrats took back the majorities in Congress after the midterm elections. In power, they quickly reinstated pay-as-you-go rules governing congressional action.[80] Democrats, in fact, campaigned on bringing back pay-as-you-go rules and against deficits in 2006.[81] But later that year the onset of the global financial crises would again shift attention away from budget deficits. Discretionary spending would increase by 23 percent between 2007 and 2009 including measures intended to prevent the spread of financial risk brought on by the crisis. The crisis itself would result in one of the worst economic recessions since the Great Depression. After President Obama was inaugurated in 2009 he would also call for additional stimulus measures that would contribute to an increase in real discretionary spending on non-defense programs by 10 percent in 2009 and 11 percent in 2010. In 2009, the deficit jumped to $1.4 trillion from $459 billion in 2008.

The first trillion dollar deficits would help to bring attention back to federal debt. However, this time the story is even more complicated. Entitlement spending was growing as the baby boom generation was reaching retirement. The Bush tax cuts had played a significant role in eliminating the earlier surpluses and had been central in the politics of the previous decade. The commitments to wars in Afghanistan and Iraq had also played a significant role in building support for the defense buildup. Meanwhile, Congress's response to the financial crises and recession had pushed non-defense spending up even higher. The response to calls for deficit reduction is never easy. However, this time, it seems that there was not a clear target with so many responsible parties.

The Return of Budget Control

The topic of health care reform was central during the 2008 presidential election. After his election, President Obama would make expanding health insurance coverage a focus of his first address to Congress and the president's budget released later that spring. Health reform would be a central focus of Congress that year and Obama needed them on board to build a budget that allowed reconciliation to be used for reform.

On February 17, 2009, President Obama signed a large stimulus, which was estimated to cost over $830 billion, named the American Recovery and Reinvestment Act.[82] Six days later, on February 23, the White House held a Fiscal Responsibility Summit aimed at discussion of the "pair of trillion-dollar deficits."[83] The first "deficit" was the gap between real and potential GDP. The second was the annual budget deficit. The event was billed consistent with standard neo-Keynesian analysis. Stimulus was needed to jump start the economy before worrying about the "unsustainable fiscal course" over the "medium to long-run." In other words, once economic recovery had been achieved, federal policymakers could turn to long-run drivers of the debt or, as OMB Director Peter Orszag observed, "[T]he path to fiscal responsibility must run directly through health care."[84] Although the event was only a White House summit and not a place to strike a grand fiscal deal, health care costs were brought up in several discussions. In fact, the Fiscal Summit is best contextualized as a step to build consensus around health care reform, which would eventually become a major legacy of Obama.

However, health care reform was viewed under the lens of sustainable fiscal policy. Republicans used this metric to criticize the various plans and Democrats used it to evaluate them. This also led to a great deal of debate around the final CBO cost estimates of the Patient Protection and Affordable Care and Health Care and Education Reconciliation Acts of 2010, together better known as "Obamacare." "Bending the cost curve" in health care came to mean not only private costs but also federal spending, especially within regards to Medicare through changes in financing. In fact, the various 2009–2010 health care reform bills were developed by Congress working closely with the Congressional Budget Office with attention paid to the deficit impact as well as insurance coverage. In the end, the Community Living Assistance Services and Supports Act (or CLASS Act), which was enacted as part of the Patient Protection and Affordable Care Act as a public long-term care option never got off the ground because of an amendment to the law that required the Medicare Office of the Actuaries to certify its financial sustainability over the long-run (which it could not).

A year later, in February 2010, Obama signed an executive order creating the National Commission on Fiscal Responsibility and Reform, also known as the Fiscal Commission or Bowles-Simpson after the bipartisan co-chairs Erskine Bowles (a White House Chief of Staff for President Clinton) and Alan Simpson (a former Republican Senator from Wyoming). The Commission was patterned after a similar commission proposed in Conrad's bill with Judd Gregg, a Republican Senator from New Hampshire, the Bipartisan Task Force for Responsible Fiscal Action Act. The Fiscal Commission included eighteen members, twelve members of Congress and six private citizens, with the goal of improving the fiscal condition of the country over the long-run.

Ultimately, the Fiscal Commission issued a report in December 2010 that recommended a number of reforms to raise revenue and reduce spending in order to stabilize the debt by 2014 and reduce the public debt from 60 to 40 percent of the economy by 2035. The Commission also recommended the establishment of a debt stabilization process based on deficit targets which would trigger legislation bringing spending and revenue policy into compliance with the fiscal goals. Other process changes recommended by the Commission included a new measure for inflation (chained-CPI) for indexing benefits of federal programs, discretionary spending limit adjustments for efforts to boost program integrity, a process to reform budget concepts, and a better automatic release system for unemployment benefits.[85] As a whole, the Commission's report was initially a flop; although, it contained many ideas that have influenced budget negotiations since its release and was advanced as the Senate Budget Committee's budget resolution in 2012 by Senator Kent Conrad, a Democrat from New Hampshire, but never passed the Senate.

In February 2010, Obama signed the Statutory Pay-As-You-Go Act into law which permanently enforces the PAYGO rules through a process of sequestration. If a bill increases the deficit as assessed by the CBO over the next five- or ten-year periods, an automatic spending reduction is applied to all non-exempt mandatory programs. But because Congress created the rule they can also turn the rule off. Statutory PAYGO initially provided exemptions for many of the tax changes that were made as part of the 2001 and 2003 Bush tax cuts, legislative overrides of the Medicare SGR that would increase spending, changes to the Alternative Minimum Tax, and reauthorizations in low-income assistance programs (such as the Supplemental Nutrition Assistance Program). Furthermore, many other bills enacted since 2010 have also been exempt of PAYGO and thus violations to increasing the deficit have not been enforced.

The 2010 midterm elections brought a renewed focus on annual budget deficits and the growth federal debt in a reaction against neo-Keynesian economic policy. As a report by the Council on Foreign Relations found, "Congressional candidates in the 2010 midterm elections found the growing U.S. debt and persistent joblessness though campaign challenges. Traditional proposals to tame unemployment – more government spending or tax cuts – were hard sells for U.S. voters worried about the country's growing federal deficits and ballooning public debt, which is expected to rise to 62 percent of gross domestic product this year. Both parties staked hopes for midterm gains on convincing voters they can both create jobs and rein in deficits."[86]

Obama proposed additional stimulus in the form of an infrastructure proposal. Republicans, on the other hand, gained steam under the Tea

Party movement whose economic policy harkened back to a form of Reaganism—reduce the size of government by cutting both spending and taxes. With Republican victory in taking back the House in those midterms came a clear focus on government debt.

The next nine months were a bit rocky. In May 2011, a bipartisan group led by Vice President Joe Biden and the House Republican Majority Leader Eric Cantor of Virginia began meeting to develop a proposal to raise the statutory debt limit, which was estimated to be exhausted August 2, while also reducing the deficit.[87] However, by late-June those talks had broken down leaving Speaker John Boehner, a Republican from Ohio, and President Obama to negotiate a final deal. The deal they eventually developed at the debt limit deadline was centered around the Budget Control Act of 2011.

The framework of the Budget Control Act (BCA) was a redline put in place by Boehner that for every dollar increase in the debt limit the House Republicans would need a dollar reduction in spending.[88] The BCA reinstituted discretionary spending limits for the period from 2012 through 2021. These limits would reduce future appropriations in each year growing to about 9 percent of CBO's estimate of such spending by 2021.[89] It also created a Joint Select Committee on Deficit Reduction (called the "Super Committee") with the goal of developing a plan by December 2011 for an additional $1.5 trillion. If the Super Committee were to fail, which they ultimately did, the spending limits would be reduced by $1.2 trillion minus debt service split equally between defense and non-defense programs. In addition, a mandatory sequestration would apply primarily to non-defense programs thus taking away some pressure from non-defense discretionary. Any breach in the limits would be enforced by sequestration.

In addition, the BCA spending limits do not apply to war funding. This has, over time, led Congress to increase the level of spending dedicated to the war (called "Overseas Contingency Operations" funding or OCO) by more than they otherwise would have to fund base defense, and even some non-defense, activities. In fact, the fiscal year 2020 budget under President Trump proposes increasing OCO funding by the entire amount of the additional adjustment under the BCA derived from the failure of the Super Committee.

By the time this book was written in 2018 and 2019, the Budget Control Act's effects have dominated discussions in Washington about federal spending. The BCA has been amended by Congress four times or roughly once every two years since 2013. Each time, Congress increases the discretionary spending limits. At first, sequestration was delayed and ultimately reduced. However, in both the Bipartisan Budget Acts of 2013 and 2015, the limits were increased by less than additional adjustment which was partly offset by mandatory spending reductions and some new revenues. Beginning in 2018, the limits were raised high enough to roll-back a portion of the initial spending limits and only about a quarter of the increase was offset. This shows that the BCA, both the initial discretionary spending limits and the additional adjustment, were perhaps too strict to be politically maintained.

What is particularly interesting about the politics of the BCA is that economy has been growing since 2010. The unemployment rate is at a 40-year low having reached 3.6 percent in May 2019. In February 2018, when the last BCA adjustment was enacted, the unemployment rate was 4.1 percent and the economy was on its fastest pace of growth since 2015. Yet, lawmakers found it impossible to live within the spending limits they established for themselves in 2011 and the deficit is expected to exceed $1 trillion by 2022.

Summary

If the historical experience was any guide one might be led to believe that we are currently in a period where fiscal restraint would be expected. In the past, voters and the politicians that they have elected have demanded some level of control over the deficit when it seems to reach a high-water mark if, for no other reason, to achieve some level of symbolic victory over the federal debt. However, the politics of the BCA demonstrates how difficult it has become to reduce spending even during periods of economic growth.

If a more recent experience is any guide, it is not uncommon for a president to propose a fiscal stimulus during a period of growth only to be pulled back by a Congress controlled by the opposing party, as was the case with both Clinton and Obama. However, when both Congress and the White House are controlled by the same party, it seems that fiscal tightening is mostly shelved regardless of any political rhetoric about budget sustainability.

President Bush campaigned on using the surplus to pay down the debt but turned to tax cuts once elected and then supported increases in domestic spending once the budget was out of balance to garner support for the military buildup. President Trump also turned to tax cuts early in his administration after campaigning on balancing the budget and producing a budget that balances but has been largely ignored by Congress. President Obama cast health care reform as entitlement reform, however, his signature legislative accomplishment expanded the federal commitment to health spending which continues to grow at an unsustainable rate.[90] The Clinton era, and its balanced budgets during a period of substantial economic growth, seems to be the only recent connection with the neo-Keynesian budget policies of the post-World War II period.

Notes

1. A. James Wagner, "Weather and Circulation of July 1974 – Heat Wave and Drought Over the Middle Third of the Country," *Monthly Weather Review* 102 (1974): 736–742.
2. See Herber (1971) for more on the policy of automatic stabilization.
3. One of the best early treatments of the Congressional Budget Act and its experience over the first five years is Schick (1980).
4. Schick, "The Congressional Budget Act of 1974 (P.L. 93–344): Legislative History and Analysis."
5. Penner and Abramson (1988) argue that the Congressional Budget Act did little to encourage Congress and the president to balance the budget or reduce the debt. Rather, political pressures have resulted in increased debt which have resulted in process breakdowns.
6. U.S. Congress Joint Study Committee on Budget Control, *Recommendations for Improving Congressional Control Over Budgetary Outlay and Receipt* Totals, Final Report (Washington: U.S. Government Printing Office, 1973).
7. Schick, "The Congressional Budget Act of 1974 (P.L. 93–344): Legislative History and Analysis."
8. Ibid.
9. Ibid.
10. Ibid.
11. Ibid.
12. Ibid.
13. Ibid.
14. Lawrence J. Korb, "An Analysis of the Congressional Budget Act of 1974." *Naval War College Review* 29, no. 4 (1975): 40–52.
15. Schick, "The Congressional Budget Act of 1974 (P.L. 93–344): Legislative History and Analysis."
16. Ibid.
17. Ibid.

18. Ibid.
19. Ibid.
20. Philip G. Joyce, "The Congressional Budget Office at Middle Age," *Working Paper, Hutchins Center on Fiscal & Monetary Policy at Brookings* (2015).
21. Congressional Budget Office, *Inflation and Unemployment: A Report on the Economy*, Report to Congress (Washington, DC: Congressional Budget Office, 1975).
22. Philip G. Joyce, *The Congressional Budget Office: Honest Numbers, Power, and Policymaking* (Washington, DC: Georgetown University Press, 2011).
23. Alice M. Rivlin, "Reform of the Budget Process," *The American Economic Review: Papers and Proceedings of the Ninety-Sixth Annual Meeting of the American Economic Association* 74, no. 2 (1984): 133–137.
24. Joyce, *The Congressional Budget Office: Honest Numbers, Power, and Policymaking.*
25. Ibid.
26. Andrew Prokop, "The Congressional Budget Office, explained," *Vox*, June 26, 2017, https://www.vox.com/policy-and-politics/2017/3/13/14860856/congressional-budget-office-cbo-explained
27. Committee for a Responsible Federal Budget, "Playing By the (Budget) Rules: Understanding and Preventing Budget Gimmicks," *CRFB.org*, February 26, 2018, https://www.crfb.org/papers/playing-budget-rules-understanding-and-preventing-budget-gimmicks
28. Benjamin R. Civiletti, *Applicability of the Antideficiency Act Upon a Lapse in an Agency's Appropriations*, Legal Memorandum (Washington: U.S. Department of Justice, 1980).
29. Ibid.
30. Ibid.
31. Ibid.
32. Ibid.
33. Gretchen Frazee and Lisa Desjardins, "How the government shutdown compared to every other since 1976." *PBS News Hour*, December 26, 2018, https://www.pbs.org/newshour/politics/every-government-shutdown-from-1976-to-now
34. Savage, *Balanced Budgets and American Politics.*
35. James M. Buchanan and Richard E. Wagner, *Fiscal Responsibility in Constitutional Democracy* (Boston, MA: Martinus Nijhoff Social Sciences Division, 1977).
36. Stephen J. Turnovsky, "Stabilization Theory and Policy: 50 Years after the Phillips Curve." *Economica* 78, no. 309 (2009): 67–88.
37. George L. Perry, "Inflation and Theory in Practice." *Brookings Papers on Economic Activity* (1980): 207–260.

38. Joseph White and Aaron Wildavsky, *The Deficit and the Public Interest: The Search for Responsible Federal Budgeting in the 1980s* (Berkeley, CA: University of California Press, 1989).
39. Savage, *Balanced Budgets and American Politics.*
40. Michael Babunakis, *Budget Reform for Government* (Westport, CT: Quorum Books, 1982).
41. William A. Niskanen, *Reaganomics* (New York, NY: Oxford University Press, 1988).
42. Savage, *Balanced Budgets and American Politics.*
43. Dennis S. Ippolito, *Uncertain Legacies: Federal Budget Policy from Roosevelt through Reagan* (Charlottesville: University of Virginia Press, 1990).
44. U.S. Treasury Office of the Assistant Secretary for Economic Policy, *The Effects of Deficits on Prices of Financial Assets: Theory and Evidence*, Economic Policy Research Paper (Washington, DC: U.S. Department of Treasury, 1984); William Dupor and Li Rong, "The Expected Inflation Channel of Government Spending in the Postwar U.S." *European Economic Review* 74 (2015): 36–56.
45. Frederic H. Mishkin, "The Causes of Inflation." *Price Stability and Public Policy* (Kansas City, MO: Federal Reserve Bank of Kansas City, 1984): 1–24.
46. Ronald, Reagan, "Address to the Nation on the Economy," *Presidential Address.* (Washington, DC: February 5, 1984). The economist Milton Friedman also believed that the government would spend what it collected and, therefore, to reduce the deficit you must reduce taxes and spending. On this point see: Penner (1991).
47. President's Private Sector Survey on Cost Control, *A Report to the President* (Washington, DC: U.S. Government Printing Office, 1984).
48. Kevin D. Hoover and Steven M. Sheffrin, "Causation, Spending, and Taxes: Sand in the Sandbox or Tax Collector for the Welfare State?" *The American Economic Review* 82, no. 1 (1992): 225–248.
49. Robert E. Lucas, Jr., "Principles of Fiscal and Monetary Policy," *Journal of Monetary Economics* 17, no. 1 (1986): 117–134.
50. Aaron Wildavsky, *The New Politics of the Budget Process* (Glenview, IL: Scott, Foresman & Co., 1988).
51. Chistina D. Romer and David H. Romer, "Do Tax Cuts Starve the Beast? The Effect of Tax Changes on Government Spending?" *Brookings Papers on Economic Activity* (2009: 139–200).
52. Peter T. Kilborn, "Reagan and the Deficit," *The New York Times*, April 26, 1985.
53. There are many histories of the Reagan years including Makin and Ornstein 1994, Rubin 2003, Ippolito 1990, Pascall 1985, and White and Wildavsky 1989.

54. Romer and Romer, "Do Tax Cuts Starve the Beast? The Effect of Tax Changes on Government Spending?"
55. (Flickinger 1987)
56. *Congressional Record*, August 7, 1987, S23169.
57. *Congressional Record*, August 7, 1987, pp. S23169-S23170.
58. *Congressional Record*, August 7, 1987, pp. S23170.
59. *Congressional Record*, September 16, 1987, pp. H24269.
60. Roy T. Meyers, "The 'Ball of Confusion' in Federal Budgeting: A Shadow Agenda for Deliberative Reform of the Budget Process," *Public Administration Review* 69, no. 2 (2009): 211–223; Alan J. Auerbach, "The U.S. Fiscal Problem: Where We Are, How We Got Here, and Where We're Going," *NBER Macroeconomics Annual* 9 (1994): 141–175.
61. Robert D. Reischauer, "Taxes and Spending Under Gramm-Rudman-Hollings," *National Tax Journal* 43, no. 3 (1990): 223–23.
62. Ibid.
63. John E. Yang, "Budget Negotiators Meet at Andrews in Cheery, Summer-Camp Like Mood," *The Washington Post*, September 8, 1990, https://www.washingtonpost.com/archive/politics/1990/09/08/budget-negotiators-meet-at-andrews-in-cheery-summer-camp-like-mood/1c28e813-e7f8-46b5-96ab-220e8c69b97c/
64. Auerbach, "The U.S. Fiscal Problem: Where We Are, How We Got Here, and Where We're Going."
65. Rosemary D. Marcuss, "Budget Rules and Tax Legislation: Experience Under the Budget Enforcement Act," *Proceedings on Taxation held under the Auspices of the National Tax Association – Tax Institute of America* (Washington, DC: Tax Institute of America, 1992): 90–96.
66. Philip G. Joyce, *The Congressional Budget Office: Honest Numbers, Power, and Policymaking* (Washington, DC: Georgetown University Press, 2011).
67. Paul. Winfree, "How Enacted Reconciliation Bills Have Changed the Deficit." *N58 Policy Research Blog*, December 29, 2017, https://www.n58policy.com/blog/2017/12/29/how-enacted-reconciliation-bills-have-changed-the-deficit
68. Besides misapplication (Gilmour 1990) suggests that the reconciliation process transfers power out of committees and into majorities that pass the resolution.
69. *Congressional Record*, October 24, 1985, pp. S14032.
70. This number is based on CBO's analysis of each bill at the time of enactment. For some bills, CBO only provides a five-year estimate. For others, it provides a ten-year analysis.
71. Meyers, "The 'Ball of Confusion' in Federal Budgeting: A Shadow Agenda for Deliberative Reform of the Budget Process."

72. Alan J. Auerbach, "Fiscal Policy, Past and Present," *Brookings Papers on Economic Activity*, no. 1 (2003): 75–122.
73. Veronique De Rugy, *Spending Under President George W. Bush*," Working Paper (Arlington, VA: Mercatus Center at George Mason University, 2009).
74. Dan L. Crippen, *Extending the Budget Enforcement Act*, Testimony before the House of Representatives Committee on the Budget (Washington, DC: Congressional Budget Office, 2001).
75. Richard W. Stevenson, "The 2000 Campaign: The Budget Issue; Bush and Gore Revise Plans To Match a Growing Surplus," *The New York Times*, June 13, 2000.
76. Peter J. Wallison, "Is George W. Bush Following the Reagan Model? A Lecture at the Ronald Reagan Library," *American Enterprise Institute*, March 19, 2003.
77. George W. Bush, "History: Presidential Statements: Address To Joint Session of the Congress--February 27, 2001," *Social Security Online*, February 27, 2001. https://www.ssa.gov/history/gwbushstmts.html#jointsession
78. Douglas Holtz-Eakin, *Estimating the Cost of the Medicare Modernization Act*, Testimony before the House of Representatives Committee on Ways and Means (Washington, DC: Congressional Budget Office, 2004).
79. Joe Richardson, *Food Stamps and Nutrition Programs in the 2002 Farm Bill*, Report for Congress (Washington, DC: Congressional Research Service, 2006).
80. Richard Kogan, "The New Pay-As-You-Go Rule in The House of Representatives," *Center for Budget and Policy Priorities*, January 12, 2007, https://www.cbpp.org/research/the-new-pay-as-you-go-rule-in-the-house-of-representatives
81. U.S. Senate Committee on the Budget Republican Staff, "The New Adventures of "Old" Pay-Go," *U.S. Senate Committee on the Budget*, February 12, 2008, https://www.budget.senate.gov/imo/media/doc/bb01-2008.pdf
82. Congressional Budget Office, *Estimated Impact of the American Recovery and Reinvestment Act on Employment and Economic Output from July 2012 Through September 2012*, Report to Congress (Washington, DC: Congressional Budget Office, 2012).
83. Cammie Croft, "Fiscal Responsibility Summit Report," *The White House Archives*, March 20, 2009, https://obamawhitehouse.archives.gov/blog/2009/03/20/fiscal-responsibility-summit-report
84. Peter Orszag, "Opening Remarks at Fiscal Responsibility Summit," *The New York Times*, February 23, 2009.

85. The National Commission on Fiscal Responsibility, *The Moment of Truth*. Final Report (Washington, DC: The White House, 2010).
86. Roya Wolverson, "Midterm Elections 2010: Spending Wars," *Council on Foreign Relations*, October 18, 2010, https://www.cfr.org/backgrounder/midterm-elections-2010-spending-wars
87. Julie Mason and Meredith Shiner, "Joe Biden begins debt talks," *Politico*, May 5, 2011, https://www.politico.com/story/2011/05/joe-biden-begins-debt-talks-054362
88. Leonard Jay Santow, *The Budget Deficit: The Causes, The Costs, The Outlook* (New York: The New York Institute of Finance, 1988) suggests that "Members of Congress want a debt ceiling for many reasons – virtually none of which has anything to do with containing the deficit." That is almost always true, of course, but in 2011 House Republicans found the debt limit to be a useful vehicle to enact spending reforms.
89. Congressional Budget Office, "Discretionary Spending Under the Budget Control Act of 2011," *Congressional Budget Office*, August 8, 2011, https://www.cbo.gov/publication/42214
90. Paul Winfree, "Causes of the Federal Government's Unsustainable Spending," *The Heritage Foundation*, July 7, 2016, https://www.heritage.org/budget-and-spending/report/causes-the-federal-governments-unsustainable-spending

References

Auerbach, Alan J. 2003. "Fiscal Policy, Past and Present." Brookings Papers on Economic Activity 2003 (1): 75–122.

Auerbach, Alan J. 1994. "The U.S. Fiscal Problem: Where We Are, How We Got Here, and Where We're Going." NBER Macroeconomics Annual 9: 141–175.

Babunakis, Michael. 1982. Budget Reform for Government. Westport, CT: Quorum Books.

Buchanan, James M., and Richard E. Wagner. 1977. Fiscal Responsibility in Constitutional Democracy. Boston, MA: Martinus Nijhoff Social Sciences Division.

Bush, George W. 2001. "History: Presidential Statements: Address To Joint Session of the Congress--February 27, 2001." Social Security Online. February 27. https://www.ssa.gov/history/gwbushstmts.html#jointsession.

Civiletti, Benjamin R. 1980. Applicability of the Antideficiency Act Upon a Lapse in an Agency's Appropriations. Legal Memorandum, Washington: United States Department of Justice.

Committee for a Responsible Federal Budget. 2018. "Playing By the (Budget) Rules: Understanding and Preventing Budget Gimmicks." CRFB.org. February

26. Accessed June 21, 2019. https://www.crfb.org/papers/playing-budget-rules-understanding-and-preventing-budget-gimmicks.

Congressional Budget Office. 2011. "Discretionary Spending Under the Budget Control Act of 2011." Congressional Budget Office. August 8. Accessed June 21, 2019. https://www.cbo.gov/publication/42214.

Congressional Budget Office. 2012. Estimated Impact of the American Recovery and Reinvestment Act on Employment and Economic Output from July 2012 Through September 2012. Report to Congress, Washington: Congressional Budget Office.

Congressional Budget Office. 1975. Inflation and Unemployment: A Report on the Economy. Report to Congress, Washington, DC: Congressional Budget Office.

Congressional Record. 1987a. August 7: S23169-S23170.

Congressional Record. 1987b. September 16: H24269.

Congressional Record. 1985. October 24: S14032.

Crippen, Dan L. 2001. Extending the Budget Enforcement Act. Testimony before the House of Representatives Committee on the Budget, Washington: Congressional Budget Office.

Croft, Cammie. 2009. "Fiscal Responsibility Summit Report." The White House Archives. March 20. Accessed June 21, 2019. https://obamawhitehouse.archives.gov/blog/2009/03/20/fiscal-responsibility-summit-report.

De Rugy, Veronique. 2009. Spending Under President George W. Bush. Working Paper, Arlington: Mercatus Center at George Mason University.

Flickinger, Richard S. 1987. "Consumer Policy: Qualified Convergence." In Political Economy: Public Policies in the United States and Britain, by Jerold L. Waltman and Donley T. Studlar, 150–181. Jackson, MS: University Press of Mississippi.

Frazee, Gretchen, and Lisa Desjardins. 2018. "How the government shutdown compared to every other since 1976." PBS News Hour. December 26. Accessed June 21, 2019. https://www.pbs.org/newshour/politics/every-government-shutdown-from-1976-to-now.

Gilmour, John B. 1990. Reconciling Differences? Congress, The Deficit and the Budget Process. Berkeley, CA: University of California Press.

Herber, Bernard P. 1971. Modern Public Finance: The Study of Public Sector Economics. Homewood, IL: Richard D. Irwin.

Holtz-Eakin, Douglas. 2004. Estimating the Cost of the Medicare Modernization Act. Testimony before the House of Representatives Committee on Ways and Means, Washington: Congressional Budget Office.

Hoover, Kevin D., and Steven M. Sheffrin. 1992. "Causation, Spending, and Taxes: Sand in the Sandbox or Tax Collector for the Welfare State?" The American Economic Review 82 (1): 225–248.

Ippolito, Dennis S. 1990. Uncertain Legacies: Federal Budget Policy from Roosevelt through Reagan. Charlottesville, VA: University of Virginia Press.

Joyce, Philip G. 2015. The Congressional Budget Office at Middle Age. Working Paper, Hutchins Center on Fiscal & Monetary Policy at Brookings.

———. 2011. The Congressional Budget Office: Honest Numbers, Power, and Policymaking. Washington, DC: Georgetown University Press.

Kilborn, Peter T. 1985. "Reagan and the Deficit." The New York Times, April 26.

Kogan, Richard. 2007. "The New Pay-As-You-Go Rule in The House of Representatives." Center for Budget and Policy Priorities. January 12. Accessed June 21, 2019. https://www.cbpp.org/research/the-new-pay-as-you-go-rule-in-the-house-of-representatives.

Korb, Lawrence J. 1975. "An Analysis of the Congressional Budget Act of 1974." Naval War College Review 29 (4): 40–52.

Lucas, Robert E., Jr. 1986. "Principles of Fiscal and Monetary Policy." Journal of Monetary Economics 17 (1): 117–134.

Makin, John, and Norman J. Ornstein. 1994. Debt and Taxes. New York, NY: Random House.

Marcuss, Rosemary D. 1992. "Budget Rules and Tax Legislation: Experience Under the Budget Enforcement Act." Proceedings on Taxation held under the Auspices of the National Tax Association – Tax Institute of America. Washington: Tax Institute of America. 90–96.

Mason, Julie, and Meredith Shiner. 2011. "Joe Biden begins debt talks." Politico. May 5. Accessed June 21, 2019. https://www.politico.com/story/2011/05/joe-biden-begins-debt-talks-054362.

Meyers, Roy T. 2009. "The 'Ball of Confusion' in Federal Budgeting: A Shadow Agenda for Deliberative Reform of the Budget Process." Public Administration Review 69 (2): 211–223.

Mishkin, Frederic H. 1984. "The Causes of Inflation." Price Stability and Public Policy. Kansas City, MO: Federal Reserve Bank of Kansas City. 1–24.

Niskanen, William A. 1988. Reaganomics. New York, NY: Oxford University Press.

Orszag, Peter. 2009. "Opening Remarks at Fiscal Responsibility Summit." The New York Times. February 23. Accessed June 21, 2019. https://www.nytimes.com/2009/02/23/us/politics/23text-summit.html.

Pascall, Glenn. 1985. The Trillion Dollar Budget: How to Stop the Bankrupting of America. Seattle, WA: University of Washington Press.

Penner, Rudolph G., and Alan J. Abramson. 1988. Broken Purse Strings: Congressional Budgeting, 1974–1988. Washington, DC: The Urban Institute Press.

Perry, George L. 1980. "Inflation and Theory in Practice." Brookings Papers on Economic Activity 207–260.

President's Commission on Budget Concepts. 1967. Report of the President's Commission on Budget Concepts. Final Report, U.S. Government Printing Office.

Prokop, Andrew. 2017. "The Congressional Budget Office, explained." Vox. June 26. Accessed June 21, 2019. https://www.vox.com/policy-and-politics/2017/3/13/14860856/congressional-budget-office-cbo-explained.

Reagan, Ronald. 1984. "Address to the Nation on the Economy." Presidential Address. Washington, DC, February 5.

Reischauer, Robert D. 1990. "Taxes and Spending Under Gramm-Rudman-Hollings." National Tax Journal 43 (3): 223–232.

Richardson, Joe. 2006. Food Stamps and Nutrition Programs in the 2002 Farm Bill. Report for Congress, Washington: Congressional Research Service.

Rivlin, Alice M. 1984. "Reform of the Budget Process." The American Economic Review: Papers and Proceedings of the Ninety-Sixth Annual Meeting of the American Economic Association 74 (2): 133–137.

Romer, Chistina D., and David H. Romer. 2009. "Do Tax Cuts Starve the Beast? The Effect of Tax Changes on Government Spending?" Brookings Papers on Economic Activity 2009: 139–200.

Rubin, Irene S. 2003. Balancing the Budget: Trimming the Herds or Eating the Seed Corn? New York, NY: Chatham House Publishers.

Santow, Leonard Jay. 1988. The Budget Deficit: The Causes, The Costs, The Outlook. New York, NY: The New York Institute of Finance.

Savage, James D. 1988. Balanced Budgets and American Politics. Ithaca, NY: Cornell University Press.

Schick, Allen. 1975. The Congressional Budget Act of 1974: Legislative History and Analysis. Report to Congress, Washington: Congressional Research Service.

Stevenson, Richard W. 2000. "The 2000 Campaign: The Budget Issue; Bush and Gore Revise Plans To Match a Growing Surplus." The New York Times. June 13. Accessed June 21, 2019. https://www.nytimes.com/2000/06/13/us/2000-campaign-budget-issue-bush-gore-revise-plans-match-growing-surplus.html.

The National Commission on Fiscal Responsibility. 2010. The Moment of Truth. Final Report, Washington: The White House.

Turnovsky, Stephen J. 2009. "Stabilization Theory and Policy: 50 Years after the Phillips Curve." Economica 78 (309): 67–88.

U.S. Congress Joint Study Committee on Budget Control. 1973. Improving Congressional Control Over Budgetary Outlay and Receipt Totals. Interim Report, Washington: U.S. Government Printing Office.

U.S. Senate Committee on the Budget Republican Staff. 2008. "The New Adventures of "Old" Pay-Go." U.S. Senate Committee on the Budget. February 12. Accessed June 21, 2019. https://www.budget.senate.gov/imo/media/doc/bb01-2008.pdf.

U.S. Treasury Office of the Assistant Secretary for Economic Policy. 1984. The Effects of Deficits on Prices of Financial Assets: Theory and Evidence. Economic Policy Research Paper, Washington: U.S. Department of Treasury.

Wagner, A. James. 1974. “Weather and Circulation of July 1974 – Heat Wave and Drought Over the Middle Third of the Country.” Monthly Weather Review 102: 736–742.

Wagner, Richard, Robert D. Tollison, Alvin Rabushka, and John T. Noonan, Jr. 1982. Balanced Budgets, Fiscal Responsibility, and the Constitution. Washington, DC: Cato Institute.

Wallison, Peter J. 2003. “Is George W. Bush Following the Reagan Model? A Lecture at the Ronald Reagan Library.” American Enterprise Institute. March 19. Accessed June 2019, 2019. https://www.nytimes.com/2000/06/13/us/2000-campaign-budget-issue-bush-gore-revise-plans-match-growing-surplus.html.

White, Joseph, and Aaron Wildavsky. 1989. The Deficit and the Public Interest: The Search for Responsible Federal Budgeting in the 1980s. Berkeley, CA: University of California Press.

Wildavsky, Aaron. 1988. The New Politics of the Budget Process. Glenview, IL: Scott, Foresman & Co.

Winfree, Paul. 2017. “How Enacted Reconciliation Bills Have Changed the Deficit.” N58 Policy Research Blog. December 29. Accessed June 21, 2019. https://www.n58policy.com/blog/2017/12/29/how-enacted-reconciliation-bills-have-changed-the-deficit.

Wolverson, Roya. 2010. “Midterm Elections 2010: Spending Wars.” Council on Foreign Relations. October 18. Accessed June 21, 2019. https://www.cfr.org/backgrounder/midterm-elections-2010-spending-wars.

Yang, John E. 1990. “Budget Negotiators Meet at Andrews in Cheery, Summer-Camp Like Mood.” The Washington Post. September 8. Accessed June 21, 2019. https://www.washingtonpost.com/archive/politics/1990/09/08/budget-negotiators-meet-at-andrews-in-cheery-summer-camp-like-mood/1c28e813-e7f8-46b5-96ab-220e8c69b97c/.

CHAPTER 8

Breaking up the Budget Process

In February 2018, the Bipartisan Budget Act (BBA) was enacted, raising the limits on discretionary spending imposed by the Budget Control Act (BCA) and suspending the statutory limit on the debt for a period of time. The BBA of 2018 also created a Joint Select Committee on Budget and Appropriations Process Reform. The Joint Select Committee comprised sixteen members from the House and Senate, represented equally by both chambers and parties. The Committee had until the end of November 2018 to issue a final report to "significantly reform" the current processes.

The Joint Select Committee was created out of frustration with the existing processes. Congress rarely passes the budgets that they require themselves to propose by the Congressional Budget Act. The recent periodic visitations of the Budget Control Act had become tedious. Members of Congress could not agree on whether earmarking is beneficial. The budget reconciliation process has migrated away from its original purposes to become like a "silver bullet" used by the majority party in the Senate to jam policy past the filibuster when they can find policy agreement with the president. Congress and administration officials spend a great deal of time each year preparing and considering budgets that either go nowhere or seemingly come together around funding deadlines and without robust input. Congress never seems to find the time to consider and pass appropriations bills before annual funding runs out. Debt has continued to

P. Winfree, *A History (and Future) of the Budget Process in the United States*, https://doi.org/10.1007/978-3-030-30959-6_8

grow as mandatory spending is obligated with little annual oversight. The government has grown extensively but has not gone through a significant reorganization in over forty years.

Policymakers, it seems, are always unsatisfied with the existing budget process. As this book details, Congress fought against the adoption of the executive budget process before finally enacting the Budget and Accounting Act of 1921. Congress tried the legislative budget in the 1940s in an attempt to regain some control they had lost. The various commissions during the twentieth century took on budget problems which led to significant innovations within the process. President Nixon complained about the congressional budget process and Congress took a stand in 1974 to place themselves in a larger role and to restrict presidential powers.

The Joint Committee had plenty of incentives to reach an agreement to reform the budget and appropriations processes. At the very least, they had created room to discuss the many divisions that have formed over the budget process. However, the Committee ultimately could not agree on a plan. This is not for lack of good ideas to reform the process. There is, in fact, no shortage of ideas to reform the budget process. Bipartisan, nonpartisan, and partisan groups have all come together around the capital city to provide guidance and things for policymakers to consider including a revision in budget concepts and new ways to budget.

In 2007, Irene Rubin, a scholar of the budget process, wrote that federal budgeting had recently become "ad hoc, fragmented and opaque… failure to prioritize has become endemic."[1] The Congressional Budget Act was a representative of its place in history as a compromise made to address the challenges of the day, but its time had come. A new set of processes were needed to meet the new challenges.

But what are those challenges? A tremendous amount of research on the budget process assumes that long-run fiscal challenges should be the primary driver. There is, and has been, a growing fiscal imbalance where the government is collecting less revenues than it spends on an annual basis. The nature and causes of structural budget deficits are obvious. As just one of many examples, the Congressional Budget Office warns each summer with the release of their long-term budget outlook that spending on Social Security, major health care programs, and interest on the debt will continue to increase as a share of the economy outpacing the growth in revenues.

Roy Meyers, the political scientist and budget scholar, has suggested that we need a return of the congressional institutionalists to foster an environment of cooperation within the legislative branch.[2] Sure enough, policymakers like former-Senator Kent Conrad have spoken on the need to put the chances of reelection success aside to deal with the challenges of the day. Cooperation is clearly necessary to achieve political consensus in our republican government.

However, cooperation may not be possible without a forcing event, like a sudden reduction in demand for U.S. debt or extensive overreach from the administration. Furthermore, the political scientist John Gilmour finds that the budget process is not very useful when policymakers cannot agree on a course of action which can end up resulting in legislated events to force action, such as the BCA's sequester.[3] The historical record has demonstrated that innovation within the budget process has often come from necessity, outside pressure, divided government, and too much power swinging to one branch or the other. Innovation from these last three causes is based on the inherent conflict associated with the period. In other words, any cooperation that seemingly leads to reform is often born from conflict. This seems to hold constant even when there is a delay in the reform from the time of the event, as was experienced with reforms that occurred after the Jackson and Lincoln Administrations.

There are very few policymakers in today's environment arguing that the long-run fiscal imbalance is not a problem.[4] Even so, the interest rate of Treasury bonds is very low and the threat of inflation seems virtually non-existent. This is offered as proof of just how obviously difficult it is to predict a crisis and even more difficult to determine how the crisis will unfold. Additionally, as countries become wealthier and play a larger role in the global economy they are less likely to have a full-blown sovereign-debt crisis (although even a small debt crisis would be very bad).[5] Therefore, it is very likely that budget policy reformers have overinvested in ideas over the last decade to plan for the long-run. Everyone knows the long-run budget scenario is not very rosy, and yet the long-run trend has been to embrace additional policies that pile onto the existing imbalance. A 20-, 30-, or even 50-year budget plan is not going to change that dynamics.

Furthermore, as the introduction of this book address, there are different roles that the federal budget assumes. The budget is supposed to reflect a transparent accounting of all spending and revenue policies. In an ideal world, this would provide policymakers and the public with information that could be used to assess whether a program worked as intended. As the federal government has grown in size and scope, those policies are now more important than ever within regards to their influence on the economy.[6] Therefore, more now than before, economic theory is critical to understanding budget policy.

However, there is not a unified set of economic principles but only a system from which to judge those principles in action. There is robust debate in the literature involving both positive and normative economics related to public finance, macroeconomics, taxes, spending, and efficacy of individual programs.[7] The political scientist Aaron Wildavsky suggested that you cannot escape normative questions in budgeting; and yet that's exactly what we often ask the budget to do. At the very least we implicitly assume that the budget is able to address both distributional and aggregational issues including differences in sophisticated economic perspectives.

In the past, there was ostensibly more agreement around the general direction of budget policy. However, important differences have always persisted even when unified around a common cause.[8] The concept of government debt is an important illustration. As both Savage's *Budget Reform Politics* and this book details, debt was generally seen as something that the federal government should seek to limit and eventually retire. Federal debt was, for Hamilton and Jefferson, reflective of differences in the type of government that each man had wanted. For Andrew Jackson, eradicating the debt was about national honor. For the progressive reformers, balanced budgets reflected efficiency. Government debt has long been thought of as a way of empowering the already powerful, the rich at the expense of the poor, as a tax on the future, and as politically unpopular. It was hard to build a political campaign around debt regardless of the economic theories on the matter.

What has changed is the economic theory of how the government relates to the economy. As James Buchanan and Richard Wagner present in *Democracy in Deficit*, the Keynesian Revolution led to the endogeneity of the government's finances within the economy. Politicians, acting in their own self-interest, have used Keynesian theory to bless deficit spending all the time—it's always time to increase spending or cut taxes.[9] Furthermore, as continued government spending becomes anticipated, private investment is crowded out by public spending in the name of keeping the economy growing. The thing that pulls policymakers back, it seems, is political pressure from the opposition.

Mr. Keynes is not alone. For Reagan's economic agenda may not have been motivated by Keynesians, but it did make budget policy central to the economy. Budgetary decisions were economic decisions. Budget policy was economic policy. However, the federal budget was no longer simply aimed at the "twin goals of economic policy"—full employment and stable prices. Rather it was aimed at "starving the beast" or promoting federalism by reducing the size of government through lower taxes and less federal spending.

Members of Congress did not have to agree on every aspect of Reagan's initial underlying economic policy to support lower taxes. They could either subscribe to the "supply-side" notion that tax cuts were not only simulative but revenue enhancing (for instance, similar to the platform of Representative Jack Kemp who said that Republicans "no longer worship at the shrine of balanced budgets") or with the notion that lower federal revenues were a positive thing in themselves.[10] However, once deficits started rising, revenue neutrality became the goal while deficit reduction through spending cuts became the administration's pursuit. Democrats in the House functioned as a credible check on reducing revenues while helping to focus policy on deficit reduction.[11]

In today's political environment the political opposition is no longer able to rely on the usual data presented to push back on growing debt. It seems that the fiscal hawks have "cried wolf" one too many times. Even recently, economists such as Larry Summers and Jason Fruman are suggesting that the deficit does not matter very much in the environment that we are in with low interest rates and seemingly lots of great stuff to spend money on.[12]

Therefore, it seems that the implicit assumption that deficits are to be avoided and debt reduction should be a primary pursuit of economic policy through the budget both share neither a political nor economic consensus.[13] As this book discusses, this did not happen overnight. Even if Reagan wanted to "starve the beast" by first cutting taxes in the early 1980s he was too late. Revenues and spending have been independent of one another since at least the 1960s. Although, historically tax cuts have been better predictors of tax increases it is not clear that holds in the current environment as the 2017 Trump tax cuts built upon an extension of the Bush tax cuts.

Buchanan and Wagner's observation is playing out yet again as politicians are inclined to cut taxes and increase spending while their appetite is fed by low interest rates and economists who bless their agnosticism over the growing federal debt. This can be true even if policymakers are not themselves inspired by economic theory. The solution proposed by Buchanan and Wagner to this problem is a fiscal rule to balance the budget and a monetary rule to grow the monetary base consistent with real output. That would work, of course, if the economic policy of government debt wasn't debatable and their perspective could garner sustained political support.

Put another way, Buchanan and Wagner attempt to resolve one of the functions of the federal budget process by imposing an aggregate fiscal rule to constrain the decision-making of policymakers. This is a rule to rule all the other rules that the politicians have a hard time living with. In some sense, it is an attempt to force Congress and the president to engage in a continual debate about the size and scope of government by paying for what they spend over some period of time. However, the imposition of these rules again assumes that economic policy has been settled when it has not in either a positive or a normative sense.[14] This is only compounded by the fact that, again, all budget policy is normative.

Furthermore, the rule may in fact backfire. In 1980, Wildavsky wrote that:

> *The [balanced budget] amendment places a ceiling on spending but not a floor. Some of its sponsors hope that eventually expenditures will comprise a significantly lower portion of GNP than it does now. I doubt it. Whatever is known about spending suggest that ceilings become floors. Too many people want too much from government to get less than they can.... Conservative congressmen will discover that it is easier to keep constituents happy and to reconcile diverse interests by spending up to (or just below) the limit.*[15]

This is exactly what has played out with the Budget Control Act. The spending limits imposed have, essentially, functioned as a floor as they have been revised upward since their enactment.

One of the main problems is that we ask the budget process to resolve too many issues that are both debatable and difficult to resolve using the current framework. Dennis Ippolito has pointed out that as the government's budget has grown it has become increasingly difficult to resolve certain issues which will result in revisiting "the perennial question of the size and role of the federal government."[16] But the same case can be made for how the overall budget fits into the economic policy of the country.

The political scientist Steven Schier has suggested that when policymakers think about economics they usually separate issues into three areas: stabilization, distribution, and allocation.[17] An economist would call stabilization simply macroeconomic policy, whereas allocation is the size of the government and distribution is the allocation of resources to different groups. We ask the federal budget process to assume responsibility over settling all of these issues.

In the 1940s, the architects of the Employment Act envisioned a National Production and Employment Budget (NPEB). Although the Employment Act did not establish an NPEB, it did establish an infrastructure for economic policy setting. The President's Council of Economic Advisors issues the Economic Report of the President each year to which the Joint Economic Committee of Congress provides a formal response. This annual process should be expanded to include a robust debate over principles of economic policy that can be used to inform the budget debate. Congress should be required to vote on these principles in the form of a concurrent resolution (similar to the budget resolution) before it can proceed to writing the budget or considering appropriations bills. Therefore, the economic policy can inform budget policymakers using some consensus whether that is to establish fiscal rules or some other framework. This will allow the process to work out some of the aggregational problems before dealing with the distributional challenges.[18] As Wildavsky wrote in response to the idea of exogenous fiscal rules, "In politics, like markets, good decisions are those on which there is agreement, not those deemed correct according to cognition by a wise man sitting astride the relevant hierarchy."[19]

Economic theory itself is not exogenous to the budget process.[20] It is very much part of the system. So too are economists who make recommendations to policymakers. Alice Rivlin wrote in 1984:

> *Budget decision making at the federal level in the United States can hardly be described as casual, haphazard, or ill-informed. The budgeting process is lengthy and elaborate. The principal decision-makers – the president and the Congress – are assisted at every stage by an army of highly trained economists and budget analysts who assemble masses of information, use sophisticated forecasting models, and have access to state-of-the-art computers. Everyone works very hard. No government in the world devotes as much time, energy, and talent to budget decision making as our's does.*[21]

What is different about today relative to the past is that we have an entire infrastructure set up around developing and executing the federal budget. However, it is critical that we structure that infrastructure a way that best channels decision-making.

Even with reforms that will help narrow what the budget process can handle it is very likely the case that the federal government has become too large and perspectives too diverse for any congressional or administrative process changes to be truly effective. As history has demonstrated, the budget process has evolved over time to address the really critical challenges of the day. We should hope that it continues to be amendable to changes when it counts.

Notes

1. Irene S. Rubin, "The Great Unraveling: Federal Budgeting, 1997–2006," *Public Administration Review* 67, no. 4 (2007): 608–617.
2. Meyers, "The 'Ball of Confusion' in Federal Budgeting: A Shadow Agenda for Deliberative Reform of the Budget Process."
3. John B. Gilmour, *Reconciling Differences? Congress, The Deficit and the Budget Process* (Berkeley, CA: University of California Press, 1990).
4. Edward M. Gramlich, "How Bad Are The Large Deficits?" in *Federal Budget Policy in the 1980s*, by Gregory B. Mills and John L. Palmer (Washington, DC: The Urban Institute, 1984). Gramlich argues that the focus on short-term deficit is irrelevant while the long-run deficit both matters and is worthy of attention. Many others have said similar things.
5. Carmen Reinhart and Kenneth Rogoff, *This Time Is Different: Eight Centuries of Financial Folly* (Princeton, NJ: Princeton University Press, 2009).
6. Herbert Stein, *Governing the $5 Trillion Economy* (New York, NY: Oxford University Press, 1989); Donald F. Kettl, *Deficit Politics: Public Budgeting in its Institutional and Historical Context* (New York, NY: Macmillan Publishing, 1992). Stein and Kettl suggest that the budget is best viewed through the lens of the economy. That is, policymakers should think about how to allocate national output rather than simply government resources.
7. Richard H. Fink and Jack C. High, *A Nation in Debt: Economists Debate the Federal Budget Deficit* (Fredrick, MD: University Publications of America, 1987). Fink and High offer a selection of differing analyses on the federal debt by economists from Adam Smith to today.
8. This is not to say that there has been agreement on methods within public finance which is a point that this book makes clear. Public finance has always been controversial even before the ratification of the Constitution.

For instance, Ferguson (1961) suggests that the main disputes prior to 1790 were between the agrarian and mercantile interests. The merchants wanted "sound money backed by specie, funded debts, government banks, and sanctity of contract," whereas the farmers wanted "fiat money, agricultural credit, and certain and painless ways of discharging public debts."

9. Gary M. Anderson, "The U.S. Federal Deficit and National Debt: A Political and Economic History," in *Deficits*, by James M. Buchanan, Charles K. Rowley and Robert D. Tollison (New York: Basil Blackwell, Inc., 1987). Anderson suggests that the Keynesian revolution contributed to the development of persistent deficits but it did not directly cause them. Rather, it was the introduction of confusion into the popular opinion that the proper deficit shouldn't be zero.
10. Albert R. Hunt, "Paul Ryan's Role Model Was Jack Kemp," *The New York Times*, August, 2012, https://www.nytimes.com/2012/08/13/us/13iht-letter13.html?mtrref=undefined&gwh=E8AA35245E856793A97B38129FF1920F&gwt=pay
11. Dennis S. Ippolito, *Congressional Spending* (Ithaca, NY: Cornell University Press, 1981). Ippolito suggested that by 1979 the liberal agenda was to neutralize budget control away from spending, whereas the conservative agenda was the control spending and eliminate chronic deficits as balanced budgets were no longer an exclusive goal.
12. Jason Furman and Lawrence H. Summers, "Who's Afraid of Budget Deficits? How Washington Should End its Debt Obsession," *Foreign Affairs*, January 27, 2019.
13. Graham C. Hockely, *Fiscal Policy: An Introduction*, 2nd ed. (New York, NY: Routledge, 1992). Hockely includes a discussion of a variety of fiscal objectives including maintaining a satisfactory level of growth, maintaining high employment, stability of money, satisfactory exchange rate and balance of payments, apportionment of taxes.
14. Gerhard Cohn and Marilyn Young, "In Search of a New Budget Rule," in *Public Budgeting and Finance: Readings in Theory and Practice*, by Robert T. Golembiewski and Jack Rabin (Itasca, IL: F.E. Peacock Publishers, Inc., 1975). Cohn and Young illustrate some practical concerns with a balanced budget amendment to the Constitution while (Wagner, et al. 1982) provides thoughts on its functionality including responses to critics including integrating the creation of rules into the political process through an Article V convention of the states.
15. Aaron Wildavsky, *How to Limit Government Spending* (Berkeley, CA: University of California Press, 1980).
16. Dennis S. Ippolito, *Why Budgets Matter: Budget Policy and American Politics* (University Park, PA: Pennsylvania State University Press, 2003). See also, Marini (1992) who argues "the inability to control the budget is

a symptom of a deeper crisis which arises from the failure of the administrative state to function effectively, or gain legitimacy, within a constitutional regime of separated powers."

17. Steven E. Schier, "Deficits Without End: Fiscal Thinking and Budget Failure in Congress," *Political Science Quarterly* 107, no. 3 (1992): 411–433.
18. Arnold J. Meltzner, "Budget Control through Political Action," in *The Federal Budget: Economics and Politics*, by Michael J. Boskin and Aaron Wildavsky (San Francisco, CA: Institute for Contemporary Studies, 1982). Meltzner suggests that, in the past, deficits have motivated budget reform; however, ultimately there needs to be some public consensus in order for there to be any sustained budget constraint as bureaucracies are too good at tampering with rules.
19. Aaron Wildavsky, *How to Limit Government Spending* (Berkeley, CA: University of California Press, 1980).
20. Alberto Alesina and Roberto Perotti, "Budget Deficits and Budget Institutions," in *Fiscal Institutions and Fiscal Performance*, by James M. Poterba and Jürgen von Hagen (Chicago, IL: The University of Chicago Press, 1999). Alesina and Perotti suggest that budget institutions are, in fact, endogenous. However, the can act exogenous to the extent that they are difficult to change.
21. Alice M. Rivlin, "Reform of the Budget Process," *The American Economic Review: Papers and Proceedings of the Ninety-Sixth Annual Meeting of the American Economic Association* 74, no. 2 (1984): 133–137.

References

Alesina, Alberto, and Roberto Perotti. 1999. "Budget Deficits and Budget Institutions." In Fiscal Institutions and Fiscal Performance, by James M. Poterba and Jürgen von Hagen. Chicago, IL: The University of Chicago Press.

Anderson, Gary M. 1987. "The U.S. Federal Deficit and National Debt: A Political and Economic History." In Deficits, by James M. Buchanan, Charles K. Rowley and Robert D. Tollison. New York, NY: Basil Blackwell, Inc.

Cohn, Gerhard, and Marilyn Young. 1975. "In Search of a New Budget Rule." In Public Budgeting and Finance: Readings in Theory and Practice, by Robert T. Golembiewski and Jack Rabin. Itasca, IL: F.E. Peacock Publishers, Inc.

Ferguson, E. James. 1961. The Power of the Purse: A History of American Public Finance, 1776–1790. Chapel Hill, NC: The University of North Carolina Press.

Fink, Richard H., and Jack C. High. 1987. A Nation in Debt: Economists Debate the Federal Budget Deficit. Fredrick, MD: University Publications of America.

Furman, Jason, and Lawrence H. Summers. 2019. "Who's Afraid of Budget Deficits? How Washington Should End its Debt Obsession." Foreign Affairs, January 27.

Gilmour, John B. 1990. Reconciling Differences? Congress, The Deficit and the Budget Process. Berkeley, CA: University of California Press.

Gramlich, Edward M. 1984. "How Bad Are The Large Deficits?" In Federal Budget Policy in the 1980s, by Gregory B. Mills and John L. Palmer. Washington, DC: The Urban Institute.

Hockely, Graham C. 1992. Fiscal Policy: An Introduction. Second. New York, NY: Routledge.

Hunt, Albert R. 2012. "Paul Ryan's Role Model Was Jack Kemp." The New York Times. August 2012. Accessed June 2019, 2019. https://www.nytimes.com/2012/08/13/us/13iht-letter13.html?mtrref=undefined&gwh=E8AA35245E856793A97B38129FF1920F&gwt=pay.

Ippolito, Dennis S. 1981. Congressional Spending. Ithaca, NY: Cornell University Press.

———. 2012. Deficits, Debt, and The New Politics of Tax Policy. New York, NY: Cambridge University Press.

———. 1990. Uncertain Legacies: Federal Budget Policy from Roosevelt through Reagan. Charlottesville, VA: University of Virginia Press.

———. 2003. Why Budgets Matter: Budget Policy and American Politics. University Park, PA: Pennsylvania State University Press.

Kettl, Donald F. 1992. Deficit Politics: Public Budgeting in its Institutional and Historical Context. New York, NY: Macmillan Publishing.

Marini, John. 1992. The Politics of Budget Control: Congress, the Presidency, and the Growth of the Administrative State. New York, NY: Taylor & Francis, Inc.

Meltzner, Arnold J. 1982. "Budget Control through Political Action." In The Federal Budget: Economics and Politics, by Michael J. Boskin and Aaron Wildavsky. San Francisco, CA: Institute for Contemporary Studies.

Meyers, Roy T. 2009. "The 'Ball of Confusion' in Federal Budgeting: A Shadow Agenda for Deliberative Reform of the Budget Process." Public Administration Review 69 (2): 211–223.

Reinhart, Carmen, and Kenneth Rogoff. 2009. This Time Is Different: Eight Centuries of Financial Folly. Princeton, NJ: Princeton University Press.

Rivlin, Alice M. 1984. "Reform of the Budget Process." The American Economic Review: Papers and Proceedings of the Ninety-Sixth Annual Meeting of the American Economic Association 74 (2): 133–137.

Rubin, Irene S. 2007. "The Great Unraveling: Federal Budgeting, 1997–2006." Public Administration Review 67 (4): 608–617.

Schier, Steven E. 1992. "Deficits Without End: Fiscal Thinking and Budget Failure in Congress." Political Science Quarterly 107 (3): 411–433.

Stein, Herbert. 1989. Governing the $5 Trillion Economy. New York, NY: Oxford University Press.

Wildavsky, Aaron. 1980. How to Limit Government Spending. Berkeley, CA: University of California Press.

Appendix

This section includes a few notes on the data presented throughout the book. Data on federal expenditures, revenue, public debt (including its composition), and government employment are from four sources unless otherwise noted. For the years before 1939 the data are from the *Historical Statistics of the United States, Colonial Times to 1970* (US Census Bureau) and the *Annual Reports of the Secretary of the Treasury's Statistical Appendices*. Data between 1939 and the present are from the *Office of Management and Budget Historical Tables* and the *Historical Statistics of the United States Millennial Edition* (Cambridge University Press). Estimates of US gross domestic product (GDP) prior to 1929 are from Johnson and Williamson ("The Annual Real and Nominal GDP for the United States, 1790–2014," MeasuringWorth) while estimates after 1929 are from the US Department of Commerce's Bureau of Economic Analysis.

P. Winfree, *A History (and Future) of the Budget Process in the United States*, https://doi.org/10.1007/978-3-030-30959-6

Index[1]

[1] Note: Page numbers followed by 'n' refer to notes.

P. Winfree, *A History (and Future) of the Budget Process in the United States*, https://doi.org/10.1007/978-3-030-30959-6

Y

CPSIA information can be obtained
at www.ICGtesting.com
Printed in the USA
BVHW040813221119
564525BV00006B/21/P

9 783030 30958